FROM RITUAL TO RECORD

From Ritual to Record

The Nature of Modern Sports

ALLEN GUTTMANN

NEW YORK

COLUMBIA UNIVERSITY PRESS

Professor Guttmann is Chairman of
the Department of American Studies,
Amherst College

Library of Congress Cataloging in Publication Data

Guttmann, Allen.
From ritual to record.

Includes bibliographical references and index.
1. Sports—Social aspects. I. Title.
GV706.5.G87   301.5'7   77-20886
ISBN 0-231-03993-X (cloth)
ISBN 0-231-08369-6 (paper)
Columbia University Press
New York   Guildford, Surrey

TO DORIS BARGEN

Preface

IN HIS INTRODUCTION to one of the first books written on the psychology of sports, the philosopher Max Scheler lamented what he saw as scholarly neglect: "Scarcely an international phenomenon of the day deserves social and psychological study to the degree that sport does. Sport has grown immeasurably in scope and in social importance, but the meaning of sport has received little in the way of serious attention."[1] That was in 1927. Fifty years later, sports remain among the most discussed and least understood phenomena of our time. One reason that sports are not understood is that familiarity has made their significance seem obvious when it is not. Another reason is that the philosophers, historians, sociologists, and psychologists who have concerned themselves with sports have only rarely written for the ordinary reader. They have communicated mainly with each other.

I hope in this present study to offer a systematic and original interpretation of modern sports and a series of speculations about what is and what is not unique about American sports. Specifically, I attempt to define the relationships that obtain among play, games, contests, and sports; to demonstrate what differentiates modern from primitive, ancient, and medieval sports; to interpret the social conditions that led to the rise of modern sports; to comment upon the distinctively American games of baseball and football, and, finally, to look into the American preference for team rather than for individual sports.

I hope also that this study will interest and persuade readers who are not specialists as well as those who are. I have sought to clarify, to explain, and to interpret. I have tried neither to mystify nor to simplify. If I have succeeded, much of the credit must go to the many colleagues and friends who have given new life to the old phrase, "community of scholars." For help of various sorts, I am grateful to Ralph Beals, Yves and Nicole Carlet, Haskell Coplin, Friederike Dewitz, Peter Graham, Robert Grose, Ommo Grupe, Herbert and Mary Jim Josephs, Gerald S. Kenyon, Hans Lenk, John Loy, Tracy Mehr, Edward Mulligan, Russel Nye, Jack Salzman, George Stade, David Turesky, Horst Überhorst, and Harold VanderZwaag. The manuscript was read critically by Doris Bargen, Jan Dizard, Frederick Errington, and John William Ward. A considerable portion of the research was subsidized by the Deutsche Forschungsgemeinschaft and by the National Endowment for the Humanities.

Allen Guttmann
January 1978

Contents

FROM RITUAL TO RECORD

Play, Games, Contests, Sports

IN HIS AUTOBIOGRAPHY, *The Four Minute Mile* (1955), Roger Bannister tells of a moment in childhood when he stood "barefoot on firm dry sand by the sea." He was overcome by a quality in the air and a beauty in the clouds, by a sense of mystic perfection: [1]

In this supreme moment I leapt in sheer joy. I was startled, and frightened, by the tremendous excitement that so few steps could create. I glanced around uneasily to see if anyone was watching. A few more steps—self-consciously now and firmly gripping the original excitement. The earth seemed almost to move with me. I was running now, and a fresh rhythm entered my body. No longer conscious of my movement I discovered a new unity with nature. I had found a new source of power and beauty, a source I never dreamt existed.

Bannister's movements were spontaneous, the sheer outburst of physical exuberance. To the degree that any human action can be described as free and unmotivated, his was. Theorists have dwelled on the biological and psychological motives behind the apparently unmotivated, spontaneous play of animals and men. There is, indeed, an entire literature which relates play to the development of motor abilities or to the mastery of unconscious phobia or to the stages of conceptual maturation. If we wished to probe for the deepest psychobiological springs of Bannister's moment of joy, we could not avoid the work of Karl Groos, Sigmund Freud, Jean Piaget, and others who have contributed to the theory of play; but we wish to go in another direction, not toward the alleged universals of human psychic behavior but rather toward some less contestable comments about modern sports as an aspect of modern society. Rather than analyzing the act of play as described by Bannister and experienced by every man, let us move to another episode in Bannister's autobiography.

It is May 6, 1954. Bannister runs again, under rather different circumstances. Although he does not underline such details in his narrative, he has entered an official race at Oxford, a race sanctioned by the established authorities of Great Britain's Amateur Athletic Union and thus, eventually, by the International Amateur Athletic Federation with which the AAU is affiliated. Iffley Road Track is of standard length, carefully tended to provide a good surface for the runners. Bannister wears a track suit and shoes which have been designed for a maximum of speed. Only this morning he has sharpened the spikes. There is an audience with certain expectations. They know what it means for a man to race against other men and, more importantly, to race against the clock.

An entire book might be written on the cultural assumptions involved in the coming together of Roger Bannister, his runner-friends Christopher Brasher and Christopher Chataway, the officials, the audience, the press, and others on that chilly, windy day in 1954. The most important cultural fact is simple enough to state and yet almost impossible to grasp. The four-minute mile. Everyone present knew that athletes had dreamed and had struggled and had always failed to run a mile in four minutes. Why had it been impossible? Looking back, we can say with certainty that it was not *physically* impossible. Miles faster than Bannister's have become routine. John Landy exceeded Bannister's achievement in a quantitative sense within weeks. There was, of course, that famous "psychological barrier" that looms as forbidding as a set of hurdles on the track. But this psychological barrier was the product of a cultural accident. It simply happened that modern sports focus on the time it takes to cover a distance rather than the distance covered in a given time. An English mile must seem an awkward distance to the metric-minded, but it happened that a mile and the world's standard chronological system of minutes and seconds combined so that English and American culture created a psychological barrier which Europeans running the 1500-meter race (.93 mi.) did not have to deal with. Except that they too, when competing in England or the United States, understood the barrier well enough to be defeated by it.

May 6, 1954. Bannister runs. He is paced by his friends Brasher and Chataway and he finishes in 3:59.4. The time is announced, registered, officially acknowledged, publicized, admired, written into the history of sports, and outdone.

The difference between Bannister's ecstatic moment on the beach and his triumphant run at Oxford's Iffley Road Track is the difference between play and modern sport. The same difference appears when we compare a child's unpremeditated leap over a bush or a rock with Dwight Stones' soaring, televised jump over the standardized cross-bar, when we compare a pebble skipped across the water of a pond with the complicated technique and awesome force of the ham-merthrow. A similar difference appears when we compare a game of catch with any one of the complex ball games played by regular teams in organized leagues in every modern country.

With the example of Bannister's two runs in mind, we can develop an elementary paradigm, a preliminary model of play, games, con-tests, and sports. For our purposes, play is any nonutilitarian physical or intellectual activity pursued for its own sake. "Play," writes Carl Diem, "is purposeless activity, for its own sake, the opposite of work."[2] Play is autotelic. Pleasure is in the doing and not in what has been done. One might say that play is to work as process is to results. Play is a realm of freedom. This definition rules out commonly ac-cepted goals like better health, character-development, improved motor skills, and peer group socialization. The definition is broad enough to include gamboling (and perhaps gambling), word play, play with numbers, chess, blind man's bluff, and football. The defi-nition excludes hunting for food and playing volleyball to fulfill a physical-education requirement. In the real world, motives are mixed. I play tennis with my wife because I love tennis and my wife, because I feel better after exercise, because I like to think of myself as an active person. Similarly, a professional like Arthur Ashe has utilitarian motives and cannot be said to play purely for the pleasure of the activity for its own sake, but he refers to a perfect shot and remarks, "Suddenly, the essence of everything you have worked a lifetime for is distilled into one shot."[3] We both play with mixed motives. Let us be strict about our definitions, about our paradigm, even as we acknowledge that the paradigm is a way to understand social reality, not a perfect replica of whatever is.

Play, in this ideal sense of the word, has been singled out as the most human of activities. From the poet Friedrich Schiller to the historian Johan Huizinga, there has been a philosophical effort to define the species as *Homo ludens,* man the player. There is even a theology of play, according to which God is the primal player whose creatures worship through imitation of *Deus ludens.*[4]

The English language differentiates, as French and German do not, between play and games. Play can be divided into two categories—spontaneous play and organized play, which we call games. The assertion seems paradoxical. How can one remain in the realm of freedom if one submits to organization? The answer is that spontaneous play may be as close as we can ever come to the realm of pure freedom, but most play is regulated and rule-bound. It remains nonutilitarian and in that sense has its own kind of freedom from the need to provide food, shelter, and the other material requirements of existence; but games symbolize the willing surrender of absolute spontaneity for the sake of playful order. One remains outside the sphere of material necessity, but one must obey the rules one imposes on oneself. Examples of games come effortlessly to mind—leapfrog, "playing house," speaking Pig Latin, chess, Monopoly, basketball. A mixed lot. The first three examples are different from the last three, but more of that in a moment.

It is useful to speak briefly of games and the way that the rules complicate the action. The rules are quite often designedly "inefficient." One does not eliminate an opponent's queen by simply reaching across the chess board and picking the piece up and dropping it into one's pocket. One does not achieve a hole-in-one by carrying the golf ball to its destination and placing it there. Bernard Suits has a helpful, if rather technical, comment on the role of rules in games:[5]

To play a game is to attempt to achieve a specific state of affairs (prelusory goal), *using only means permitted by rules* (lusory means), *where the rules prohibit use of more efficient in favor of less efficient means* (constitutive rules), *and where such rules are accepted just because they make possible such activity* (lusory attitude).

The reference to the prelusory goal places an apparent stress on winning, a stress which is certainly compatible with the ethos of sports as articulated by Vince Lombardi but which runs contrary to our present emphasis on the activity rather than the outcome. What is the goal of leapfrog other than the pleasures of leapfrog?

This leads to another necessary distinction, another branch in a series of dichotomies. As everyone knows, leapfrog and basketball are different kinds of games. They both have rules, as spontaneous play does not, but the rules provide for a difference which is often overlooked even in fairly rigorous discussion. Leapfrog is not a contest and basketball is. Of course, one can turn almost any activity into a contest, but leapfrog and ring-around-the-rosie are games which are complete in themselves without a won-lost outcome. Definitions of "game" which insist that there must be a winner discard information relevant to the large area of organized play which is not competitive. There are rules to "playing doctor," but winning and losing are not defined.

The importance of contests in our society makes it difficult to realize that there are literally thousands of games that are not contests. Japanese *kemari*, for instance, is a game often called "football" by Western observers because the ball is kicked with the foot, but the ceremonial object of the game is to keep the ball in the air and the participants are in no sense contestants. Kicking the ball while standing in an area whose four corners are marked by a willow tree, a cherry tree, a pine tree, and a maple tree, the players act out their sense of universal harmony.[6] No one wins, no one loses. Of a similar game in Micronesia, an anthropologist has written, "There is an overall lack of interest in the competitive possibilities of the sport. The emphasis is on gracefulness and skill."[7] Our games are not like *kemari*. The importance of contests in modern society can be glimpsed from etymology. The term "athlete" derives from the Greek words *athlos* ("contest") and *athlon* ("prize"). For Americans, whose

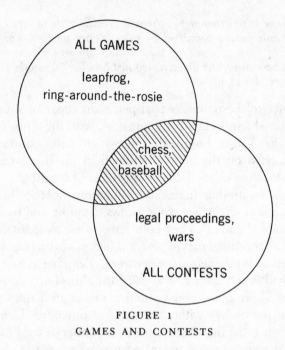

FIGURE 1
GAMES AND CONTESTS

children's games have largely been replaced by adult-organized contests, the games of noncompetitive peoples like the Navajo are likely to seem quaint, even "childish," a response which tells us something important about ourselves.

Contests are infinite in their variety. Chess is one example, basketball is another. It is important, however, to remember that the contests which concern us now are subcategories of the world of play. Perhaps a Venn diagram is useful (see figure 1). Playful contests are the intersection of two sets—all games and all contests. There are clearly games which are not contests and contests which are not games in our technical sense. ("War games" and the "game theory" of military strategists are not subcategories of play except to the degree that the men involved begin to enjoy the activity for its own sake.) Johan Huizinga's classic and enormously influential book *Homo Ludens* (1938), is seriously flawed by his inclusion of legal contests and even warfare under the rubric of play. "Contest means play . . . there is no sufficient reason to deny any contest whatsoever the character of play."[8] Huizinga's misconception is not groundless. There is the logical possibility that warfare can become autotelic, an end in itself, waged for the sheer pleasure of the activity. In fact, the line between the medieval tournament and the medieval battle was not very finely drawn. At the Battle of Brémule in 1119, three men were killed; at the tournament at Neuss in 1240, sixty died.[9] The ostensible purposes were different, but who can say for sure that the knights involved did not approach the battle more playfully than the tournament? Similarly, lawyers involved in a legal action have been known to take such pleasure in their roles that the courtroom became, in an extended sense, their playground. Nonetheless, the distinction between contests that are and are not games is a crucial one. Huizinga's confusion of the two detracts considerably from the value of his work. Roger Caillois's comment on *Homo Ludens* is correct: "The work is not a study of games but rather research into the fecundity of the play-spirit in the domain of culture, more precisely, into the spirit which resides in a certain kind of games, those of regulated competition."[10] By ignoring the distinction between games that are and are not contests, by assuming that all contests are games, Huizinga managed to write a fascinating but fundamentally obfuscating book on poetry, religion, play, warfare, art, music, and politics.

Having defined play, games, and contests somewhat more carefully than Huizinga did, we can now make a final dichotomization and define sports as "playful" physical contests, that is, as nonutilitarian contests which include an important measure of physical as well as intellectual skill.[11] (Although we shall speak of "physical contests," it is hard to imagine a sport completely devoid of intellectual skill.) In our sense, chess is certainly a contest but it is not, despite inclusion in *Sports Illustrated*, a sport. Whether automobile racing and similar "motor sports" are sufficiently physical to warrant the name sports is debatable, as is the status of horse racing. Horse races are, indeed, a special problem. Is the contest mainly between the horses or the jockeys? Pausanias, the second-century Greek traveler to whom we owe much of our knowledge of ancient sports, tells of an Olympic race won by a mare after the rider had been thrown. The horse's owner was declared the winner.[12] Similarly, modern bets are placed on the horses and the animal is clearly the *protagoniste d'action*—at least in French sports pages.[13] Fortunately, we need not decide disputes of this sort. The essential point is that we have a clear definition with which to make whatever discriminations are justified by the empirical data. What to call a horse race is uncertain, but we can be sure that the whaling industry, which at least one prominent historian defiantly classified as sport, must be excluded.[14] We can also avoid the disarmingly acknowledged embarrassment of James A. Michener's *Sports in America* (1976), where spectators, bettors, and athletes are all counted as sportsmen. Michener comments, "It galls me to classify sedentary spectators as sportsmen, but they are entitled to the designation."[15] Not really. Michener's initial instincts were right. Watching a physical contest is not really very much like engaging in a physical contest. Betting comes closer, but not close enough.

If we step back for a moment, we can see that we have a series of dichotomies. How does our paradigm (figure 2) compare at this point with the classifications presently employed in anthropological research? In a fascinating series of articles, John M. Roberts, Brian Sutton-Smith, and their associates have developed a tripartite classification of games into (1) games of physical skill, which may or may not include elements of strategy and chance, (2) games of strategy, which may or may not include elements of chance, and (3) simple games of chance.[16] This taxonomy does not distinguish between games that are and are not contests, which leads Roberts and Sutton-Smith to the questionable conclusion that there are primitive societies with no games at all.[17] Noncompetitive games they refer to as pastimes. Their emphasis is upon competitive games of all sorts, not solely on sports.

Using data like that collected in the Cross-Cultural Survey Files and Human Relations Area Files at Yale University, Roberts and Sutton-Smith have sought to establish correlations between kinds of games and kinds of cultures, that is, between games and political and economic roles, religious beliefs, kinship systems, child-rearing practices, sexual behavior, etc. "Games of physical skill," they write, "whether considered separately as pure physical skill or as physical skill and strategy jointly, show significant relationships with reward for achievement and frequency of achievement."[18] Games of strategy correlate statistically with a high degree of political integration and

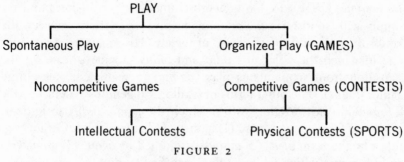

FIGURE 2
PLAY, GAMES, CONTESTS, SPORTS

with a rigorous demand for obedience in children. In "chance cultures," we find that early sexual satisfaction is low, anxiety of various sorts is high, warfare is prevalent, harsh natural environments are characteristic, settlements are not fixed, nurturance is uncertain, and first-cousin marriages are forbidden.

In the many valuable contributions of this anthropological school, there is a stress on games as contests, a stress which is theoretically consistent with the work of Sigmund Freud, whose influential book, *Beyond the Pleasure Principle* (1924), treats games as efforts at mastery. Roberts and Sutton-Smith remark that the "conflict hypothesis of game involvement holds that players become initially curious about games, learn them, and ultimately acquire high involvement in them because of specific psychological conflicts."[19] Games are in this sense therapeutic. Different kinds of games represent different approaches to the mastery of psychological conflict: "Games are . . . models of ways of succeeding over others, by magical power (as in games of chance), by force (as in physical skill games), or by cleverness (as in games of strategy)."[20] The underlying assumptions of this approach are revealed in a subsequent comment. In games, children learn the "necessary arts of trickery, deception, harassment, divination, and foul play that their teachers won't teach them, but which are most important in successful human interrelationships in marriage, business, and war."[21] In the struggle for mastery, games are analogues to jokes—as Freud saw them.

The French anthropologist Roger Caillois has worked in a fashion somewhat similar to that of Roberts and Sutton-Smith. In *Les Jeux et les hommes* (1958), he too concerns himself with all games and not simply with sports. He too attempts to find correlations between the kinds of games and the structure of society. His scheme is a complex one in which the poles of *paidia* and *ludus* provide a scale for the transition from spontaneous play (*paidia*) to regulated, rule-bound games (*ludus*). The other terms of Caillois's ingenious system provide a four-fold categorization within which the *paidia-ludus* scale operates. The four categories are (1) games of chance, which Caillois signifies by the term *alea*, (2) contests, signified by *agon*, (3) *mimickry*, and (4) games which incite vertigo, signified by *ilinx*. As examples of the four categories at the level of *paidia*, Caillois offers coin flipping, races, childish imitations, and children's swings. As examples at the level of *ludus*, he offers lotteries, chess, theatre, and mountain-climbing. Armed with this paradigm, Caillois sets forth to establish not a sociology of games but rather a sociology derived from games, not a "sociologie des jeux" but a "sociologie *à partir* des jeux."[22] His design has the grandeur that one associates with French anthropology.

Caillois shares with Roberts and Sutton-Smith the assumption that particular kinds of games are highly significant and can, therefore, be related to the nature of the social order. He writes that[23]

primitive societies . . . are those under the sway of masks and possession, that is, of mimickry and ilinx. Conversely, the Incas, the Assyrians, the Chinese or the Romans are examples of ordered societies with offices, careers, codes, calculations, and controlled and hierarchical privilege, societies where agon *and* alea, *that is, merit and the accidents of birth, appear as elementary aspects of culture and as complements of the game of society.*

Structured games mirror structured society.

Without attempting to criticize Roberts, Sutton-Smith, or Caillois in detail, we can express a degree of doubt about their approach and, simultaneously, indicate the rather different path we mean to pursue. While it is certainly plausible to say that people drawn to a game like chess are different in their personalities from those who toss a pair of dice and trust in fate, it is much riskier to characterize an entire epoch or even a single tribe by the presence or absence of *agon* or *alea*. The more specific the allegedly characterizing game, the riskier the enterprise. The modern sport of archery, for example, differs considerably from the archery of the Zen master concerned for mystic unity with the universe. In fact, modern archery differs appreciably from the sport of archery among the English of Shakespeare's day. Similarly, the tombs of Beni Hassan in Egypt, dating from pharaonic times, depict very nearly the entire gamut of wrestling holds used in today's intercollegiate matches. In other words, it is doubtful that the kind of game, determined by anthropologists, matters as much as the cultural perception of the game on the part of the players themselves. We can learn a great deal from careful attention to the games a society emphasizes, but the "same" game is likely to vary greatly in its meaning from one cultural context to another. I shall emulate Roberts, Sutton-Smith, and Caillois and attempt in chapters 4 and 5 to indicate some reasons why baseball and football are peculiarly American games, but I shall be more concerned with the variation of the "same" sports over time. I shall be less intent on *whether* the sport appears than with *how* it appears.

Let us return to our preliminary paradigm, which is nearly complete, but not quite. If we go back to the point of our classificatory departure, to play itself, we can ask if play is the only alternative to what can be characterized as the world of work. Clearly it is not. At the very least, we must add the arts to the list of activities ideally pursued for nonutilitarian ends. One hesitates to make this point because, once again, there is an entire literature devoted to the question of sports' relationship to the fine arts. Pierre Frayssinet's subtle, informative, provocative book, *Le Sport parmi les beaux-arts* (1968), is an extended argument for the inclusion of sports within the more prestigious (for some) category of the arts.[24] Similarly, Roland Barthes has described the Tour de France as an epic and no one can deny that modern dance and the musically accompanied floor exercises of women's gymnastics resemble one another.

What speaks against the inclusion of sport among the arts? The distinction between play and art may lie in the theory of expression. Although not all students of aesthetics are likely to agree with the formulation, the arts can be conceived of as modes of expression which, in their untruncated form, assume the communication of the artist with an audience. Art may not always communicate morally, although literature often does, but art must communicate something—a sense of form and color, an awareness of patterned sound, an interpretation of human movement. The artist needs his audience which, regrettably, he is sometimes forced to do without. Play, however, needs no audience because play expresses an exuberance that need not be communicated. The activity is, as we have said, for its own sake. Games, contests, and even sports do acquire audiences and no one familiar with modern professional team sports is unaware of the intimate financial relationships between sports, live audiences, and the television networks. Nonetheless, sports have existed, do exist, and will continue to exist in situations without an audience. In fact, the athlete who displaces his attention from the activity to the audience, who performs for the fans, violates the code of sports and frequently suffers under the mockery of purists. "Grandstanding" is not admired within what Erving Goffman calls the "back region," where the insiders interact with one another. Using Goffman's distinction between "front" and "back" regions, Alan G. Ingham and Michael D. Smith comment, "In the front regions, since he is exposed to his teammates, authority figures, and spectators, the athlete has to handle the problem of whether to play or display."[25]

Roland Barthes' account of professional wrestling demonstrates clearly this distinction between sport and art. The activity engaged in by professional wrestlers looks somewhat like the activity of college wrestlers, but the feigned struggle is not really a contest. It is rather a kind of folk-art, a melodramatic allegory of good and evil. "What is offered to the public," comments Barthes, "is the grand spectacle of Pain, of Defeat, and of Justice."[26] Collegiate wrestlers may or may not gapple in public, but the grunters and groaners of "le catch" need their audience thrilling to the visible triumph of good and the audible punishment of evil.

Sports can become symbolic actions. The crowd at the World Series or at Wimbledon often responds to the contest as if it were an allegory. Nonetheless, we must recall that a race between two children or a domestic game of tennis or a single duffer's attempt to get around the golf links in par are all instances of sport, regardless of whether or not there are spectators to allegorize the activity. In the last example, at least, the ardent wish is undoubtedly for absolute solitude.

Having offered in sketchy and abstract form a preliminary paradigm of play, games, contests, and sports, having tentatively suggested a distinction between the domain of these activities and that of the fine arts, I must confront a question no serious student of sports seems able to avoid. Huizinga insists in *Homo Ludens* that play always "proceeds within its own proper boundaries of time and space according to fixed rules and in an orderly manner."[27] Caillois agrees: "Play is essentially a separate occupation, carefully isolated from the rest of existence and generally occurring within precise limitations of time and place. . . . In any event, the domain of play is a universe apart, closed and protected—a pure space."[28] In response to Huizinga we have already decided that fixed rules belong to games and not to the spontaneous form of play, but what of the separation of time and space? Although we can conceptualize a universe in which the utilitarian and the nonutilitarian are totally compartmentalized, in which work and play are distinct realms which never interpenetrate, we often experience work and play in their impure forms. Moments of play appear unpredictably in the most unlikely places, even upon the gallows, and the most ecstatic flights of child's play can suddenly droop into dull compulsion. "Let's keep playing," says one child. The other agrees reluctantly, out of a sense of obligation. The first plays on, the second only seems to. Do they occupy separate times and spaces? We have a marvelous ability to transform almost any tedious or unpleasant task into a game; we have a less admirable capacity to corrupt pure play by ulterior motives that can range from the innocent maintenance of physical fitness to the maiming of an opponent in order to secure the winner's share of the take. In the film *Cool Hand Luke*, a group of convicts bewilders the guards by increasing the tempo of their road-work, by running back and forth in eager performance of their imposed task, by laughing, by turning punishment into play. There is in this situation no formal contest because the guards are not included among the players, but their bewilderment is in fact the rational point of the apparently irrational game. Had the convicts begun the game purely for their own amusement, like children suddenly captivated by a whim, the activity would have been a nonutilitarian one phenomenologically indistinguishable from the utilitarian work that was done.

Huizinga was concerned with contests rather than with play or noncompetitive games. It is probably the case that the movement from play through games and contests to sports involves an increasing degree of spatial-temporal separateness. The more highly structured the event, the more precisely demarcated and set aside from ordinary time and space; but even the most strictly conventionalized "ludic frame" can be broken. In his many guises, the "spoilsport" stands ready to dispell the illusion and to allow the rainbow world of play to "fade into the light of common day."[29]

Having responded to the questions raised by Frayssinet and by Huizinga, let us return once again to our paradigm in which sports are "playful" physical contests. Our paradigm is a tool, a heuristic device, a helpful model. Not only is it ahistorical, we have preferred it to the more directly, more grandly historical paradigms developed by Roberts, Sutton-Smith, and Caillois. Our paradigm is a necessary abstraction, but in order to understand what is modern about modern sports, which is one of our two related purposes, we must understand what was not modern about the sports of earlier times. Having been somewhat philosophical for a few pages, we must now become historical.

II

From Ritual to Record

ONE WAY TO understand a phenomenon is to see it against the background of what it is not. When Mark Twain was informed that Albert Spalding's touring baseball teams had played an exhibition game in the Hawaian Islands, he marveled at the cultural contrast: [1]

I have visited the Sandwich Islands . . . where life is one long, slumberless Sabbath, the climate one long, delicious summer day. . . . And these boys have played baseball there!—baseball, which is the very symbol, the outward and visible expression of the drive and push and rush and struggle of the raging, tearing, booming nineteenth century! One cannot realize it; the place and the fact are so incongruous; it's like interrupting a funeral with a circus.

Funeral and circus are not the most precise metaphors, but the Gestalt of modern sports does appear in sharply delineated contrast against the background of primitive, ancient, and medieval sports.

Seen in this fashion, the distinguishing characteristics of modern sports, as contrasted with those of previous eras, are seven in number. They are easy enough to name, but their implications, ramifications, mutual relations, and ultimate significance require precise and somewhat extended analysis. Like other cultural facts, they are likely to be taken for granted and to be thought of as self-evidently "natural" by members of the culture while they seem strange to those who approach them from the outside. Stated now in their most abstract form, simply as a means to indicate the direction of the anlysis, the seven characteristics are

secularism,
equality of opportunity to compete and in the conditions of competition,
specialization of roles,
rationalization,
bureaucratic organization,
quantification,
the quest for records.

It is not likely that the student of Max Weber or Talcott Parsons will respond with alarm to such a list of characteristics, but very few Americans have attempted what might be called the historical sociology—or the sociological history—of sports. European scholars, especially the Germans, have been much more extensively involved in the serious study of sport as a social phenomenon. It is time to draw upon both American and European work in order to advance the discussion beyond its present boundaries.

1. THE SACRED AND THE SECULAR

Primitive cultures rarely have a word for sport in our sense.[2] If we hold strictly to our definition of sport as a nonutilitarian physical contest, we may be tempted to say that primitive men had no sports at all. Carl Diem's monumental world history of sports begins with the bold assertion, "All physical exercises were originally cultic."[3] Plentiful evidence exists to document the claim that primitive societies frequently incorporated running, jumping, throwing, wrestling, and even ball playing in their religious rituals and ceremonies.

Ethnographers have done a great deal of work on the games of the American Indians, especially of the Plains Indians who were the last to fall under the cultural influence of their conquerors. In his enormous compendium, Stewart Culin writes:[4]

Children have a variety of other amusements, such as top spinning, mimic fights, and similar imitative sports, but the games first described are played only by men and women, or youths and maidens, not by children, and usually at fixed seasons as the accompaniment of certain festivals or religious rites. . . . In general, games appear to be played ceremonially, as pleasing to the gods, with the object of securing fertility, causing rain, giving and prolonging life, expelling demons, or curing sickness.

Culin's collection of ethnographic information does not, with rare exceptions, actually elucidate the religious nature of the games, but an excellent example is available from a later account.

The Jicarilla Apaches of the Southwest used "sports" in conjunction with solar-lunar symbolism as part of a yearly fertility rite. Apache myth dramatizes the delicate balance between the two main sources of food among Plains Indians. Animal sources were associated with the sun, vegetable sources with the moon. "The sun is connected with the animal and the moon with the fruit because the sun is a man and the moon is a woman."[5] This dualistic conception of natural order is one that Claude Lévi-Strauss and many other anthropologists posit as an inevitable facet of *la pensée sauvage*. Writing about the Timbira Indians of Brazil, Käthe Hye-Kerkdal emphasizes the connection between the sport and the world-view: "Athletic contests and the dualistic social organization of primitive peoples can be characterized as two different representations of a polarized picture of the world (*eines polaren Weltbildes*)."[6] The enactment of the dualistic myth which interests us at present is a kind of relay race in which all males participated at least once between puberty and marriage. One side represented the sun, the other side the moon. The race was governed by complicated rituals. Abstinence fom meat and from sexual intercourse was required prior to the race. The track was called "the Milky Way" after the heavenly path over which the sun and the moon had originally raced. The "Milky Way" connected two circles around whose circumference small holes were dug, clockwise, into which the leaders of the two sides, praying all the while, dropped pollen. Trees were then planted in the holes. This and other rituals were accompanied by drums representing the sun and the moon, by flags, dances, songs, a feast. The race itself was on the third day of the festival, at which time a fire was ignited in the center of each circle. The boys were painted, pollened, adorned with feathers, and led to their circles by two young girls carrying an ear of corn in one hand, an eagle feather in the other (symbolizing the two sources of food). Four old men paced out the track, then came the race itself. The ceremony was clearly more important than the question of winning or losing. The leaders ran first, followed by the others in no particular order. Some ran four or five times, but everyone ran at least once. Dances and another feast followed the conclusion of the race.[7]

A second example of cultic sport is not, strictly speaking, drawn from a primitive society, because the Zulu soccer players of Durban, South Africa, are members of a transitional culture between tribal and modern social organization. Their game, soccer, is the most widespread of modern ballgames, but their perception of the game assimilates it to a way of life anything but modern. Zulu soccer teams play by the rules of the International Football Association and the desire to perform well can lead to behavior which directly violates Zulu custom. A coach or trainer, for instance, may strike an older player—a clear instance of an imperative of modern sport overriding a traditional tabu. Other aspects of the "soccer culture" are contributions of the Zulus themselves. There is a preseason and a postseason sacrifice of a goat. Pregame ritual requires that players, coaches, and dedicated supporters of the team spend the night before a game together—sleeping in a huge group around a camp fire. All are naked, but there are no sexual relations. A witch doctor, called an "Inyanga," makes incisions in the knees, elbows, and other joints of the players (very much like the medicine man in the ritual ball game of the Cherokee Indians). The players are also given a purifying emetic. On the day of the game, there is a procession, a movement in tight formation with each man touching those adjacent to him. The Inyanga administers magic potions. When the team is unsuccessful, it is the Inyanga, rather than the coach or manager, who is replaced.[8]

My examples demonstrate the concurrence of sport and religious cult, but Carl Diem's comment implies not merely the possibility but also the inevitability of this concurrence. His generalization forces an implied question upon us. Is sport among primitive peoples invariably a part of religion or is there an independent sector where sports are simply a part of secular life? The question supposes that primitive people have a secular life, which some authorities deny, arguing instead that primitive religious life was coterminus with culture. The question has a special significance in light of our preliminary paradigm of play–games–contests–sports. If we decide that sports among primitive peoples were always sacred, always part of cult, then we are forced to the somewhat curious conclusion that they had no sports at all in our sense because their physical contests were religious in nature and thus in an extended sense utilitarian. They were for an ulterior purpose—like assuring the earth's fertility—rather than for the sheer pleasure of the activity itself.

But is Diem right? I think not. From ethnographic reports we can document many instances of cultic sports, but we cannot meaningfully stretch the term "religion" to the point where all human behavior falls within the sphere of the sacred. Children wrestling or casting spears at a target? It is difficult to think of their actions as part of a cult. Although Käthe Hye-Kerkdal's account of the arduous "log-races" of the Timbira Indians of Brazil makes clear the cultic significance of many of the races, some of them seem to have been secular activities pursued for their own sake.[9] Dogmatic proclamations of negative universals ("Primitive peoples have no secular sports") are unwise. Nonetheless, Diem's overstatement contains an important truth—sports, as opposed to "physical exercises," may indeed have entered the lives of primitive adults primarily in conjunction with some form of religious significance. It is a fault of our own pervasive secularism that we tend to underestimate the cultic aspects of primitive sports.

Among the most thoroughly documented and intensively studied of all religious sports was the ball game of the Mayans and Aztecs, whose complex civilization we can classify as ancient rather than primitive. Although my subsequent discussions of ancient sports will concentrate on classical antiquity rather than on the distant pasts of China, India, and other "non-Western" cultures, the prominent place of the Mayan-Aztec ball-court game in anthropological literature, plus the intrinsic interest of the activity, justify the use of this example.

Behind the game itself was the myth of twin brothers whose names appear in various transliterations. The brothers left their mother's house in order to challenge the gods of the underworld in a game of football (actually soccer of sorts). They lost and paid the mythically predictable price of defeat—death. The head of one brother was placed in a tree, where a young girl happened upon it. From the mouth of the head spurted a stream of seeds which impregnated the girl, who removed to the house of the twin's mother, where she bore children. They grew to youthful manhood and challenged the gods at football and, again predictably, won. Whereupon the heads of the twins rose to the heavens and became the sun and the moon.[10]

The archeological evidence for this sun-moon myth can be found in the more than forty ball courts which have been located in an area stretching from Arizona to Guatamala and Honduras. Considered as symbols of the heavens, the ball courts are invariably within a temple complex, the best preserved of which is at Chichén Itzá in Yucatán. In Aztec times, the game itself was under the protection of the goddess Xochiquetzal, but the stone rings through which the ball seems to have been propelled were carved with the symbols of Quetzalcoatl, the famed plumed serpent. To these and other gods, thousands of human sacrifices were offered annually, some of them in direct connection with the ball game. Whether the losing players or the winning ones were sacrificed is unclear, but we can safely assume that the requirements of the contest *qua* contest doomed the losers rather than the winners. In either event, the archeological evidence indicates clearly that the game was quite literally for life or death. Each of the six reliefs at the great ball court of Chichén Itzá shows the decapitation of a player. On the whole, details about the actual playing of the game are meager and much disputed, but Spanish observers of the sixteenth century clearly saw the religious nature of the activity and one of them noted, "Every tennis-court was a temple."[11] The Spanish authorities banned the game—if game it was.[12]

Although Greek sports may be conceived of as the ancestors of modern sports, the physical contests of Olympia and Delphi were culturally closer to those of primitive peoples than to our own Olympics. The relative familiarity of Greek culture and the revival of specific track and field sports in our own time act to obscure fundamental similarities between the sports of the Athenians and those of the Apaches and Aztecs. The problem is only in part a lack of information. Book XXIII of the *Iliad*, containing the funeral games celebrated in honor of the slain Patroclus, is merely the first, and most important, of numerous literary texts which are the heritage of every educated person. Athletic encounters depicted on Greek vases remain a part of the aesthetic experience of Western man and Myron's *Discus Thrower* must rank among the best known statues ever sculpted. Although our knowledge of Greek sports is marked by many lacunae, the problem is less one of information than of interpretation.

The Olympic games, like the Pythian, the Isthmian, the Nemean, and the Athenaic, were sacred festivals, integral aspects of the religious life of the ancient Hellenes. In the words of one scholar, "The Olympic games were sacred games, staged in a sacred place and at a sacred festival; they were a religious act in honor of the deity. Those who took part did so in order to serve the god and the prizes which they won came from the god. . . . The Olympic games had their roots in religion."[13] The games at Olympia were in homage to Zeus. Those of Corinth—the Isthmian games—were sacred to Poseidon, while Apollo was worshipped by the runners and wrestlers of Delphi and Nemea. (See table 1.)[14]

Table 1
Greek Athletic Festivals

Festival	Place	God Honored	Branch or Wreath	Intervals (years)	Founded (B.C.)
Olympic	Olympia	Zeus	olive	4	776
Pythian	Delphi	Apollo	bay	4	582
Isthmian	Corinth	Poseidon	pine	2	582
Nemean	Nemea	Apollo	parsley	2	573

The exact history of the origins of the Olympic games is unknown and in all likelihood never will be known. It is thought that Olympia was first sacred to Gea, goddess of the earth. Greek legend told also of Pelops ("producer of abundance") and of his suitor's victory in the chariot-race against Oenomaus, father of Hippodamia. It was said that Herakles inaugurated the games at the tomb of Pelops, who was considered to have been brought back to life by the sacrifice of a boy. Defeat in an athletic contest was thus the symbolic substitute for sacrificial death. (Contemporary football coaches who liken defeat to death are better anthropologists than they realize.) Since Herakles had been a Minoan fertility god whom the conquering Greeks demoted to a demi-god and hero, the fertility myth is the common thread of every version of the founding of the games. By classical times the games were marked by a kind of syncretism—the altar of Gea remained as one of the four at Olympia, the funeral rites of Pelops were celebrated on the second day of the games, and the great sacrifice to Zeus took place on the third day. The purpose of the games remained cultic, religious. The athletic events were "held in order to persuade the god to return from the dead, to reappear in the form of a new shoot emerging from the dark womb of the earth into the light of day."[15]

The time of the games was as sacred to the Greeks as the place. The games occurred at the time of the second or third full moon after the summer solstice, and three heralds went forth to announce an Olympic truce. The athletes gathered at the nearby town of Elis and spent thirty days in final preparation for their exertions, after which came a two-day procession with much religious ceremony to the actual site on the river Eurotas. Because of the sacred nature of the games, women were excluded even as spectators, except for the priestess of Demeter. The games expanded over time from the simple stade race (one length of the stadium) in 776 B.C. to an elaborate program of foot races, chariot races, boxing, wrestling, a combination of boxing and wrestling known as the *pankration*, discus and javelin throwing. There were contests for boys as well as men and, from 396 B.C., contests for trumpeters and heralds. According to most accounts, the fifth and last day was devoted entirely to religious ceremony. There was a banquet, the gods were solemnly thanked for their sponsorship of the games, the winners were awarded olive branches cut from the sacred grove of Zeus by a boy whose two parents were still alive. The religious character of the Olympic games was never in doubt, nor was that of the other "crown" games (thus named because the victors were crowned with olive, bay, pine, or parsley wreaths).

With this information in mind we can return to the contention of Frayssinet that sports are forms of artistic expression. "The study of various Greek religious ceremonies teaches us that one can always please the gods by offering them . . . music, dance, poetry, drama and athletic contests."[16] The "crown" games, and many hundreds of local games, were indeed a way to please the gods, but this fact should not incline us to the conclusion that sports are one with music, dance, poetry, drama, and the other arts. The relationship of sport and art among the Greeks was the opposite of that suggested by Frayssinet. To the degree that Greek athletic festivals were religious ritual and artistic expression, they had a purpose beyond themselves and ceased to be sports in our strictest definition of the term. The closer the contests came to the status of art, the further they departed from that of sport.

The Olympic and other "crown" games were sacred festivals, and athletic events were often endowed with religious significance; but we can nonetheless detect among the Greeks the emergence of sports as a more or less secular phenomenon too. The remark of a German scholar is relevant. "When one speaks in this context of 'secularization,' one does not mean that an originally religious phenomenon becomes worldly but rather that an athletic game (*sportliches Spiel*), originally laden with religious significance, concentrated itself upon its own essential elements—play, exercise, competition."[17] This is what happened. Sports gradually became a part of the ordinary life of the *polis* as well as a means of worship. That Greek society generally valued physical excellence is obvious from any examination of Hellenic civilization. Cities gloried in the athletic victories of their citizens, rewarded the victors materially with large pensions and other benefits, honored them in legend, in the form of statues, and in some of the greatest poetry ever written (the Olympic odes of Pindar, for instance). Socrates, who had participated in the Isthmian games, admired physical excellence and scorned those who took no pride in their bodies. Even Plato, who never wavered from his conviction that the world of pure ideas was of a higher order than the sphere of the corporeal, had been a wrestler in his youth and had won prizes at the Pythian, Nemean, and Isthmian games. And in *The Republic* he insisted upon the importance of gymnastic exercises for both men and women. Ordinary citizens emulated the achievements of the most gifted and no city was without its athletic facilities. We can be sure that those who exercised in the gymnasium did not neglect to offer libations to the gods, but we can nonetheless detect the secularization of sport.

Roman society continued and accelerated the tendency. The Romans were given neither to athletic competitions nor to athletic festivals. They believed in physical fitness for the ulterior end of warfare. In his classic study of sports in antiquity, E. Norman Gardiner wrote, "The only athletic events which interested them at all were the fighting events, wrestling, boxing, and the pankration."[18] Roman moralists tended to mock the degeneracy of those who revealed an interest in Greek athletics. "The Greek principle of a harmonious development of the body, and a striving for bodily beauty and grace, was considered effeminate."[19] Not even Scipio Africanus, the famous conqueror of Hannibal in the Third Punic War, was immune from the verbal darts of his fellow citizens when he appeared at the gymnasium in Greek clothing. Not even the imperial prestige of Augustus was sufficient for him to establish "isolympic" games patterned on the Greek model. Such festivals as existed were usually occasions for Roman spectators to watch Greek athletes from Pergamon, Antioch, or Alexandria. More typical for Roman tastes than races or the discus were the gladiatorial combats which date from the funeral celebrations for the father of Marcus and Decimus Brutus in 264 B.C. It is common knowledge that gladiatorial spectacles reached bestial enormity by imperial times. Whatever religious significance remained was apparently overshadowed in the eyes of the mob accustomed to bread and circuses and blood.

In their secularism as in most of their other characteristics, modern sports are closer to the Roman than to the Greek model. It is, indeed, precisely this pervasive secularism which made modern sports suspect in the view of many religious leaders of the seventeenth through the nineteenth centuries. After long and stubborn opposition to the allegedly misplaced emphasis on the body symbolized in Greek athletics, both Catholicism and Protestantism have worked out a *modus vivendi*, a kind of concordat, with modern sports. Theologians now repudiate the harsh condemnations of earlier generations and blame Platonism and Neo-Platonism for the ascetic strain in traditional Christianity. Churchmen now seek eagerly to establish the harmony of modern sports and Christian doctine.[20] The Cathedral of St. John the Divine in New York has a stained-glass window depicting baseball and other modern sports, the Fellowship of Christian Athletes endeavors to leaven the hard ethos of football and basketball and hockey with the words of Jesus, and in a popular song of the 1970s, the singer asks, in a refrain, that Jesus drop kick him "through the goal-posts of life."[21]

There is, however, a fundamental difference between obligatory pregame lockerroom prayers and the worship of the gods by means of an athletic festival. For the Jicarilla Apache running between the circles of the sun and the moon or the Athenian youth racing in the stadium built above the sacred way at Delphi, the contest was in itself a religious act. For most contemporary athletes, even for those who ask for divine assistance in the game, the contest is a secular event. The Sermon on the Mount does not interfere with hard blocking and determined tackling. Religion remains on the sidelines.

Unless sports themselves take on a religious significance of their own. One of the strangest turns in the long, devious route that leads from primitive ritual to the World Series and the *Fußballweltmeisterschaft* is the proclivity of modern sports to become a kind of secular faith. Young men, and many no longer young, seem quite literally to worship the heroes of modern sports. Journalists, referring to the passion of the Welsh for rugby or the devotion of Texans to football, speak of sports as the "religion" of the populace. "Sport," says an Australian authority, "is the ultimate Australian super-religion, the one thing every Australian believes in passionately."[22] Pierre de Coubertin, founder of the modern Olympic games, spoke reverently of the "religio athletae" and the French version of Leni Riefenstahl's monumental documentary film of the 1936 Olympics was entitled *Les Dieux du stade*. Michael Novak's ecstatic homage to the joy of sports contains a reference to baseball, football, and basketball as a "holy trinity." He goes on to maintain that sports are "secular religions, civil religions. . . . The athlete may of course be pagan, but sports are, as it were, natural religions."[23] If we shift our attention from philosophic ecstasy to sophomoric irony, we can consider the name given by the students of Notre Dame University to their library's mosaic of Christ with upraised arms: "Six Points."[24]

Whether or not one considers the passions, the rituals, and the myths of modern sports as a secular religion, the fundamental contrast with primitive and ancient sports remains. The bond between the secular and the sacred has been broken, the attachment to the realm of the transcendent has been severed.[25] Modern sports are activities partly pursued for their own sake, partly for other ends which are equally secular. We do not run in order that the earth be more fertile. We till the earth, or work in our factories and offices, so that we can have time to play.

2. EQUALITY

The first distinguishing characteristic of modern sports is, therefore, that they are far more secular than primitive and ancient sports. The second characteristic of modern sports is equality in two senses of that complex concept: (1) everyone should, theoretically, have an opportunity to compete; (2) the conditions of competition should be the same for all contestants. In actual practice, there are numerous inequalities, which will occupy us at some length when we consider not the conceptual model but the contemporary state of affairs. Nonetheless, the principle is clear. Modern sports assume equality. For primitive societies, however, participation is likely to be on the basis of membership in a caste or kinship group. In Max Weber's classic formulation, ascription rather than achievement governs. For the Jicarilla rite described earlier, whether or not a young man has reached puberty is decisive, not his swiftness of foot. The young girls who accompany the runners to the circles of the sun and moon must be virgins, a status indifferent to the achievement principle.

The relationship between equality and the achievement principle is a vital one.[26] Swiftness of foot and strength of hand are less relevant for primitive sports than membership in the proper group, because these sports are often not really contests at all. In many of them, the outcome is determined by religious necessity, not by athletic ability. There is no need to guarantee everyone a chance to "make the team," because the team was made aeons ago, by the gods, who divided the village into two opposed moieties. There is no need to equalize the conditions of competition, because the outcome too was more likely than not determined by the gods rather than by the relative skill of the participants. The dominance of ascription over achievement is rarely complete. When the wrestlers of two clans approach each other and grapple, they are presumably involved in a struggle for physical mastery as well as in a complex religious ceremony, but we must be attentive; they crack their sinews because the gods demand the effort—even when both of them know that one of them is destined to win.

Examples are helpful and Raymond Firth has provided us with a classic one. Among the Polynesians there was a kind of sacred dart or spear game known variously as *teka* (Maori), *tika* (Samoan), or *tinga* (Fijian). *Tapu* ("sacredness") belonged to the game, which was probably a fertility rite. The two sides consisted of approximately twelve to twenty players each, drawn from families and clans so that a man was invariably on one side or the other. Curiously, the two sides are denominated "bachelors" and "married men" although both sides are now (i.e., at the time of Firth's visit) actually constituted without regard to marital status. It is apparent that the fertility rite which originally governed the selection of the sides had, by 1930, faded from prominence. It is also clear that the new principle of selection was based on ascription rather than on some notion of equal competition like that embodied in the technique known to every modern child— choosing sides by letting the two captains pick in turn until the talent has been allotted.[27]

Just as the Zulus of Durban exemplify a curious mixture of primitive and modern traits in their approach to football, so do the Eskimos of Point Hope in Alaska enable us to see the contrast between teams chosen by ascription and by achievement. Although the Eskimos of the village speak English, worship in the Episcopalian Church, wear more American than traditional clothing, and seem greatly to enjoy the game of baseball, which they play by modern rules, they have also preserved their fondness for an older game roughly like soccer. In this traditional football game, the goals are several hundred yards apart and the ball is kicked across the goal (not into a net). Men, women, and children play and the sides are made up of the "land people" versus the "point or sea people." The land people kick the ball toward the sea, which lies to the west of the village, and the sea people kick the ball landwards. It is, of course, the kinship system that divided the players into land and sea people. Finally, according to the old rules, only elderly men and women were entitled to pick the ball up and throw it. Age has its compensations, at least in this primitive society.[28]

Among the ancient Greeks, achievement counted for more and ascription for less than among primitive peoples, but it was by no means assumed that everyone should be allowed to compete. The elegies of the poet Propertius and statues now standing in the Louvre, the Vatican Museum, and the National Museum in Athens prove that Greek art did not totally neglect female athletes, but women were barred from Olympia and most other games. When women did compete, it was separately, as at the Heraean games which followed the far more important Olympic festival. Similarly, Greek sports were closed to slaves and to "barbarians," i.e., to all who were not Greek. Within these parameters, however, each man—no matter what his social rank—was free to prove himself a worthy competitor at his chosen event. The classical scholars M. I. Finley and H. W. Pleket indicate how extraordinary this equality was: "Every competitor had the same formal rights, under the same rules, and could claim the prize if he won; only his own skill and strength mattered. In a world of built-in inequalities, that was a significant rarity."[29] Legend has it, probably wrongly, that the first winner at the earliest recorded Olympic celebration in 776 B.C. was a cook.[30]

Equality of the conditions of competition was important to the Greeks and they went to considerable trouble to avoid certain inequalities. Men were separated from boys on the basis of size and physical maturity rather than chronological age. A boy who had matured rapidly competed among the men and not among the ephebes, against whom he might have had an unfair advantage. The finest example of the concern for fair competition is probably in the matter of oiling and dusting. All Greek athletes rubbed themselves with olive oil before the contest. Wrestlers were then sprinkled with a fine powder, to make the struggle something other than a slippery mismatch. To insure that neither wrestler had the advantage of an undusted patch of skin, they sprinkled each other. Curiously, however, the Greeks did *not* divide wrestlers or boxers into classes by weight or size, as we do.

During the events of an athletic festival, officials watched for possible unfairness, which they apparently punished forthwith. Numerous vases contain pictures of the officials whipping athletes who had committed an infraction of the rules. Needless to say, primitive sports, with their frequent lack of emphasis on winning or losing, were supervised by ritual adepts rather than by officials.

To the degree that Roman athletic sports were modeled on Greek, they accepted the principle of equality of terms of competition, but it is apparent that gladiatorial contests were organized on different principles. In the arena, swordsmen fought men armed with nets and tridents, men fought animals, and the audience lusted for ever more improbable encounters which depraved emperors hastened to provide. In 90 A.D., the emperor Domitian titillated the populace with a combat of dwarves against women.[31] By this date, the gladiators were almost always slaves rather than citizens, a complete reversal of the Greek view of participation.

The Roman fondness for inequality in gladiatorial combats provides us with an unexpected clue to the status of such different sports as bull-fighting and mountain-climbing. The first sport is very old. Murals discovered by Sir Arthur Evans in ancient Crete depict a kind of acrobatic bull-fight which was probably a part of religious ritual.[32] The second sport is startlingly recent—the Alpine Club of London was founded in 1857 and the Matterhorn was first scaled in 1865—and apparently without conventional religious connotations. Neither sport makes any pretense of equality of conditions of competition. If we imagine the contest to be one of man against nature in the form of the charging bull or the forbidding peak, then the inequality is obvious. If we take a more abstract view and imagine the contest to be a mediated one of man against man, both tested by the same natural difficulty, it is equally obvious that the natural difficulty is not always the same. Some bulls are less fierce than others. Even when the same face of the same mountain is scaled, the conditions change with the weather, with the season. And the glory harvested by a first ascent can never be repeated by subsequent climbers, who must find new peaks to conquer.

There is little doubt that modern sports now embody the principle of equality, which is carried far beyond the point reached by the Greeks. Theorists can comfortably assert that sports are rationally organized "on the basis of the universalistic criterion of achievement," but the tenet of equal access to the contest has consistently limped behind the much more completely institutionalized tenet of equal conditions of competition.[33] Because our present confusions apropos of the amateur rule derive from medieval notions beyond which even Greek sports had evolved, it is necessary to look attentively at the slow development of the tenet of equal access to the contest.

In medieval times, jousts and tournaments were limited to the nobility. Knights who sullied their honor by inferior marriages—to peasant girls, for instance—were disbarred. If they were bold enough to enter a tournament despite their loss of status, and were discovered, they were beaten and their weapons were broken. Peasants reckless enough to emulate the sport of their masters were punished by death.

In the evolution of medieval society toward modern modes of organization, the strict inequality of feudal sports lingered on. The game of court-tennis—an ancestor of our lawn-tennis—was forbidden to servants and laborers in 1388 and in 1410.[34] The game was an aristocratic and regal passion. Henry VIII had his private facilities at Hampton Court. In this instance, class clearly mattered more than sex, for women were not excluded and a certain Margot de Hainault was mentioned in 1427 as superior to the best male tennis-players of Paris.[35] In 1541, six years after Henry VIII repeated the decree restricting tennis to noblemen and property-owners, bowling was prohibited except for noblemen and those "having manors, lands or tenements, to the yearly value of one hundred pounds or above."[36] James I repeated the ban in 1618. Feudal restraints were found even in the colonies. In Virginia in 1674, a tailor was fined because he dared to race his horse against a gentleman's.[37] Nor can we say that class restrictions are wholly absent from our own society. In the regulations for the Henley Regatta of 1879, we read, "No person shall be considered an amateur oarsman or sculler . . . Who is or has been by trade or employment for wages, a mechanic, artisan, or laborer."[38] (Among those excluded from Henley was the father of Princess Grace of Monaco.)

In an unusually fine essay, Eric Dunning and Kenneth Sheard have analyzed the split in British sport which took place in 1895 when dissident clubs of the Rugby Football Union broke away and formed the openly professional Rugby League. The immediate conflict was over the rigid amateurism of the Rugby Football Union, which not only banned cash payments for time lost from work but also threatened to expel players or clubs receiving medals. The deeper disagreement was, however, on the nature of sport as a social institution. The bitterness of the controversy derived largely from upper-class and upper-middle-class fears that "their" game was falling into the hands of lower-middle-class elements, especially in the industrial north of England. "In other words, even though the public school élite tended to rationalize their ethos in sport-specific terms and claimed they were interested solely in preserving the 'essential character' of sport, class and regional hostility and resentment over the loss of their erstwhile dominance played an important part."[39] The amateur rule was an instrument of class warfare.

An American observer of 1895 found the class divisions of English sport perfectly sound:[40]

Why there should be such constant strife to bring together in sport the two divergent elements of society that never by any chance meet elsewhere on even terms is quite incomprehensible, and it is altogether the sole cause of all our athletic woe. . . . The laboring class are all right in their way; let them go their way in peace, and have their athletics in whatsoever manner best suits their inclinations. . . . Let us have our own sport among the more refined elements, and allow no discordant spirits to enter into it.

As late as 1960, an English authority defended the exclusion of mechanics, artisans, and laborers as "the only way to keep the sport pure from the elements of corruption. . . . It is argued, with much show of truth, that the average workman has no idea of sport for its own sake."[41]

The attempt to limit sports to gentlemen of means still survives in the anachronistic amateur rule. The rule derives partly from medieval conceptions of social hierarchy, partly from the Renaissance ideal of the courtier who was skilled at many activities but supreme (by dint of hard practice) at none of them, partly—as we have seen—from the class relationships of nineteenth-century society. Since no one seriously contends today that participation in sports should be limited by class membership, the first and third of these justifications for the amateur rule are ludicrously inapropos. The second justification, rooted in the notion that someone who simply seeks diversion at an activity should not be asked to compete with someone else for whom it is a way of life, is much more difficult to deal with. One might argue that the exclusion of the highly trained and specialized athlete preserves equality of competition, but this argument is specious because (1) it is exactly this inequality of athletic ability that sports are all about in the first place and (2) the present amateur rule does not exclude the highly trained and specialized but rather those who openly receive payments in money. It is certain that the criterion of pecuniary compensation does not distinguish between those who devote a moderate portion of their lives to sports and those for whom sport has become a way of life. There is no way in which the present amateur rule enhances equality in what the Germans call *Höchstleistungssport* ("sport at the highest level of achievement"). Western nations must eventually abolish the amateur-professional distinction in its present form because it has long since become anachronistic and because it is corroded by hypocrisy and mocked by the practice of Communist nations whose "amateurs" devote at least as much time to sports as do our "professionals."

Exclusion on the basis of class is clearly an anomaly within the structure of modern sports. Exclusion on the basis of race is just as clearly anomalous. It is, nonetheless, common knowledge that racism has hindered the development of modern sports in the United States, South Africa, and many other countries. Although fourteen of the fifteen jockeys who rode in the first Kentucky Derby of 1875 were Negroes, blacks were soon forced out of this profitable occupation, from which they continue to be almost completely blocked. Although numerous blacks boxed well enough to have been contenders for the heavyweight championship, it was not until Jack Johnson's defeat of Tommy Burns in 1908 that the color bar was lowered enough to allow a black fighter to compete for the mantle of John L. Sullivan, Gentleman Jim Corbett, and Bob Fitzsimmons. Although

Moses Fleetwood Walker and several other blacks played in professional baseball in the 1880s, Negroes were gradually excluded and
left with no alternative but to begin their own leagues, which flourished, floundered, and rose again from dormancy until the memora-
ble moment in 1947 when Jackie Robinson stepped onto the field to
play ball for the Brooklyn Dodgers. Although William H. Lewis and
William Tecumseh Sherman Jackson played football for Amherst
College in the 1890s, the National Football League rejected black
athletes until the 1940s.[42]

By 1970, 24.5 percent of all major-league baseball players, 33.7
percent of all NFL football players, and 54.3 percent of the National
Basketball Association were black.[43] Afro-Americans earned more
money on the average than their white counterparts, but discrimination and inequality remained in forms more subtle than lower pay
or outright exclusion. Black athletes still find themselves "stacked"
into certain positions (outfielders in baseball, running backs in football) and they seldom have opportunities to move into managerial
positions.[44] They also continue to be underpaid in proportion to their
ability.[45] Nonetheless, compared to the situation in the 1920s—the
so-called "Golden Age of Sports"—the importance of race has dimin-
ished. Under intermittent pressure from abroad, there have also been
changes in South African sport, which had been even more exclu-
sionist than American in that blacks and whites had been prevented
from mixed competition either in South Africa or abroad.[46]

Although Jews are not really a race, Nazi policy considered them
to be one and the possible exclusion of Jews from the Olympic games
of 1936 became a heated political controversy in the years just prior
to the games. Rather devious political maneuvering on the part of
Avery Brundage prevented the AAU from carrying out a threatened
boycott, and outright duplicity on the part of the Nazis enabled them
to promise to allow German Jews to try out for their team and then to
bar all except the fencer Helene Meyer who, as a "half-Jew," still had
German citizenship. Among those excluded was Gretel Bergmann, a
highjumper who had come within an inch of the world's record; her
best of 1.6 meters was ignored and Elfriede Kaun, who cleared 1.54
meters was chosen in her place.[47]

Exclusion on the basis of sex has been the third anachronism preventing the emergence of modern sport in its pure form. Although men's greater physical strength and quicker reaction time (from age five to age fifty-five) make direct competition with women unsuitable in many sports, the logic of the development of modern sports demands at the very least that women be granted separate-but-equal opportunity for involvement in sports. In actual practice, the exclusion of women from sports, i.e., from physical contests as opposed to physical education or play, has lasted longer than the exclusion of blacks. The first gymnastic facility for German women was established in 1832, but the first important gymnastics competition was staged in 1913.[48] As late as 1909, Prussian girls who contested the highjump and the longjump were judged for their grace and style as well as for height and distance.[49] Pierre de Coubertin opposed female participation in the Olympics and they were barred from official competition in most sports until the swimmers were admitted in 1912 and the track-and-field athletes in 1928. Weighing the pros and cons of "Olympics for girls," a contributor to *School and Society* wrote in 1929 that competition is natural to males but, "In woman it is profoundly unnatural." The author was opposed to the "masculinization" of girls. "Natural feminine health and attractiveness, whether physical, emotional or social, certainly are impaired if not destroyed by the belligerent attitudes and competitive spirit . . . which intense athletics inevitably fosters."[50] In 1930, the Women's Division of the National Amateur Athletic Federation petitioned the International Olympic Committee and requested that women be dropped from the program for 1932.[51] In the view of the Women's Division, such strenuous athletic contests were physically and psychologically unhealthy.

The prejudice against women athletes derived from Victorian attitudes about porcelain-doll femininity rather than from the fearful kind of discrimination that barred blacks from competition with whites. It was not direct hostility against women so much as overprotectiveness. A leading German scholar opined in 1853 that an "Amazon-like physical development runs directly counter to the true concept of womanly worth and grace."[52] More than a century later, a prominent British sportswriter and novelist came to the same conclusion.[53] It will probably be at least another generation before the term "Amazon" drops out of use as a pejorative term for athletic women.

There were women, even in the 1890s, determined to defy conventions of femininity and to urge competitive athletics for women, but female coaches and administrators of women's sports were frequently among the sharpest critics of women's involvement in real contests.[54] In 1922, the Women's Division favored "Play Days" and "Sports Days" rather than intercollegiate meets, i.e., gala gatherings with more emphasis on sociability than on athletic achievement. Gradually, in the 1950s and 1960s, the women in charge of women's sports began to accept the idea of intercollegiate and even of national competition. The founding of the Association for Intercollegiate Athletics for Women (1971) may be considered a sign that most female coaches and physical-education administrators have decided to accept if not actively to promote the principle of equal access to competitive sports. Changes in attitudes have been accompanied by changes in the law. The Equal Opportunity Act of 1972 empowered enforcement of Title VII of the Civil Rights Act of 1964 and Title IX of the Education Act of 1972 outlawed sex bias in education, including physical education. Legal action has opened the Boston Marathon to women and has brought men's and women's physical-education budgets somewhat closer to parity—so that men's sports now rarely receive fifty times what women's sports receive at the same university or in the same school district.[55]

In the Communist societies of Eastern Europe, the effort to achieve equality for women's sports has from the first been a matter of governmental policy. Despite official propaganda and the availability of facilities attached to factories and offices, the actual rate of participation for ordinary women is approximately the same as in Western societies—the male-female participation ratio is rarely lower than 2–1.[56] At the international level, however, the extraordinary accomplishments in women's gymnastics, in track and field, rowing, and swimming, amply demonstrate the possibilities of modern sports for women as equality of opportunity is realized.

The stellar achievements of Colette Besson, Billie Jean King, and Kornelia Ender remind us that equality of opportunity is not the same as equality of results. When *all* have had their chance, we shall know who is the best of all. In fact, the more equal the chance to participate, the more unequal the results will be. For men and for women, the distance between the ordinary athlete and the international champion is greater every year. There is an irony here which Günther Lüschen has expressed well: "While everywhere else in the modern world . . . there is at least an ideological tendency towards the elimination of social rank, sport contains an element of hierarchical social differentiation whose precise and objective gradations are scarcely to be found in any other ranking system."[57] Inequality of results is an essential characteristic of modern sports, which is often used to justify inequality in other areas, like education, where there is less equality of opportunity and in the conditions of competition.

3. SPECIALIZATION

Whatever may have been the case among the earliest men, primitive societies known to modern ethnography show elements of specialization of function. The specialization of New Guinean sports is different from that of the National Football League, but the difference is one of degree. Still, the difference is remarkable.

In fact, the difference between the sports of primitive societies and the athletics of classical antiquity is nearly as remarkable. It did not take the Greeks long to discover that some men were physically equipped to run and others to wrestle or throw the discus. "Before the close of the fifth century," wrote E. Norman Gardiner, "the excessive prominence given to bodily excellence and athletic success had produced specialization and professionalism."[58] The combination of prowess demonstrated by the pentathlon was in itself an indication that there were different specialties to be combined in a single test of more general ability. In the long course of Greek civilization, specialization did indeed lead to professionalization in the sense that athletes were officially remunerated and in the more important sense that they were able to devote themselves fully to their sports. Amply provided for by their enthusiastic fellow citizens, the athletes were freed from economic necessity and encouraged to make the most of their physical talents. Athletic festivals came to be dominated by professionals whom traditionalists like the dramatist Euripides abhorred. In his fragment *Autolycus,* he raged:[59]

Of all the countless evils throughout Hellas none is worse than the race of athletes. . . . Slaves of their belly and their jaw they know not how to live well. . . . In youth they strut about in splendor, the idols of the city, but when bitter old age comes upon them they are cast aside like worn-out cloaks.

The dramatist's disgust, aimed partly it seems at the ingratitude of the citizens vis-à-vis the ex-athlete, did no more than satire ever has to arrest the progressive professionalization of athletics. Five centuries later, in second-century Pergamon, the medical philosopher Galen was even more emphatic on the subject of professionalism:[60]

Beneath their mass of flesh and blood their souls are stifled as in a sea of mud. . . . They have not health nor have they beauty. Even those who are naturally well proportioned become fat and bloated: their faces are often shapeless and unsightly owing to the wounds received in boxing and in the pankration. They lose their eyes and their teeth and their limbs are strained.

Throughout the Roman Empire, the ubiquity of athletic professionalism helped to reduce the status of sports among moralists and philosophers, not because it was ignoble to receive money but because specialization distorted the many-sided development of the citizen. But there is no reason to think that the thousands who jammed the Circus Maximus in Rome to cheer on their favorite charioteer did not react as worshipfully as the contemporary millions who idolize Pelé, George Best, Franz Beckenbauer, and the other heroes of modern sport.

The sports of the medieval and early modern periods were probably a good deal less specialized than those of Roman times. The Renaissance ideal of the courtier, as propagated by Baldissare Castiglione and others, emphasized the harmonic cultivation of many skills rather than the intense concentration upon a single strength. Among the peasantry, specialization probably went no further than the selection of the physically powerful to represent the group at wrestling or lifting. The undifferentiatedness of medieval sports is especially clear in the village game which eventually became modern soccer.

In medieval football, there was room for everyone and a sharply defined role for no one. The game was played by the entire village or, more likely still, by one village against another. Men, women, and children rushed to kick the ball and the devil took the hindmost. From the vantage point of a church tower, the players must have looked like a swarm of bees as they battled fiercely for possession of the ball. In a fine article, Eric Dunning comments on the marked lack of specialization in what he calls the "folk-games" of the medieval and early modern periods:[61]

These games were relatively undifferentiated in the following three respects: (1) elements of what later became highly specialized games such as rugby, soccer, hockey, boxing, wrestling, and polo were often contained in a single game; (2) there was little division of labor among the players; and (3) no attempt was made to draw a hard and fast distinction between playing and spectating roles.

The Middle Ages had their acrobats and tumblers and *jongleurs*, but they were not a period of athletic specialization.

What a contrast we see in modern sports! American football players are divided into twenty-two positions, not counting the "special" teams, which are restricted to placekicks, kickoffs, kickoff receptions, etc. An exchange of roles is possible but not common. A defensive lineman occasionally intercepts a forward pass and lumbers goalward in a moment of glory, but he quickly resumes his accustomed role. What is true of football is true of other modern sports. Baseball is an interesting example. Characterized from its invention in 1845 by a division of labor into nine separate playing positions, the game, at least in the American League, has recently edged toward a still higher degree of specialization akin to that found in football—the pitcher has become exclusively defensive and has been replaced offensively by the Designated Hitter. Will baseball eventually evolve into football's two-platoon system? Traditionalists shudder, but the natural interruption between halves of innings allows the possibility and the entire thrust of modern sports suggests that the possibility will one day be acted upon.

Specialization upon the modern field of play is paralleled by an intricate system of supportive personnel. Sociologists speak of primary, secondary, and tertiary involvement and discuss the roles of owners, managers, coaches, trainers, scouts, doctors, recruiters, referees and umpires, schedulers, linesmen, groundsmen, ticket-takers, pop-corn sellers, spectators, journalists, and even sports sociologists. Intercollegiate athletics, which began when students from Oxford and Cambridge and Harvard and Yale and Amherst and Williams began to challenge each other in rowing, rugby, and baseball, now involve departments of physical education and athletics staffed by a myriad of professionals trained in special graduate programs in sports administration.

Given the internal logic of modern sports, specialization and professionalization are inevitable. To an extent, they are the same thing. As we indicated in our comments on equality and the amateur rule, the crucial factor in professionalization is not money but time—how much of a person's life is dedicated to the achievement of athletic excellence? In other words, to what degree does a person specialize in such excellence? Since athletic achievement in a variety of sports is increasingly incompatible with top-level performance in any one of them, specialization tends to be narrower and narrower. Although I shall continue to defer to common usage and employ the term "professional" to describe those who openly receive pecuniary compensation, the professional is, in fact, any athlete specialized to the point where some single athletic excellence is for some extended period of time his main purpose in life. There are thoughtful arguments to the effect that we should consider those who pursue sports for the pleasure of the activity to be amateurs and those motivated by ulterior ends as professionals, but we have preferred to make this distinction the basic theoretical one between play of all kinds and the world of work.[62]

Specialization results from the characteristically modern stress on achievement which leads, in turn, to the desire to liberate the athlete from the bothersome, distracting details of economic necessity, whether this liberation is by means of a wealthy parent, a generous patron, an athletic scholarship, a government grant, or a straight salary. Despite the *Sturm und Drang* of the tedious controversies over the amateur rule, the plain fact is that world-class competition is usually incompatible with an ordinary vocation. *Someone* has to pay for Dorothy Hamill's icy figures and for Fran Tarkenton's scrambled patterns.

4. RATIONALIZATION

There must be rules of competition, even in the most primitive sports, simply because sports are by definition games, i.e., organized, rule-bound play. One might even plausibly argue that the ritual race of the Apaches had more rules and stricter enforcement than a modern game of soccer played by a group of schoolboys. Anthropologists have, after all, long since modified the Rousseauian notion of the perfect freedom of the Noble Savage; we realize that the primitive world is often one of totem and tabu, with hundreds of limitations and restraints. What sets the rules of modern sports aside from those of primitive peoples is less the number of rules than their nature. The origin and status of the rules are different. Modern games are rationalized in Max Weber's sense of *Zweckrationalität*, i.e., there is a logical relationship between means and ends. In order to do this, we have to do that. The rules of the game are perceived by us as means to an end. More importantly, new rules are invented and old ones discarded whenever the participants decide that ludic convenience outweighs the inertia of convention. The rules are cultural artifacts and not divine instructions. All parties to the scholarly disputes about the nature of the Mayan-Aztec ball games assume that the rules were traditional and sacred. Their origin was obviously unknown. They were not changed at yearly congresses called for that purpose.

Consider, in contrast, the invention of basketball by James Naismith on December 21, 1891, at the Y.M.C.A.'s training facilities in Springfield, Massachusetts. The very fact that we can name the inventor, the date, and the place signals the modernity of the game. Naismith responded to a challenge from Luther Gulick, head of the International Training School. Young people needed some sort of winter game that might be played indoors. Naismith experimented with various possibilities and then came up with basketball.[63]

His invention was an instant success. His colleague, the soon-to-be-famous Amos Alonzo Stagg, introduced the game to the University of Chicago in 1893. That same year, W. O. Black took the game to Stanford. The first intercollegiate game (Hamline College versus the Minnesota School of Agriculture) was played in February 1895. The following year, the Y.M.C.A. had a national tournament. By

1901 there was an intercollegiate league. Five years earlier, the
Y.M.C.A. had introduced the game to China. By 1915, it was popular in every modern society, and in many not so modern ones.

In this period of amazingly rapid ludic diffusion, the game was
continually transformed, one might even say tinkered with, with all
the connotations of Eli Whitney, Thomas Edison, and Henry Ford.
Naismith's first teams consisted of nine men each because his physical-education class had eighteen students. Within five years, five-
man teams became the norm. The pivot was allowed in 1893 and the
dribble in 1896 (although the dribbler wasn't allowed to shoot from
1901 to 1908). The wild scrambles for out-of-bounds balls ended in
1913 when the present rule was introduced to bring the ball back into
play. But a rule-by-rule account of the major transformations and the
minor adjustments of the game is unnecessary. The point is significant but simple. The game was a conscious invention, a cultural ar-
tifact to be designed, used, redesigned. Basketball represents the
triumph of ludic rationality.

The rules are, moreover, universal. The rules are now more complicated than on that marvelous December day when the inventive
Mr. Naismith nailed the peachbaskets to opposite ends of the Springfield gymnasium, but these complicated rules are accepted everywhere. The rules of the Polynesian dart game are also complicated
but they vary from place to place, whereas the rules of basketball are
basically the same in Tashkent and Topeka.

How does the well-known superstitiousness of many professional
athletes relate to this pronounced emphasis on rationality? If we continue to draw examples, for the moment, from basketball, we observe
that one of the game's most famous and successful coaches, UCLA's
John Wooden, performed an invariant pregame ritual. Before every
contest, he won the favor of the gods by turning to wink at his wife
(who always attended the game and always sat behind him), by pat-
ting the knee of his assistant coach, by tugging at his socks, and by
leaning over to tap the floor. No one can maintain that this ritual
represents a rationalistic approach to sports, but one must note that
Wooden's odd behavior did not interfere with the course of the game.
Had his superstition violated the canons of rationality relevant to the
game itself, had he, for instance, chosen his starting players on the

basis of their zodiacal signs, it is difficult to believe that the UCLA Bruins would have won seven straight NCAA championships.

Basketball was created as a modern sport. It is instructive to consider how hunting, which is a premodern sport, became archery, which is now thoroughly modern. Rationalization is the key. Hunting began, of course, as a utilitarian occupation. We can safely assume that cave men pursuing their prey with stones or clubs or spears thought more of their larders than of the pleasures of the chase. But hunting became a sport in Assyria and in Egypt, in China and in India, in Greece and in Rome, in every ancient civilization. It was the most popular aristocratic sport in the Middle Ages and it continues to attract followers from every class. Like bull-fighting, hunting tends to ignore the principle of equality of the conditions of competition. The lion-hunter has more prestige than the farm boy who bangs away at squirrels and lions are by no means all alike. My lion was fiercer than your lion and was shot under more dangerous circumstances. Whatever George Orwell may have said in *Animal Farm*, all animals are not equal. How shall we transform hunting into a modern sport? The answer, of course, is to create an "animal" which symbolizes the equality of all animals, i.e., a target. The target is of a standard size. It stands in one spot and it does not roar. With the target, we can rationalize hunting into archery or pistol-shooting. Rationalization is the key to the development of all sports which utilize a target. Shooting at a bull may be more satisfying than shooting at a bull's eye, but it is less modern. A similar rationalizing process has turned the cavalryman's prancing mount into the gymnast's horse.

In respect to the rationalization of the rules, Greek sports lay somewhere between primitive and modern habits. Despite the best efforts of classical scholars, we still know less than we would like about the rules of Greek and Roman sports. There is, for instance, a variety of explanations of the scoring system for the pentathlon and the leading authority on the subject has recently revised his earlier views.[64] There is, however, one aspect of rationalization which nicely illuminates the cultural difference between antiquity and modern society. As indicated earlier in the brief discussion of equality in the conditions of competition, Greek athletes competing directly against one

another probably used the same discus or javelin. But the standard-
ization of equipment stopped at precisely that point. The discus
hurled at Delphi in honor of Apollo was not the same size and
weight as that flung at Athens in honor of the goddess. In fact, the di-
ameters of discuses which have come down to us vary from 5.5
inches to 13.5 inches and the weights from 3 to 15 pounds. The
stade race was standard at athletic festivals, but the "stade" was not an
invariant length. We know that a 400-meter track in Montreal is—
within a few centimeters—the same length as one in Munich or
Moscow, but the Greek stade varied from festival to festival. At
Olympia, the stade was 192.27 meters, at Delphi 177.5 meters, at
Epidaurus 181.3 meters, and at Pergamon 210 meters. The Greeks,
and certainly the Romans, were technologically sophisticated enough
to have standardized these distances, but they chose not to.

The Greeks did rationalize sports in another way. They seem to
have been the first people more or less scientifically to study the techniques of athletic events and to explore the physiological basis of
achievement. Other peoples produced manuals and accumulated
lore, but the Greeks generated a whole branch of science, now
mostly lost, that parallels our own production of manuals, guides,
and scholarly papers in sports medicine and sports psychology. A
comment by Aristotle is especially revealing: "We argue about the
navigation of ships more than about the training of athletes, because
[navigation] has been less well organized as a science."[65]

Although the boys' games of primitive peoples include physical activities which prepare them for the adult roles of hunter and warrior,
primitive adults do not seem to practice in order to improve their
hunting skills. The Ifugao of the Philippine Islands "thinks he hits or
misses according to the will of his gods and the forces of magic. From
the time he was a boy, he does not practice his spear-throwing,
makes no effort even to keep in form. Almost all the practice he gets,
his whole life long, is from the throwing" in boyhood and youth.[66]
The Greeks did more than practice. They trained. The distinction is
important. Training implies a rationalization of the whole enterprise,
a willingness to experiment, a constant testing of results achieved.
For the athlete, there was a special diet with much more meat than
was customary. There was the tetrad or four-day cycle of preparation,

concentration, relaxation, moderation (i.e., easy exercises, strenuous effort, recovery, technical exercises). There was a whole way of life concentrated on the single goal of athletic excellence.

We have taken what they initiated and have, in our usual way, gone to what sometimes seems like an extreme. The scientific study of physiology and psychology in the university provides us with technical information to be utilized by coaches and trainers. In the United States, the relationship between scientific research and actual *praxis* is relatively informal. The results of laboratory investigation are published in monographs or in special journals like the *Research Quarterly* where the information is available for those who wish to apply it. For decades coaches ignored scientific studies which demonstrated that weight-training did not render athletes "muscle-bound." Today, however, coaches who seek to "keep up" lecture ten-year-old hockey players on the relative merits of aerobic and anaerobic exercises. In Germany and in Eastern Europe generally, the scientific study of sports is rationalized to an even greater extent than in America. There are special institutes to carry on research and the application of scientific discoveries to training schedules and to athletic events is much quicker than here. One reason for the astonishing success of East Germany at the 1976 Olympics was that physiological research is taken more seriously than in the United States. Their *Sportwissenschaftler* are able to identify prospective champions, to isolate them for intensive training, and to prepare them psychologically for the moment of competition. Kornelia Ender's potential as a champion swimmer, for instance, was first discovered by means of a blood test. There has been a reaction against the ruthlessly rationalized training of athletes, who have been described by some as "robots," but there is an unquestionable line of development here which extends from the first manuals of ancient Greece through Renaissance books on the art of fencing to the complex facilities of Leipzig, Prague, Warsaw, and Moscow. West Germany's efforts rival those of the Communist countries, and the United States will almost inevitably strive to close this new "gap." It is highly unlikely that the tendency toward increased rationalization will be halted by the protests of men and women who cherish the day when sports were avocations.

5. BUREAUCRATIZATION

Who in actual practice decides the rules of modern sports and who administers the complicated system of research? The answer is obvious. A bureaucratic organization. Once again, we need but to remind ourselves of Max Weber's analysis of the distinctions between a primitive hierarchy of prescribed behavior and a modern bureaucracy of functional roles. We can be sure that the rules of primitive sports changed slowly and that the changes were probably introduced by ritual adepts. Sportswriters today may refer to the heads of the National Football League or the National Collegiate Athletic Association or the Fédération Internationale de Natation as the "high priests" of sports, but the insult is metaphorical. Alvin "Pete" Rozelle, Willi Daume, and even Lord Killanin of the International Olympic Committee are elected administrators of extensive bureaucratic organizations. One of their many functions is to see that the rules of the game really are universal.

Needless to say, primitive societies are not characterized by bureaucratic organizations of any kind, let alone a sports bureaucracy. Once again, we can turn to the Greeks for intimations of the modern. Prolific as they were of institutional forms, they may be said to have had a nascent form of sports bureaucracy. The Athenians and others with democratic tendencies elected officials or selected them by lot. Each Greek city had its *gymnasiarch* or ruler of the gymnasium. Athletic competitions were usually administered by an *agonathete*. How much of the administration remained in priestly as opposed to secular hands is hard to say. What is certain is that the germs of sport bureaucracy flowered in Roman times. The most famous administrator was Herodes Atticus, whom the emperor Hadrian appointed as *athlothete*, who endowed the great stadium in Athens.[67] It was, incidentally, this stadium which the Greeks renovated in order to stage the first of the modern Olympic games in 1896.

The most remarkable form of Roman sports bureaucracy was the guild or *xystos* (note the frequency of Greek terms) of athletes, an organization imperial in scope, with elected leadership, detailed rules and regulations, entrance requirements, codes of proper conduct, and even the material paraphernalia—like membership certificates—that we associate with modern sports administration.

The absense of bureaucratic organization among primitive peoples and its presence among the Romans should astonish no one, but the ubiquity of such administrative forms in every modern society ought to give one more pause than it generally does. As in many areas, England led the way. The Marylebone Cricket Club, founded in 1787, gradually became the ultimate authority in all matters pertaining to cricket. By the early nineteenth century, the MCC had successfully standardized the game, with precise regulations for the weight of the ball, the width of the bat, the distance between wickets, the dimensions of the wicket, etc.

Except for anomalies like baseball and American football, every major modern sport has its international organization which, in turn, supervises dozens of national affiliates. The first of these was the Union Internationale de Courses de Yacht (1875). By 1959, there were seventy-three such organizations, the strongest of which, the Fédération Internationale de Football Association (FIFA) had, in 1964, 126 national organizations as members.[68] The international federations cooperate closely with the International Olympic Committee and the various national Olympic committees. There are, of course, numerous occasions for jurisdictional squabbles and ugly confrontations as well, but the point is that there is an intricate bureaucratic web covering the globe.

The first national sports organizations were born in the middle of the nineteenth century, in England. By the end of the century, international organizations proliferated, and the International Olympic Committee had been born (in 1894). In the twentieth century, almost every modern nation has created a governmental sports bureaucracy to aid, abet, regulate, or replace the voluntary associations of the nineteenth century. Even Czarist Russia had its Office of the General Supervisor for the Physical Development of the Peoples of Russia.[69] Here, the United States is once again exceptional in that we have no Minister of Sports, nor, it must be added, are our amateur athletes governed by a single voluntary association. It is, however, all but certain that a single governing authority, private or public, will soon emerge. The recent report of the Presidential Commission on Olympic Sports (1977) is a step in that direction.

One of the most important functions of the bureaucracy is to see that the rules and regulations are universal. Another is to facilitate a network of competitions that usually progress from local contests through national to world championships. Of more immediate interest is still another function of sports associations, namely, the ratification of records. The International Amateur Athletic Federation (IAAF) was founded in 1913 and began in the very next year to publish its official list of world records.[70] But the very concept of a record, which is the last and most uniquely modern characteristic of modern sports, depends upon the penultimate characteristic—quantification.

6. QUANTIFICATION

There can hardly be an American, a Frenchman, or a Japanese who did not, as a child, while playing alone, count the numbers of consecutive times that he or she tossed a ball into the air and caught it again. If one can throw, one can count. One *must* count. It is a childish game that is far more typical of modern than of primitive society, where quantification is not a *modus vivendi*. Nimrod was a mighty hunter of Biblical times, but it is typical of our world that Rowland Ward's *Records of Big Game* (1892) is referred to as "Nimrod's slide-rule."[71]

We need not exaggerate. The Polynesians of Tikopia scored their dart game with a complicated system and similar systems existed for calculating points in many ancient ball games, but modern sports are characterized by the almost inevitable tendency to transform *every* athletic feat into one that can be quantified and measured. The accumulation of statistics on every conceivable aspect of the game is a hallmark of football, baseball, basketball, hockey, and of track and field sports too, where the accuracy of quantification has, thanks to an increasingly precise technology, reached a degree that makes the stopwatch seem positively primitive. (The stopwatch itself is often taken as a symbol for the development of modern sports. It was invented *ca*. 1730 as an instrument to time races.) Electronic timers measure in hundredths and even thousandths of a second and these differences are perceived by the spectators and by the athletes themselves as intensely significant. Was it merely an accident that the founder of the International Amateur Athletic Federation—Sigfrid Edstrom—was an engineer?

Newspapers publish daily statistics on the most popular team sports—baseball, football, basketball, and hockey in the United States, soccer in most other modern societies. The quantified results of golf and tennis matches are usually given coverage in newspapers. Sports such as track and field, gymnastics, and weightlifting have their specialized journals which print column after column of statistical information. In East Germany, perhaps the most bureaucratized and quantified of all countries, the government publishes an annual *DDR-Bestenliste der Kleinsten*, which gives the year's best athletic achievements for children in the first four years of elementary school.[72] Most sports also have their encyclopedias. At least one theorist suggests that sport be defined as that physical activity which can be measured in points or in the c-g-s system (centimeter-gram-second).[73]

The statistics of the game are part and parcel of the statistics of modern society. The Earned Run Average and the Gross National Product, Yards Gained Rushing and the Grade Point Average. We live in a world of numbers. Computers inform us of the successful batter's new average before he arrives breathlessly at second base, just as computers provide us with data on the Dow-Jones Average and the felony rate in twenty-five metropolitan areas. When the tabulation of gold, silver, and bronze medals seems inadequate for comparisons among nations at the Olympic games, the dedicated statistician quickly derives a logarithmic formula: $P = 100\,(1 - \log x/\log n)$, where $P =$ the number of points, $x =$ the placement of the athlete or team, and $n =$ the number of contestants in the event.[74] First place receives 100 points (because the log of one is zero) and last place receives no points (because $\log n/\log n$ is one), while fourth place out of five contestants earns 13.86 points and the more impressive showing of fourth out of fifty reaps 64.56 points. The physiologist who devised this system has also invented tables of equivalence which compare incomparables like the highjump and the discus throw—an extension on his part of the idea behind the point system of the decathlon. It is his assertion that Bob Beamon's fantastic longjump of 8.90 meters (29 feet) is the equivalent of a mile run of 3:43.3 seconds.[75] We live in a world of numbers.

The Greeks did not. Pythagoras, Archimedes, Euclid, and others made great contributions to mathematics, especially to geometry, but Greek civilization was not obsessed with the need to quantify. For them, man was still the measure of all things, not the object of endless measurements. To wear the victor's leafy crown, to be the best of those who had on that cloudless day contested for glory and fame at Olympia or Corinth—that was sufficient. How far was the discus thrown? How fast did the runner traverse the distance? No one knows. In all the literary remains of Hellenism there are only scattered epigrams which give us the numbers. It is said that Phayllus of Croton jumped 16 meters (55 feet) and threw the discus 29 meters (95 feet). The second achievement is unimpressive, the first is impossible. The epigram was probably satirical, but modern searches for a plausible explanation for that jump led to the invention of the triple jump, an event of very doubtful authenticity.[76]

Why don't we know how fast the runner ran? We are tempted to respond that the Greeks lacked accurate chronometers. This may be the correct answer, but I suspect that it may have been the other way around—the Greeks had no accurate chronometers because they didn't care how fast the runner ran. Why don't we know how far they jumped or threw the javelin? We certainly cannot respond in this instance that the Greeks lacked the means of measurement. Their technology was more than adequate for them to have marked off a rope and used it to ascertain the distance. The significant point is that they simply didn't care. Whether or not the victor of one Olympiad sent his javelin farther than the one thrown four years earlier seems to have been a matter of indifference. Similarly, the winner of the discus throw at the Panathenaic festival may or may not have outdistanced the winner at Nemea or Pergamon. We shall never know. No wonder then that discuses varied in size and weight. Comparability beyond the circle of athletes gathered together for the event was never sought and quantification of the results was unnecessary. The closest approach to our modern sense of quantification was in the numeration of achievements. Just as Herakles performed ten labors, Milo of Croton was famed for five victories at Olympia, six at the Pythian games, ten at the Isthmian games, and nine at Nemea.

It was this characteristic—the numeration of achievements—which the Romans seized upon and developed *almost* in the spirit of modern sports. The Romans do not seem to have attempted to quantify Greek sports, for which they had little enthusiasm anyway. There was, understandably, little reason to quantify a gladiatorial combat, but the chariot races of Rome and Constantinople were another matter. The races were not, to the best of our knowledge, timed. We have as little idea of the winner's speed as we do of a Greek runner's swiftness, but the Romans became fascinated with counting the number of first places, second places, first places won from behind, etc. There is, for instance, an inscription to Gaius Appuleius Diocles, whose career began in 122 A.D. In four-horse chariot races, he started 4,257 times, won 1,462 times, came in second 861 times, and third 576 times. But our sources are too few and uncertain to sustain the kind of assertions that we can make about modern sports. Does *occupavit et vicit* mean to have taken the lead and kept it to victory? We cannot be sure.[77] There was a second kind of quantification which began under the Greeks and continued into Roman times. Professional athletes frequently boasted that they were the first to have won seven victories at seven different festivals or three times in a row at this or that famous site. It is still a long way from this type of scoring to the lengthy statistical appendices with which modern biographies terminate, but the first steps were taken. We celebrate our Olympics and imagine ourselves the heirs of ancient Hellas, but we are probably closer in this as in other matters to the howling crowds of "Blues" and "Greens" that cheered on the charioteers of Constantinople.

When the Olympics were revived in 1896, an American observer noted that gymnastics were not especially popular because they were not "real" athletic contests amenable to precise measurement.[78] He underestimated the urge to quantify which characterizes our society. In our cultural universe, even those contests which resist quantification are modified to bring them into conformity with the dominant mode. It is easy enough to mark off the length of a track or of a swimming pool into the appropriate metric distance and to time the runners or the swimmers electronically, but how can one rationalize and quantify a competition in gymnastics, in aesthetics? The answer now seems obvious. Set up an interval scale and a panel of judges and then take the arithmetic mean of their subjective evaluations (excluding the highest and lowest scores). Nadia Comaneci scored exactly 79.275 points in Montreal, neither more nor less. The ingenuity of *Homo mensor* must not be underestimated.

7. RECORDS

Combine the impulse to quantification with the desire to win, to excel, to be the best—and the result is the concept of the record. Primitive sports are not entirely devoid of the instinct to identify the unsurpassed. Our Tikopian dart throwers set down a stone to mark a cast mightier than the rest, and other tribes have commemorated fabulous achievements—which may indeed have been the progeny of fable rather. than of measurement. Archery seems to have been among the first sports for which records were set. A Turkish inscription from the thirteenth century praises Sultan Mahmud Khan for a shot of 1,215 arrow-lengths and a seventeenth-century miniature portrays archers on Istanbul's *Okmeidan* ("Place of Arrows"), where shots of astounding length were recorded.[79] Among the Japanese, records for the number of arrows shot under various stringent conditions were set at least as early as the seventeenth century.[80] But the modern record is the child of the modern mania for quantification. The Greeks had no concept of records in our sense of the term. According to the classicists M. I. Finley and H. W. Pleket, there was not even a way for the Greeks to say "to set a record" or "to break a record"; the noun *"record"* made the verb *"record"* (an abbreviation as in "fastest recorded time"') dates from the 1880s.[81]

What is a record in our modern sense? It is the marvelous abstraction that permits competition not only among those gathered together on the field of sport but also among them and others distant in time and space. Through the strange abstraction of the quantified record, the Australian can compete with the Finn who died a decade before the Australian was born. The record becomes a psychological presence in the mind of everyone involved with the event, as it was at Iffley Road Track in 1954 when Roger Bannister ran the first four-minute mile. The record is a number in the "record book" and in the upper-right-hand corner of the television screen, it is a stimulus to unimagined heights of achievement and a psychic barrier which thwarts our efforts, it is an occasion for frenzy, a form of rationalized madness, a symbol of our civilization. In a lyrical moment, a French athlete of the 1920s hoped that his daughter would "one day recite the litany not of our battles but of our records, more beautiful than the labors of Hercules."[82]

The mass media of the United States worked themselves into a lather of profitable ecstasy as Henry Aaron gradually approached and finally surpassed Babe Ruth's lifetime record of 714 home runs. *Pravda* shows the same perspective. In an editorial of August 6, 1950, it was said, "Many sport records set up several years ago have not yet been surpassed. It is the task of our young athletes to break these records and establish new, incomparably better ones."[83] Five years earlier, *Pravda* had announced cash payments of 25,000 rubles to "amateur" athletes who set new world records.[84] The results of such encouragement can be seen in the gradual domination of the Olympic games by athletes from the Soviet Union and the other Communist nations.

We have already observed that the quantification of the aesthetic makes possible scores for figure skaters and divers and gymnasts. The fact of quantification generates the quest for records even in these ballet-like sports. A score of ten in Olympic competition represented, at the moment when Nadia Comaneci approached the uneven parallel bars in Montreal, a hitherto unrecorded and unanticipated "perfection." Seven times she achieved "perfection" and *that*, the magical number seven, becomes a record which surpasses Nelli Kim's attainment of the same score only once. We marvel at Nadia Comaneci's achievement and assume in the innocence of our quantification that her movements were a finer aesthetic-athletic performance than Ludmilla Tourescheva's in 1972. Was not Nadia's total of 79.275 better than Ludmilla's 77.025? We know that John Walker has run a mile faster than any human ever recognized by the International Amateur Athletic Federation. Because a record is a record, we think we know that Nadia's brilliant performance was the best ever. The Mayans and Aztecs had their superstitions, we have ours.

What will happen to our obsessive quest for records when athletes finally do begin to reach, as eventually they must, the limits of human possibility? What will happen when there is no Kornelia Ender or Dwight Stones to sate the public's orgiastic demand for world records? Toward the end of his remarkable book, *De la Gymnastique aux sports modernes* (1965), Jacques Ulmann contrasts the spirit of Greek sports with that of the modern world: "Greek gymnastics was inseparable from a conception of the body which was itself conditioned by a metaphysics of finitude. The sport of modern man is associated with a philosophy, sometimes diffuse, sometimes coherent, i.e., the theory of progress."[85] The "Idea of Progress" is an idea whose history the scholar J. B. Bury was able to trace back to the eighteenth century, an idea which became dominant in the minds of nineteenth-century thinkers. The theory or idea of progress is a linear concept which assumes that every improvement can be improved upon. Johnny Weissmuller astonished the world in 1924 when he swam 400 meters in 5:04.2 seconds. Today, his winning time would not earn him a place in the women's finals. We expect that the present women's record for 100 meters freestyle will drop from the 55.65 seconds set by Kornelia Ender, but it is humanly impossible for the record to drop to 30 seconds. Somewhere in that interval it must come to rest. What will happen when it does?

Perhaps an example from the history of Japanese sports will be instructive. In the ancient religious center of Kyoto there is a temple, Sanju-Sangen-Do, which is surrounded by a gallery. Between the eaves of the temple and those of the gallery there is an aperture of 4.54 meters. In the seventeenth century, a contest was inaugurated—"Oyakazu." The point of Oyakazu was to see how many arrows an archer could shoot through this aperture, without touching the gallery, in a period of twenty-four hours. The contest dates from 1606 and was still known in 1842, but interest dropped off drastically after April 16, 1686, when a certain Daichachiro Wasa scored 8,132

successes with 13,053 arrows. A modern Japanese historian comments, "As people found it difficult to break the record, the Oyakazu
gradually went out of vogue."[86] It may be, of course, that the modern historian's interpretation is anachronistic—after all, the activity
continued for another 156 years—but the *interpretation* is in itself
highly suggestive of the extraordinary place that the concept of the
record holds in our modern world. What will happen when athletic
championships no longer yield their harvests of new records, when
every sport has its Daichachiro Wasa? Will we accept sports in the
Greek sense, content with the dramatic contest of man against man
(or woman against woman), or will we imagine new ways to satisfy
the Faustian lust for the absolutely unprecedented athletic achievement? We must, with uncharacteristic patience, wait and see.

8. THE CHARACTERISTICS OF MODERN SPORTS

The seven distinguishing characteristics of modern sports have been
discussed. The uniqueness of modern sports can now be summed
upon in typically modern tabular form (table 2). These characteristics
are not simply a random set selected impressionistically or on an *ad-
hoc* basis. When we look back from the last of them, from the quest
for records, we can see that they are interrelated. They interact systematically. We might even invent a (false) teleology and assert that,
in order to achieve records, the other characteristics were necessary.

Table 2
The Characteristics of Sports in Various Ages

	Primitive Sports	Greek Sports	Roman Sports	Medieval Sports	Modern Sports
Secularism	Yes & No	Yes & No	Yes & No	Yes & No	Yes
Equality	No	Yes & No	Yes & No	No	Yes
Specialization	No	Yes	Yes	No	Yes
Rationalization	No	Yes	Yes	No	Yes
Bureaucracy	No	Yes & No	Yes	No	Yes
Quantification	No	No	Yes & No	No	Yes
Records	No	No	No	No	Yes

The modern quest for records is certainly unthinkable in its present form without quantification. It is also impossible, after a certain point reached by the untrained body, to achieve new records without specialization and rationalization. But specialization and rationalization usually imply bureaucratic organization, without which world championships cannot be staged nor rules established nor records duly certified. The spectacular achievements of Montreal and Innsbruck were the culmination of years of effort by thousands of people. The specialization, rationalization, and bureaucratization of modern sport also assume certain kinds of equality of opportunity. The quest for records would be farcical if the fastest runner or the most skillful fencer were barred from competition because of occupation or skin color or religion. Finally, the very notion of quantified achievement is probably more compatible with the standards of a secular system than with one closely oriented to the transcendent realm of the sacred. This is a difficult notion to grasp and perhaps even an unpalatable one, but it may be that the dynamics of athletic achievement commence with the secularization of society. When qualitative distinctions fade and lose their force, we turn to quantitative ones. When we can no longer distinguish the sacred from the profane or even the good from the bad, we content ourselves with minute discriminations between the batting average of the .308 hitter and the .307 hitter. Once the gods have vanished from Mount Olympus or from Dante's paradise, we can no longer run to appease them or to save our souls, but we can set a new record. It is a uniquely modern form of immortality.

Capitalism, Protestantism, and Modern Sport

MODERN SPORT, a ubiquitous and unique form of nonutilitarian physical contests, took shape over a period of approximately 150 years, from the early eighteenth to the late nineteenth centuries. Speaking historically, we can be reasonably precise about place as well as time. Modern sports were born in England and spread from their birthplace to the United States, to Western Europe, and to the world beyond. The origins of modern sports have been chronicled in hundreds of books and articles and particular sports have had their industrious historians, but only a handful of scholars, mostly Europeans, have attempted to *explain* the rise of modern sports. The most persuasive explanations have been stimulated by the insights of Karl Marx and Max Weber, neither of whom wrote very much about sports.

1. A MARXIST INTERPRETATION

Marxist interpretations of the rise of modern sports begin with the materialist conception of history. In the Marxist view, sports are invariably related to the organization of the modes of production. Even in the Stone Age, "Physical exercises . . . were originally one with the means of production (Arbeitsprozeß)." [1] Men ran, heaved rocks, and cast spears in order to improve their skills as hunters. Survival depended on physical prowess. What was true of the "sports" of the Stone Age remains true, in different circumstances, today. Marxist historians have consistently analyzed the rise of modern sports from this materialist perspective. Medieval sports mirrored feudal society and modern sports are the product of Liberal capitalism, that is, of bourgeois society. There is enough truth in this interpretation to reward an investigation of it. I shall, for the rest of this section, write from their point of view, without constant qualifications such as "from a Marxist perspective." My criticisms appear in section 3.

Medieval sports served the interest of the feudal nobility which was the effective ruling class of the Middle Ages. [2] Sports were of many kinds; even the peasants had their rude games, their running, wrestling, fighting with staves, their rough-and-tumble version of what eventually became modern soccer. The sports of the peasantry tended to be those which kept them physically fit for the strenuous tasks of agricultural labor. Sports were one means to maintain their labor power (Arbeitskraft) at a suitably exploitable level.

The sports of the nobility also bore the marks of their origins in the world of work. On the one hand, there were hunting, fishing, and hawking—all of which were pastimes open to ladies as well as to lords, all of which were injurious to the lower orders of society who were often dependent on hunting or fishing to supplement their diets or who suffered economically when their rulers pursued game through cultivated areas. Frequently, the right to hunt or hawk was restricted to the nobility. Poachers were cruelly punished. In addition to the "field sports" which evolved directly from the world of productive work, there were sports immediately related to the realities of political power. There were tournaments and jousts, the first a miniature battle between a large number of armored horsemen, the second a combat between two mounted knights. In a world based on rule by physical force, play itself symbolized the relationship between classes. The tournament was mock warfare, sport, a demonstration of martial ability, and a subtle warning to those who might dream of a more egalitarian social order.

The class relationships of capitalist society are governed by different modes of production from those of the Middle Ages. Different social imperatives led to different kinds of sports and, more importantly, to different conceptions of the nature of sports.

The gross disparities in the distribution of wealth obtained from industrial and financial capitalism led to increased differentiation in the kinds of sports enjoyed by the rich and the poor. The lords of the land became landlords, and they laid aside the weapons of a feudal age. Sports lost their directly political function—it is impossible to crush a rebellion with a golf club—and certain sports became the expression of a leisured class.[3] Golf and tennis continued to be the prerogative of the ruling class, but there was no longer any need to confine them to the wealthy by royal edict or by threats of dire punishment. Economic cost sufficed. Tennis, for instance, requires an expensive court and must be learned slowly, which often implies professional lessons and always means the investment of considerable time. The traditional clothing of tennis, immaculate "whites," was a subtle reminder to upstarts that proper dress was in itself beyond the means of most people. For the very rich, for whom even golf and tennis had become too popular, there was always polo or yachting. Consider, for example, The Book of Sport, published in New York in 1901. This sumptuous, lavishly illustrated tome contains essays on golf, court-tennis, racquets, hand-fives, squash, lawn-tennis, polo, fox-hunting, yatching, and coaching. Of the last, driving about in horsedrawn carriages, Oliver H. P. Belmont opined, "No sport which requires the perfection of skill and dash and the exercise of nerve will ever be abandoned by Americans."[4] Absent from The Book of Sport was any mention of the sports that most Americans played.

In capitalist society, sports like soccer and baseball are reserved for the laboring classes. These sports have as their major goal the maintenance of a maximally productive work-force. "What happens or is allowed to happen in the worker's leisure time is determined by the necessity, in a capitalist society, for labor power (Arbeitskraft) to be reproduced."[5] It is also necessary to provide some kind of compensation for the cramped physical conditions of assembly-line production, lest illness reduce the worker's labor power to zero.

The sports of the elite are means of socialization by which the rulers can develop those traits of character and leadership necessary for dominion at home and abroad. The sports of the proletariat, on the other hand, are vehicles for a different sort of socialization. They tend to be team sports which inculcate subordination and acceptance of authority, authority symbolized most immediately in the person of the coach. They initiate youth into the routines of the industrial system and they act to divert potentially revolutionary energies from politics.

It was inevitable, therefore, that England, the homeland of industrial capitalism, was also the birthplace of modern sports. The astonishing readiness of the English to wager money on horse races, foot races, and boxing was commented upon by many observers. In the words of an eighteenth-century French commentator on English customs, "The probability of life, and the return of ships, are the objects of their arithmetic. The same habit of calculating they extend to games, wagers, and everything in which there is any hazard."[6]

This readiness to wager on horses, cocks, bears, ships, and pugilistic butchers paralleled the increased willingness to risk venture capital in the development of England's expanding industry. From the eagerness to risk and wager came the need to measure time and space. The capitalist's ledgers are close kin to the scorecard. We suddenly enter the world of the bookkeeper and the bookie.

In the nineteenth century, public schools like Rugby, Eton, Harrow, and Winchester joined with Oxford and Cambridge to create an ethos of fair play, good sportsmanship, and business acumen. Thomas Hughes' famous novel, *Tom Brown's Schooldays* (1857), is the dramatic embodiment of the regnant values of Thomas Arnold's Ruby School, where the sons of the middle class learned the lessons of bourgeois Liberalism. To Oxford and Cambridge went the graduates of the public schools. From Oxford and Cambridge the energetic British soldier, civil servant, or businessman went forth to Vancouver, Madras, Cape Town, or Melbourne. And brought with him the marvels of modern sports.

As early as 1830, Englishmen resident in Germany founded the Hamburg Rowing Club. Within five years after Major (Ret.) Walter Wingate invented lawn tennis in 1873, the exciting new game had spread to Germany, the United States, Brazil, India, and Australia.

The British founded the Dresden Football Club in 1890 and the following year they founded the White Rovers at Paris. Three years later, the son of an English family living in Brazil brought soccer to São Paulo. In 1896, the son of Hungarian immigrants to England visited his relatives and introduced soccer to Hungary. A similar story can be told about a dozen other sports, from rugby to badminton. We can sense the force of the British model when we note that the Hamburg Sport Club of 1880 held its races in English distances, and when we see that the most famous athletic clubs of France tended to have English names, like le Racing-Club de France (1882).

Table 3
The Diffusion of Modern Sports
(By year of organization)

	English	U.S.	French	German	Swedish
Football Assoc.	1863	1913	1919	1900	1904
Amateur Swimming Assoc.	1869	1878	1889	1886	1904
Bicyclists Union	1878	1881	1881	1884	1900
Metropolitan Rowing Assoc.	1879	1872	1890	1883	1904
Amateur Athletic Union	1880	1888	1887	1891	1895
Lawn Tennis Assoc.	1888	1881	1889	1902	1906

The receptivity of a nation to the ecological invasion of modern sport is in itself an index of that nation's industrial development. Despite the accidents of historical transmission and all the other uncertainties of such an investigation, it is nonetheless remarkable how the spread of modern sports organizations correlates with the rise of industrialism. According to W. W. Rostow's study *The Stages of Economic Growth* (1960), the first five nations to "take off" into the stage of sustained economic growth were Great Britain, France, the United States, Germany, and Sweden. Table 3 clearly demonstrates that the first nations to industrialize were also the first to establish national organizations for modern sports, in almost the same order.[7] By concentrating on *national* organizations, I have sought to minimize the distortions caused by such factors as a group of British businessmen setting up a single soccer club totally out of character with the indigenous sports of the host country. If we calculate Kendall's coefficient

of concordance, which will be 1.0 if the sequence is always England-
America-France-Germany-Sweden and 0 if the sequence is always
reversed, the coefficient of concordance is quite high, .637, which
strongly suggests *some* relationship between the pace of industrialism
and the spread of modern sports.[8]

In the early nineteenth century, modern sports were—like capitalism itself—a progressive force, more democratic than the medieval
sports they superseded, but the development of industrial capitalism
led to forms of exploitation which were even grimmer than those of
feudalism. Sports began to play an increasingly conservative and re-
actionary role. One sign of this has been the intense commercialization of sports everywhere outside the orbits of the Soviet Union
and the People's Republic of China. The tendency to transform
human behavior into transactions of the marketplace has made sports
into a matter of profit and loss. The structure of amateur sports
demands on ticket sales to college games and to meets sponsored by
sports organizations like the AAU. The sporting goods and recreation
industries are large and complex. The structure of professional sports
is openly rather than covertly commercial. Corporations and
wheeler-dealer millionaires own teams and take advantage of the tax
laws to profit economically while complaining all the while of the
unprofitability of their franchises. Major-league baseball depends on
the Supreme Court's special exemption from antitrust legislation
while other professional team sports must limp along with depreciation allowances on their players, with enormous revenues from commercial television, with stadiums donated by gratefully bilked munic-
ipalities, and with the leverage of extralegal rather than wholly legal
monopolies. The result? Teenagers sell themselves into semibondage
for millions of dollars, "amateur" athletes earn enough *sub rosa* to
grumble about their losses when they become professionals, drug-
abuse accompanies the desperate desire to share in the winner's
bonus. All in all, an unattractive picture.[9]

In addition to commercialism, Western sports have increasingly
been vehicles for the inculcation of militarism, nationalism, and imperialism. In the 1920s and 1930s, the leaders of sports were ready to
welcome Fascism. The French novelist Henry de Montherlant wrote
Les Olympiques (1920, 1938) and *Le Songe* (1922) in which ath-
leticism was a metaphor for a Fascist view of the world. Edmund

Neuendorff, leader of the *Deutsche Turnerschaft,* congratulated Hitler on becoming chancellor and affirmed that the German gymnastics movement marched side by side with Hitler's Storm Troops.[10] The 1936 Olympics, staged in Berlin under Hitler's aegis, symbolize the marriage of Nazism and modern sports. Since World War II, the United States and the nations of Western Europe have continued to use sports as a means to indoctrinate the masses with the virus of militarism, nationalism, and imperialism. On the occasion of the founding of East Germany's national sports organization, the *Deutscher Turn- und Sportbund* (1957), its president announced, "The DTSB incorporates social democracy in sports and finds its firm basis in the principle of democratic centralism. In West Germany, on the contrary, democracy is ground under foot. A small group of imperialists and militarists rules over the majority of the people. These conditions are mirrored in sport."[11] Nearly twenty years later, in the new era of détente, East Germany's chief theoretical journal for sports studies, *Theorie und Praxis der Körperkultur,* continued to denounce the militarism and imperialism of bourgeois sports.[12]

The final stage of historical development comes with the emergence of socialism, which eliminates the exploitative relationship between the capitalist and the worker. Since the mode of production is transformed, it is inevitable that sports too are transformed. In the Soviet Union and in the nations of Eastern Europe, sports continue to be a means of socialization (in the psychological sense), but the lessons learned are utterly unlike those of the past. In addition to their recreational function, sports are elements in national security and economic productivity. In the Soviet Union there is an entire system of physical culture, beginning with compulsory exercises for preschool children and including organized sports within the schools and universities as well as in factories and offices, regular "Spartakiades" which involve tens of millions of contestants throughout the entire area of the USSR, seven levels of athletic achievement ranging from "Youthful Achievement Second Class" to Honored Master of Sport," advanced research at dozens of university-centers, and constant supervision by governmental and party authorities. Ideologically, the system can be traced back to the Third Congress of Komsomol (Young Communist League) in October 1920, when, in Lenin's presence, the delegates resolved that[13] *the physical education of the younger generation is an essential element in the overall system of the Communist upbringing of young people, aimed at creating harmoniously developed people, creative citizens of Communist society. Today, physical education also has direct practical aims: (1) preparing young people for work; and (2) preparing them for military defense of Soviet power.*

In line with this policy, Ministers of Sport and Tourism urge the people of every Communist country to maintain their physical fitness through calisthenics and sports in order to raise the level of industrial output and to contribute to the defense of socialist society. The importance of this theme is reflected in constitutional provisions. Article 18 of the Constitution of the German Democratic Republic affirms, for example, that "Physical education (*Körperkultur*), Sports, and Tourism are elements of socialist culture and further the citizen's all-around physical and spiritual development."[14] A less official but scarcely less prominent goal is competition with athletes from capitalist nations in order to demonstrate the superiority of the socialist way of life.

Under socialism, sports are available as never before to both sexes, to all races, and to all classes. "Universal sport," comments a leading Polish sociologist, "requires the removal of all kinds of social divisions. . . . Sport for all assumes the abolition of every social, national, class-linked, sexual, and racial discrimination."[15] Sports cease to be associated with nationalism and imperialism. They contribute to the creation of what Marxists refer to as "New Socialist Man." "As is generally known, the Soviet Union is successfully resolving the task of an all-round development of man."[16] Sports are an integral part of that success.

This, briefly, is the historical development of modern sports as interpreted by Marxist scholars. Before evaluating this interpretation, it will be helpful to examine the work of the Neo-Marxists.

2. THE NEO-MARXIST CRITIQUE

The Marxist interpretation of the rise of modern sports begins in more or less objective analysis and ends in polemics. The closer the discussion comes to the present, the less disinterested, the more passionate. The Neo-Marxist critique commences with the fundamental criticism of Western sports made by Marxist scholars and extends the criticism into a wholesale indictment not simply of the alleged perversions of sport under contemporary capitalism but of the very idea of sports. While Marxist theorists condemn the alleged militarism and imperialism of West-German sports, while American radicals such as Jack Scott and Harry Edwards expose the authoritarianism and racism of the "sports establishment" of the United States, the Neo-Marxists are still more radical. They reject not merely the abuses of the institution but the institution itself. They hold that sports in their *ideal* form—sports as described by coaches, physical educators, and administrators—are a perversion of the human spirit.

The theoretical sources of Neo-Marxism lie partly in Marx, especially in the early, more philosophical writings, and partly in Freud, whose theory of the unconscious is a necessary element in the argument that workers (or athletes) who seem satisfied with the status quo are victims of "false consciousness," i.e., they do not really understand their own interests. Institutionally, Neo-Marxism flourished in the 1920s at Frankfurt's *Institut für Sozialforschung*, where Theodor Adorno, Max Horkheimer, and Herbert Marcuse labored in fruitful collaboration. Although none of the great figures of prewar Neo-Marxism has devoted an entire book to the phenomenon of sports, passages in Adorno's *Prismen* (1955) and *Erziehung zur Mündigkeit* (1970) have been an important stimulus for Bero Rigauer, Gerhard Vinnai, Jean-Marie Brohm, and other spokesmen for the Neo-Marxist critique of sports which sprang up in Germany and France in the 1960s.

As in the previous section, it is important to understand the Neo-Marxist position before we attempt an evaluation of it. Once again, I shall synthesize from their point of view and hold my own criticisms in abeyance.

Of the seven characteristics of modern sports, the Neo-Marxists are quite ready to accept the first two—secularism and equality—but specialization represents the beginnings of evil. Consider, for instance, the field-goal kicker of an American football team. Is there a more absurd symbol of specialization in modern sports? Is he an athlete or a figure from a film by Charlie Chaplin? Can he be held up as an example of *mens sana in corpore sano?* Does he feel a surge of animal pleasure as his foot meets the ball and his five seconds of "play" come to an end? Consider, similarly, the single-minded dedication necessary to become the world's best highjumper or hammer-thrower. Consider the months and the years of rigorous training, the abnegations, the self-discipline, the asceticism, the cultivated one-sidedness. How different is the highjumper or the hammer-thrower from the exploited bolt-tightener on the assembly line? Marx wrote in *Die Deutsche Ideologie* (1845–1846) of the whole man, of the fully developed human capable of an infinite variety of activities:[17]

As soon as the division of labor sets in, each man develops a certain exclusive range of activity, which is imposed on him, which he cannot avoid or escape. He is a hunter, a fisherman, or a herder, or a critic, and he must remain what he is, if he doesn't want to risk his livelihood, but in the communist society of the future, where no one is restricted to a limited range of activity, it will be possible to do one thing today, another tomorrow, to hunt in the morning, to fish in the afternoon, to be a herdsman in the evening, to criticize one's meal—without becoming a hunter, a fisherman, a herder, or a critic.

The Neo-Marxist extends the list of limited identities—hunter, fisherman, herder, critic, sprinter, left tackle, relief pitcher, goalie.

Simultaneously with the advent of specialization, man becomes mechanical, the athlete is metamorphosed into a cog in the machinery of sports. "The champion," writes a French critic, "is fabricated in the image of the worker and the track in the image of the factory. Athletic activity has become a form of production and takes on all the characteristics of industrial production."[18] A German scholar makes a similar point: "Man becomes an interchangeable part on the playing field as in the office and the factory. . . . Man becomes a kind of machine and his movements, controlled by apparatus, become mechanical."[19] The final result of specialization is, paradoxically, a mechanical perfection with no human quirks to hinder replacement or substitution.

Rationalization in sports is equally incompatible with spontaneity and inventiveness. There is no modern sport which does not have codified rules and regulations, but why shouldn't we play whatever game we want to play, in whatever manner and spirit we choose? The rule-boundedness of modern sports is thus the athletic equivalent of a paint-by-the-numbers kit.

There is more to rationalization than the coercion of the spontaneous impulses of *Homo ludens*. Bourgeois theorists boast that sports offer a model of fair play through adherence to the rules of the game. The Neo-Marxists maintain that society's rules are exploitative, grossly unfair, and immoral. Sport helps to socialize us into accepting rules which are inherently unjust and unfair and into assuming falsely that justice can be subsumed under fair play. "The individual is compelled to follow 'the rules of the game' upon which he has had no influence and through which the privileges of the ruling class are preserved."[20] The real task is to realize the class nature of society's rules and regulations. They are rational means to an irrational end, namely, the maintenance of the repressive power of the capitalist class.

Bureaucratic organization? The phrase itself reeks of inhumanity. Individual athletes become helpless pawns in the hands of a power structure composed of retired athletes, government functionaries, or wealthy businessmen with an interest in (and frequently a profit from) sports. Decisions are made in an authoritarian way by officials accountable to no one, certainly not to the athletes whose lives they callously manipulate. Edicts are handed down and there is neither discussion nor appeal. "The individual athlete shrinks into the object of alienated centralized administration."[21] The AAU and the NCAA struggle for power and the helpless athlete finds himself barred from contests, suspended, thwarted, humiliated.

Quantification? The living, breathing person, the simple, separate person praised by Whitman and evoked by Wordsworth and the German Romantic poets disappears into the abstraction of numbers. "Into all human relationships, into all sectors of social life, capitalism begets quantification."[22] In a capitalist society, the human personality becomes a salary, a serial number, a batting average. Despite the elegant rhetoric about playing the game rather than thinking about the numbers, the spectator's attention becomes fixed in a relentless search for quantification. There is no time left for considerations of grace, no room for fair play, no chance to respond to the kinesthetic sense of physical exuberance. The phenomenon of alienation, by which the worker disappears into the fetish of the commodities he produces, can be seen most clearly when the individual athlete vanishes into the abstraction and becomes the ten-second man or the .300 hitter. Jimmy Brown, surely one of football's greatest running backs, reveals as much when he admits, "I hold more than a dozen records and as a result have been turned into a statistic."[23]

The extreme form of this tendency is, as we have seen, the emphasis on records, on the most repressive form of quantification. The fetish of achievement is no longer satisfied by victory in the contest itself. In capitalist society, even the winner of the race becomes a loser when his time disappoints the crowd's expectations. What are the Olympic games or the Super Bowl without a harvest of records? The quest for records fuels the drive for more intense specialization, for longer, harder, more physically punishing training. The result is that almost everyone, except the handful of athletes who set the (always temporary) records, is left with a sense of frustration and failure.

To the Marxist critique of sports under capitalism and to the rejection of the distinguishing characteristics of modern sport, the followers of Adorno and Marcuse add specific charges about the insidious function of sports. The most important charge is that sports are designed as sexual sublimation. Sports release sexual impulses in the form of aggression. If these impulses had been left repressed, they might have exploded in the form of political revolution, which is, of course, the outcome to be avoided if capitalism is to survive. Sexual repression is, according to Marcuse, a necessary part of capitalism, but sports provide a safety valve when the repression becomes excessive. Sports drain off repressed sexual energy which cannot, for whatever reason, be profitably utilized by the economic system. Through the psychological mechanism of identification, the spectators join vicariously in the sublimation achieved by the players on the field.

The precise form of this sublimation is important. Sexual repression produces aggression and it is aggression that is directly released through sports, aggression which might otherwise destabilize the entire system of political control. "The aggression derived from sexual repression can thus be released (kompensiert) through the athletic achievements and competitions."[24] Unfortunately, the transformation of sexual energies into physical aggression is imperfect. Sexuality appears in sports as sexuality—but only in the forms of perversion, as sadism, masochism, narcissism, and homosexuality. "The erotic life of the athlete demonstrates a strange schizophrenia; in its physiological aspects, it is heterosexual, but in its psychic aspects it corresponds to the erotic dispositions of early childhood, and it is accordingly homosexual."[25] The athlete's wife may satisfy his lust, but his teammates are the objects of his love. Football, argues Paul Hoch, is "America's Number One fake-masculinity ritual," an ironic, unconscious display of the very perversions that athletes and spectators most despise.[26]

In short, sport is "the capitalistically distorted form of play."[27] Sport is not an escape from the world of work but rather an exact structural and functional parallel to the world of work. Sport does not offer compensation for the frustrations of alienated labor in capitalist society; it seduces the luckless athlete and spectator into a second world of work more authoritarian and repressive and less meaningful than the economic sphere itself. Capitalist society is essentially achievement-oriented and competitive and sports present to us the purest model of that society—and that is just what is wrong with sports. What society needs is not greater pressure for more achievement, but freedom from the incessant demands for achievement, from the "inhumane absurdity . . . of the will to win."[28] What society needs is not sports but play, not the *Realitätsprinzip* but the *Lustprinzip*. Sport represses, play emancipates. Under Communism, sport will disappear and play will resume its rightful place.

3. A CRITIQUE OF CRITIQUES

I should never have begun this book if I were not convinced of the proposition that there is a relationship between sports and society. The question is, what kind of relationship? One way to answer the question is to examine the characteristics of modern sport and to demonstrate that they are to a remarkable degree the characteristics of modern society as described by Max Weber and Talcott Parsons. This we have attempted in chapter 2. Another way to answer the question is to examine the historical process by which modern sports evolved out of the folk-games and aristocratic sports of the Middle Ages. The Marxists and the Neo-Marxists agree that the evolution of modern sports can be explained by the development of industrial capitalism. Supported by the undeniable fact that England was the birthplace of both modern sports and the industrial revolution, the theory has a great deal to recommend it, but I am prepared to advocate an alternative explanation. It is important, however, that we know exactly why we cannot accept the Marxist and the Neo-Marxist interpretations *in toto*.

The Marxist claim that the nature of sport is determined by the means of production is not persuasive. Despite its wealth of detailed information, this analysis remains vague about the exact relationship between a given sport and a given economic system. The joust between the armored knights on horseback was undeniably an aspect of the feudal order, but the mode of production was essentially agricultural, as it had been for centuries and as it would for centuries remain. Since an agrarian economy preceded and followed the sport, the connection between the joust and agricultural labor is by no means clear. If it is argued that jousts and tournaments are martial exercises which relate directly to the status of the ruling class which ruled by direct physical force, then the argument has shifted from economic to political-military determinants. This turn in the argument leads to other problems. If the political purposes of the ruling class are the clue to the kinds of sports in medieval society, then we must ask why the English ruling class persistently emphasized *archery* as the preferred sport for the yeomanry. Was it sensible to encourage the disadvantaged to practice the very weapon which was to end the supremacy of the mounted knight?

More vague and less persuasive still are the arguments made about the specific kinds of sports practiced in the modern world. Generalizations must be challenged by specific questions. What is the exact relationship between industrial capitalism and the game of soccer? The game itself can be traced back to medieval times. It is popular today in countries which remain almost entirely agricultural as well as in the most industrial cities of Europe. It is popular in Poland, Czechoslovakia, and other Communist nations which are, indeed, highly industrialized but which can scarcely be called capitalist. If the game of soccer by its internal structure contributes to the exploitation of the working class, then it is difficult to see that the enthusiastic players of the Soviet Union are exempt from the same exploitation as those of São Paulo and Liverpool. If it is argued that the social context makes the difference, then it is the social context that matters and not the kind of sport. The humane society makes all sports humane. But to admit this is to abandon the thesis that different kinds of sports reflect different modes of production.

Similarly, it is true that empirical studies of rates of participation give statistical support to the common-sense observation that kinds of sport vary with social class.[29] We can go further and establish the fact that English soccer is, indeed, more popular among factory workers than among professionals while the contrary is certainly true for cricket, but it remains difficult to perceive the necessary connection between these correlations and the socialization of the players to rule or be ruled. If there were something about American football which encouraged the players to accept their inferior lot in life, why was the game popular at Harvard, Yale, and Princeton at a time when it was scarcely known among the working class? Long after the establishment of the National Football League in 1920, American football continued to be regarded as typically collegiate, and today the sport continues to be considerably more popular among managers and executives than among factory workers.[30] If the game inculcates subservience and docility, the ruling class, led by none other than Richard M. Nixon, has victimized itself. Marxist and Neo-Marxist interpretations of the values transmitted through particular kinds of sports are the product of ideology rather than the result of careful empirical analysis.

Equally unpersuasive is the allegation that Western sports have been schools of nationalism and imperialism. If it is true that American or Italian athletes and sports administrators are more militaristic and nationalistic than their counterparts in Cuba or Yugoslavia, then the explanation must lie elsewhere than in the kinds of sports because, once again, the kinds are essentially the same. It is, of course, theoretically possible that athletes in the West are manipulated into the adoption of undemocratic values while those of the East are encouraged in the opposite direction, but considerable empirical evidence points to the conclusion that militarism and nationalism are more strongly associated with the sports of Communist than with those of non-Communist countries.

While the United States Army and the armies of Western Europe commonly introduce sports into their leisure-time programs, the organization of sports in the Soviet Union and its allies has frequently taken a directly military turn. The twelve "friendly armies" of the Warsaw Pact nations compete in sports, just as the soldiers of NATO do.[31] Civilians learn military along with athletic skills. Motorcyclists in the sports clubs of the Soviet Union learn to drive quickly and well; they also learn to drive with "gas masks, throwing grenades, and shooting, all from the motorcycle."[32] The Russians award the GTO badge for men ("Ready for Work and Defense") for physical fitness in eight categories. Six of the categories are pacific enough, but the seventh calls for proficiency in shooting and the eighth offers a choice: one can throw a discus, a javelin, a shot, or a hand grenade.[33] While critics of American sports point to military metaphors like the "long bomb" in football, Chinese sports include marksmanship, running the obstacle course, bayonet charges, grenade throwing, parachuting, and anti-aircraft defense—all for civilians.[34] In 1960, the East Germans awarded the "touristic" pentathlon badge for children from twelve to fourteen years of age. The five sports of the pentathlon were the eight-kilometer orientation run, the obstacle course, throwing clubs at a target, long-distance swimming, and shooting with air guns.[35] In a speech, the East-German Minister of Education reminded his audience:[36]

It is no accident that Friedrich Engels placed great weight on the premilitary education of youth through gymnastic exercises. We have up to now underestimated the importance of premilitary education. . . . We must overcome the pedagogic pacifism in physical-education classes. These classes must become a part of the premilitary education of our youth.

Finally, athletes from Communist countries are far more likely than their Western counterparts to say that they compete for their homelands. The Chinese credit their achievements to the inspiration of Chairman Mao, the East-Germans to the model of Walter Ulbricht, and the Cubans to the exemplary leadership of Fidel Castro. In the words of an East-German "Master of Sport," "The finest and most beautiful aspect of achievement-sport (*Leistungssport*) is the possibility of representing one's country in a national or international competition."[37] Quite naturally, much is made in Communist publications and broadcasts of their athletes' success in international competition.[38] Given the Communists' emphasis on the symbolic social significance of athletic superiority over capitalist nations, this attitude should surprise no one.

The claim that Western nations have organized their sports in a militaristic and nationalistic manner must be taken *cum grano salis*, but there is another accusation whose truth we must acknowledge. Western sports, especially American sports, are commercialized to an extent unknown elsewhere. What the state does in the Soviet Union or Bulgaria, what the private club does in West Germany or France, a combination of schools and private enterprise does in the United States. And the line between "big-time" college sports and the openly professional sports leagues is often a faint one, difficult for foreigners to trace and impossible for the NCAA to enforce. Nonetheless, we must not mistakenly assume that commercialization is solely responsible for all the ills of modern sports. There are many evils specific to commercialism: the neglect of sports that do not prove profitable, excessive costs which limit access to facilities that should be available to all, the mutilation of televised games and meets by advertisements, and the manipulation of scheduling in order to cash in on "prime-time" television audiences. Most of the diseases of modern sports, however, have infected all modern societies and cannot be associated simply with commercialization: an overemphasis on winning, cheating, the use of drugs, the training of small children for highly competitive sports, and the tendency to turn every form of play into some kind of contest.

This brings us back to the fundamental postulate of chapter 2. The characteristics of modern sports are essentially invariant in every modern society, whether that society is Liberal, socialist, or Communist. Differences do exist, and they will occupy us in chapters 4–6, but these differences are minor in comparison with those distinguishing modern from primitive, ancient, and medieval sports. This fact seriously undercuts the Neo-Marxist critique. It is true that American and French sports are characterized by a high level of quantification, but this social fact cannot be explained simply by capitalism when an equally high if not higher level of quantification exists in Poland and the Soviet Union. It is true that bureaucratic organization governs the competitive sports of West Germany, but we must be permitted considerable skepticism when a leading East-German sociologist asserts, "It is a fundamental principle of socialist democracy that the athletes themselves should work out, discuss, agree upon and finally realize their plans and intentions for the further development of sporting activities." [39] Fundamental principle it may be, but the principle of "democratic centralism" has made present practice in Eastern Europe even more bureaucratic than that of Western Europe—and capitalism cannot be the reason. It is true that Western sports institutionalize the achievement principle and frequently carry it to extremes, but achievement is also the proud slogan of Communist nations: "Everywhere in our social life the achievement principle increases in strength. . . . Achievement-sport mirrors the humanistic character of our socialist physical culture." [40] If capitalism accounted for the stress on achievement rather than on ascription, then Marxism must have found a more than adequate substitute. To a degree unknown in the West, the sport psychology of Eastern Europe is devoted to the scientific study of motivation, a study itself motivated by the intense desire to raise levels of athletic achievement. [41]

No wonder, then, that the West-German Neo-Marxists have concentrated their critical fire on the West rather than on the specialization, rationalization, bureaucratic organization, quantification, and quest for records in the Communist world. Their theoretical model simply cannot cope with the institutional reality of Communism. Final proof of this can be observed in the *Marxist* response to Neo-Marxism. Communist scholars have repudiated the entire Neo-Marxist critique of sports with much the same impatience that Lenin showed for "infantile Left-Wing deviationism." They have denounced the Neo-Marxists as "left-radical Trotskyites" whose work contains "political weaknesses and errors deriving from the anti-Marxism and anti-Leninism of their basic assumptions." [42] Meanwhile, French Neo-Marxists have not hesitated to carry the logic of their argument to the ineluctable conclusion that Communist sport is as bad (almost) as capitalist sport. The French have excoriated the Parti Communiste Français for its worship of the heresy of modern sports. The PCF has found words with which to defend itself. The ideological pot boils. [43]

That the Soviet Union cannot be excluded from any rational criticism of modern sports, however, does not imply that modern sports cannot be rationally criticized. It is one thing to say that the Neo-Marxists are wrong to explain every abuse in terms of capitalism and another to say that there are no abuses. The crux of the matter for us is whether the abuses represent the distortion of modern sports or the very essence of the phenomenon. Are sports a modern curse? Do they alienate the athlete from the product of his labor? Are they a form of sexual sublimation?

When we move from the world of play and noncompetitive games to the world of contests, we have made an important transition, have crossed a kind of ludic Rubicon. The cooperative Japanese ball game kemari has neither winners nor losers, but modern sports are by definition structured to produce a won-lost outcome. Ties are possible, but the entire tendency of modern sports is to eliminate them by extra innings in baseball, by "sudden-death" overtimes, by rematches, by some device that will end the ambiguity. From the psychological need to win, a thousand distempers grow. Here are the roots of what psychiatrist Arnold Beisser calls "the madness in sports." [44] It is the desire to win at all costs which eats away at the simple pleasures of play, which leads ultimately to illicit violence and the use of drugs. When eight-year-old hockey players skate out on the ice and begin by prearranged plan to "take out" the star of the opposing team by breaking his ankle with their hockey sticks, the "achievement principle" has clearly gone too far.

Let us grant this. Let us also note that the structure of modern sports makes it all but inevitable that half the participants in any contest will lose. In leagues and in championship meets, the proportion of losers necessarily rises. When the Olympic race has been won, the victor receives the gold medal and all the others have lost, but the losers live with their disappointment. They quote Pierre de Coubertin on the rewards of participation. Unless we take the sportsmanlike quotation to be utter hypocrisy, we must conclude that winning isn't always everything. There must, in other words, be some psychological mechanism which enables all of us to endure defeat and to live with the fact that not everyone can be the best. While the stress on athletic victory is often destructive, especially when children are the actors involved, it may be that sports are a valuable means to socialize us into a world where disappointment and frustration are inevitable. I am not anxious to overpraise the "good loser" of Victorian homily, but I insist that the winner cannot be the only one who profits from the contest. Defeat is simply too common for it to be as destructive to the psyche as some have claimed.

Similarly, the allegations of alienation in sports have been hyperbolic. To the thesis that modern sports alienates the athlete from himself, Hans Lenk has countered that there is less alienation in sport than elsewhere in the modern world. Sports remain a subdivision of the realm of freedom in that the athlete chooses whether or not to participate. It is precisely in this freely chosen world of sports that one *can* identify with "the product of one's work," i.e., with one's performance as an athlete. In the achievements of sports one can experience a sense of wholeness denied elsewhere. Here, as in the arts, one submits to a discipline which liberates. "Athletic achievement is . . . unambiguously one's *own*, contrary to the achievements of assemblyline production."[45] On the field of sports, one's achievements are intelligible to everyone, as those of the physicist are not, and one can win recognition beyond the circle of specialists. It is the athlete who is able, in Erving Goffman's sense of the term, to "present himself" to others.[46]

The alleged extinction of personality within the abstraction of the record is also an overstatement. If the athlete is a colorless person, it is probably true that his moment of glory will last only as long as his record, but it is also true that the recognition received by such a colorless person would have been unattainable elsewhere. Better fleeting glory than none at all. It is, moreover, undeniably the case that the fame of many athletes has survived despite the fact that their achievements have been surpassed. Hans Lenk asks the right question: "The records of Nurmi or Zatopek or Wilma Rudolph have been surpassed and forgotten, but have the names and the image of personality

CAPITALISM, PROTESTANTISM, MODERN SPORT 77

disappeared along with the records?"[47] Quite obviously not. The names of Jim Thorpe and Babe Ruth and Big Bill Tilden may not last so long as those of Milo of Croton and Theagenes of Thasos, but the relationship between records and personality is clearly a complicated one.

Unless we are to assume that men and women are so victimized by "false consciousness" that they have lost all awareness of their own emotions, we must pay attention to what people say about their athletic experiences. Let us be distrustful of the published biographies and autobiographies of famous athletes, most of which exude enthusiasm for the world of sports. Let us look at the carefully assembled evidence in Michel Bouet's phenomenological study, *Les Motivations des sportifs* (1969) and at the painstaking empirical investigations of Hartmut Gabler, whose quantitative studies of swimmers must be among the most thorough ever conducted.[48] The results are clear. From Bouet's protocols, gathered from 1,634 sportsmen and sportswomen, sports appear to be means of "feeling that one exists," "discovering oneself," "realizing oneself," "finding an expression of the self," "knowing oneself," "communicating nonlinguistically," "obtaining recognition from others," and "dominating others." (Bouet is too honest to censor out the unpleasant motivations.) Sports "offer to man a chance to prove his existence to others in an authentic manner."[49] Gabler's psychological tests are less dramatic, but they ought to suffice against the popular notion that athletic achievement is correlated with neurotic personality.[50] Since we began our inquiry into the nature of modern sports by quoting Roger Bannister's description of a magical moment of spontaneous play, it is perhaps appropriate to single him out from among the thousands of athletes who have tried to communicate what they felt about sports. Bannister tried to portray his emotional state as he neared the end of the first four-minute mile:[51]

I had a moment of mixed joy and anguish, when my mind took over. It raced well ahead of my body and drew my body compellingly forward. I felt that the moment of a lifetime had come. There was no pain, only a great unity of movement and aim. The world seemed to stand still, or did not exist. . . . I felt at that moment that it was my chance to do one thing supremely well. I drove on, impelled by a combination of fear and pride.

And when it was over, when the time was announced, Bannister grabbed his friends Brasher and Chataway "and together we scampered round the track in a burst of spontaneous joy."[52]

Although athletes are sometimes thought to be rather inarticulate, it is truly remarkable how many of them have attempted to express themselves in poetic form, especially in the pages of professional physical-education journals like Quest. The poems are almost invariably attempts to communicate what is, of course, essentially incommunicable—the joy of physical action. In her book of poems, My Skin Barely Covers Me (1975), ex-swimmer Barbara Lamblin dramatizes both the joy of sports and the destruction of that joy by an excessive stress on winning.

Barbara Lamblin is not alone. Many athletes have become disillusioned with the practice and even with the ideals of modern sports. Some have testified to a sense of victimization and alienation.[53] The Neo-Marxist insists that athletes avowing a sense of alienation experience reality while the voices of affirmation speak from "false consciousness." There is, ultimately, no way to resolve a disagreement of this sort. A similar impasse awaits us in the rocky terrain of psychoanalysis. What can we reply to the charge that repressed heterosexual energy is sublimated into homosexual athletic aggression? Like much psychoanalytic theory, the Neo-Marxist interpretation of sexuality and sports is impossible to invalidate. The best response seems to be that Victorian sexual morality did look to sports as a substitute for sexual activity. Strenuous play and a cold shower tamed the savage adolescent. But modern sports have long since freed themselves from Victorian views of sexuality. Whatever coaches and physical educators may now say in their public statements, athletes have made it abundantly clear that heterosexual activity is a perquisite of the sporting life. What Babe Ruth did on the sly, screened by the cooperation of moralistic journalists, Wilt Chamberlain and "Broadway Joe" Namath now do openly, even boastfully. Let a runner give what seems to be the almost universal opinion: "Athletes love physical expression, and sex is one of the best forms of it."[54] To the evidence of predominantly heterosexual behavior, the Neo-Marxist countercharges that the heterosexuality of the athlete is inauthentic, a "repressive cosmetics-and-commodity sexual pseudo fulfillment."[55] The argument has become positively ptolemaic. Such indictments cannot be answered.

Ironically, the Neo-Marxist radicals have not ventured to defend the rights of homosexuals in sports. For that, we can turn to a remarkable American novel by Patricia Nell Warren, *The Front Runner* (1975), but the Neo-Marxist will find cold comfort in a book which celebrates both the joy of sports and the homosexual love of an Olympic champion and his coach.

At least one aspect of the Neo-Marxist critique is susceptible to an empirical test. The argument that sports function to render apathetic and to divert from political activity can be invalidated by the evidence. Numerous studies have demonstrated a strong correlation between active and passive sports participation. Those who participate directly in sports are more likely than nonparticipants to be spectators, both in person and through the electronic media.[56] Since active participants are invariably a minority of the total population of a society, this does *not* mean that most spectators are also active participants. They *are*, however, more likely to be participants than their fellow citizens who avoid the spectator's role. Even in soccer, where the ratio of active to passive participation is much lower than in most other sports, studies have shown that as many as two-thirds of the spectators in the stadium are themselves active players.[57] An even larger number of empirical studies have indicated that active participation in sports is positively correlated with various other cultural activities, including involvement in politics.[58] This last point is especially important. The best data now available tend strongly to disprove the charge that an interest in sports "infantalizes" or "cretinizes" the athlete or the spectator.

We can carry the discussion further. If sport *in general* is repressive, alienating, and apathy-inducive, which is the Neo-Marxist thesis, then we must conclude that the ruling class of modern society has decided to alienate itself rather than those whom they most oppress. There is overwhelming evidence to demonstrate conclusively that managers and professionals participate in sport at higher rates than members of the working class; the educated participate at a higher rate than the uneducated; men participate more than women.[59] These relationships hold for Communist as well as non-

Communist countries and they hold more strongly for highly competitive than for more recreational sport. If sport is an engine of alienation, we can only conclude that the advantaged have turned it upon themselves rather than upon the disadvantaged.

A final comment on the Neo-Marxist critique. The preference for play rather than for modern sports is one which the "New Left" shares with Johan Huizinga, who more than a generation ago lamented that the instinct for play had atrophied "with the increasing systematization and regimentation of sport."[60] The preference for play is part and parcel of a Romantic rejection of the basic characteristics of modern society. On this issue, the Neo-Marxist position is much closer to the conservatism of *Homo Ludens* than to the radicalism of *Das Kapital*.

4. A WEBERIAN INTERPRETATION

The critique of the Marxist and Neo-Marxist critiques brings us once again to the fact that there is undoubtedly some relationship between the rise of modern sports and the development of modern society. What relationship? The answer must, inevitably, be a generalization of a rather large order. Such generalizations are certainly subject to close scrutiny and hard questions about detailed interactions, but there is at least one interpretation which does not founder upon the shoals of blatant contradiction of theory by fact.

The entire discussion of the difference between primitive and modern sports (chapter 2) was informed by what I refer to in shorthand as a Weberian view of social organization. Max Weber's analysis of the transition from traditional to modern society has its analogues in Ferdinand Tönnies' classical formulations of *Gemeinschaft* and *Gesellschaft* ("community" and "society"), in Sir Henry Maine's theory of the movement from status to contract, and in Talcott Parsons' distinction between particularistic and universalistic modes. My choice of the term "Weberian" is motivated partly by convenience.

One great advantage of the Weberian model is that it enables one to see in the microcosm (modern sports) the characteristics of the macrocosm (modern society)—secularism, equality, specialization, rationalism, bureaucratic organization, and quantification. These six characteristics, plus the quest for records which appears even more strikingly in sports than in the rest of the social order, are interdependent, systematically related elements of the ideal type of a modern society. They derive from the fundamental Weberian notion of the difference between the ascribed status of traditional society and the achieved status of a modern one.

Another advantage of the Weberian interpretation is that it does not reduce explanation to the economic determinism which is Marxism's ever-present beast in the jungle. The trouble with economic determinism in this particular case is that the explanatory factor, industrialization, does not explain enough. Although the first nations to industrialize were, indeed, the first to develop national organizations for modern sports, other countries, like Bulgaria and Cuba, have reached impressive levels of athletic achievement without extensive industrialization (not to speak of industrial *capitalism*). Industrialism no longer seems to be the key, if it ever was.

A recent statistical study by Hilmi Ibrahim attempts to correlate national success in Olympic competition, on a points-per-capita basis, with industrialization as measured by Robert Marsh's Index of Societal Differentiation, which ranks nations by the percentage of their nonagricultural labor and the level of their energy consumption. With these admittedly imperfect variables, Ibrahim found that nations high on Marsh's scale have done well at the Olympics, but less industrialized nations have often done better, especially in recent years.[61] Using Ibrahim's data, we can calculate the Spearman rank-order correlation for Olympic success and industrialization. If the rank order in the first category is the same as in the second, the correlation is 1.0. If the order is reversed, the correlation is -1.0. For the top five medal-winners in 1968, the correlation of athletic success to level of industrialism was actually $-.8$.

Economic factors remain, however, absolutely essential to any satisfactory interpretation of the nature of modern sport. In every modern society, for instance, the middle class is overrepresented in its active and passive participation in sports. This overrepresentation cannot be unrelated to economic factors like wealth and income and occupational category. Marxist scholarship has alerted us to this relationship. But it is also true of modern sports that the young are more intensely involved than the old, men more than women, the educated more than the uneducated, Protestants more than Catholics, and the upwardly mobile more than the downwardly mobile. Class is important, but age, sex, education, religion, and mobility are also important factors which cannot be neglected if we seek to comprehend the nature of modern sports. Once again, the common thread that ties these factors together is the emphasis on achievement. If status is awarded on the basis of age or sex or religious affiliation, then social mobility—if there is any—will hardly be a function of achievement and the educational process will not stress individual effort as the route to success. Obviously, we do *not* now and never will live entirely in what the psychologist David McClelland calls "the achievement society." Not even in the achievement-oriented world of sports are the influences of ascribed status completely absent. Coaches will always play favorites and officials will never be completely unbiased. But the Weberian model is more congruent with social reality than is any other model. The congruence is especially close in modern sports.

  For a Weberian interpretation, however, the relation of sports to religion is a particularly sticky wicket, just as the relationship between economics and religion proved to be a classical problem in Weber's own sociological work. We know that modern sports spread from Protestant England and that they spread more quickly to Protestant than to Catholic countries (although France is an important exception here). We also know that Protestants are more likely than Catholics to be involved in sports and also more likely to be athletes of international calibre (which is not to deny that Catholics are overrepresented in some sports, like American professional football). Tables 4 and 5, taken from studies by Günther Lüschen and Hans Lenk, demonstrate the overrepresentation of Protestants in German sports and in Olympic competiton.[62] Given such data, we are tempted to seize upon Weber's own concept of "secular asceticism" and to explain disparities in the rate of participation and achievement by the self-discipline of physical training, which is therefore the equivalent of the deferred gratification necessary for the accumulation of capital and the reinvestment of profits.[63]

Table 4
Sport and Religion in West Germany

	General Population (%)	Members of Sports Clubs (%)	Members Involved in Track & Swimming (%)	Members in High-Level Track & Swimming (%)
Protestants	52	60	67	73
Catholics	44	37	31	26
Others	4	3	2	1
Number		1,880	366	111

Table 5
Sport and Religion at the Olympic Games

	Share of Olympic Gold Medals (%)	Share of World's Religious Population (%)
Protestants	54.5	7.6
Catholics	40	23.6
Mohammedans	1.6	15.5
Buddhists, Shintoists	1.2	7.3
Jews	1	.4
Others	1.6	45.4

Unfortunately for this line of reasoning, we quite properly think of the English and American Puritans as among the most Protestant of Protestants and we know that the Puritans were bitterly hostile to sports. John Bunyan's autobiography dramatizes his conversion to righteousness at the very moment when he wickedly indulged in a "game of cat" (an ancestor of baseball). The Puritans of Massachusetts and Connecticut "banned dice, cards, quoits, bowls, ninepins, 'or any other unlawful game in house, yard, garden, or backside,' singing out for special attention 'the Game called Shuffle Board, in howses of Common Interteinment, whereby much precious time is spent unfruitfully.'" [64] The interdiction of shuffle board does not suggest a strong disposition toward sports.

James I of England urged in his Book of Sports (1618) that the people of his realm should not be disturbed "from any lawfull Recreation; Such as dauncing, either men or women, Archeries for men, leaping, vaulting or other harmless Recreation . . . ," but the Puritans of the Commonwealth had the hangman burn the king's book.[65] Dennis Brailsford, in a history of sport and society from Queen Elizabeth to Queen Anne, sums up the Puritan view: "The Puritans saw their mission to erase all sport and play from men's lives."[66] This may sound like Macaulay's quip that the Puritans banned bear-baiting not because of the pain suffered by the animals but because of the pleasure experienced by the spectators, but Brailsford's study is a meticulously researched piece of scholarship. Other historians have commented on the sudden revival of English sports in 1660 when Charles II, "the Merry Monarch," returned to restore the banished pleasures of the stage and the turf.[67] There is ample evidence of Protestantism's reluctance, before the twentieth century, to look favorably upon modern sports.[68]

This hostility poses one problem. Another arises when we ponder the enthusiasm for modern sports in the Soviet Union and in Japan, two nations quite definitely out of the orbit of Protestantism, nor can we explain the achievements of Polish, Cuban, Bulgarian, and Hungarian athletes by references to Protestantism any better than by assertions about the imperatives of capitalist development. The clue of this explanatory labyrinth may well be found in Robert Merton's famous essay, "Puritanism, Pietism, and Science" (1936). In this essay, Merton demonstrated that Protestants were much more likely than Roman Catholics to have been partisans of the "new science" of the seventeenth century:[69]

Empiricism and rationalism were canonized, beatified, so to speak. It may very well be that the Puritan ethos did not directly influence the method of science and that this was simply a parallel development in the internal history of science, but it is evident that through the psychological compulsion toward certain modes of thought and conduct this value-complex made an empirically-founded science commendable rather than, as in the medieval period, reprehensible, or at best acceptable on sufferance.

The implication for our present purpose is that the correlation between Protestantism and participation in sports disguises the fundamental causal relationship between these two dependent variables and the independent variable which acts upon them. The basic explanatory factor is the scientific world-view, a world-view which has since been espoused by the Japanese and by every Marxist society. Indeed, Marxists like to think of themselves as the only scientific philosophers.

In other words, the mathematical discoveries of the seventeenth century were popularized in the eighteenth century, at which time we can observe the beginnings of our modern obsession with quantification in sport. During the Age of the Enlightenment, we can see the transition from the Renaissance concept of "measure," in the sense of moderation and balance, to the modern concept of measurement. The movement is philologically visible in German as well, i.e., from *Maß* to *Messen*.[70] The emergence of modern sports represents neither the triumph of capitalism nor the rise of Protestantism but rather the slow development of an empirical, experimental, mathematical *Weltanschauung*. England's early leadership has less to do with the Protestant ethic and the spirit of capitalism than with the intellectual revolution symbolized by the names of Isaac Newton and John Locke and institutionalized in the Royal Society, founded during the Restoration, in 1662, for the advancement of science.

This interpretation was suggested by Hans Lenk: "Achievement sport, i.e., sport whose achievements are extended beyond the here and now through measured comparisons, is closely connected to the scientific-experimental attitudes of the modern West."[71] The suggestion was further developed by Henning Eichberg in *Der Weg des Sports in die industrielle Zivilisation*.[72] Equipped with this insight into the role of the scientific *Weltanschauung* in the rise of modern sports, we can satisfactorily account for the post-World-War-II surge of athletic achievement in the nations of Eastern Europe, where the vestiges of premodern social organization and ideology were suddenly, even ruthlessly, challenged by a relentlessly modern attitude.

To the degree that religious tradition induces a nonscientific or even an antiscientific orientation, the transition from folk-games to modern sports will be inhibited and retarded, but the reason for this inhibition and retardation has less to do with the positive in religious faith than with the negative assessment of modern science. This can be seen in the case of Canadian sport, where the French population has been drastically underrepresented. In France itself, Roman Catholicism interacted with the rise of mathematical science in such a manner that the French, from the time of Descartes and Pascal to that of Poincaré and de Broglie, have made great contributions to the natural sciences. In France itself, modern sports appeared early and developed fairly quickly (despite the opinion of some that sport "has made no real impression on the soul of the French nation").[73] In Canada, however, Catholicism seems to have encouraged a kind of parochial antagonism to the modern world, a negativism which appears in the statistics on sports participation. Although roughly 30 percent of Canada is ethnically French, this group has provided only 8.1 percent of the 4,297 athletes representing Canada at the Commonwealth, Pan-American, and Olympic games. Since we know that economic factors play an important role in rates of participation in modern sports, we cannot simply say that religion alone is responsible for this striking disparity, but it would be a mistake to discount the powerful influence of the Catholic Church in Quebec and the Maritime Provinces. The sociologists whose empirical study I have just cited offer the following explanation for Quebec's athletic backwardness: "Among French Canadians, the traditional mentality has long rested on an agricultural ideology and on a vision of the world which is essentially religious, which venerates the past."[74]

The persuasiveness of this explanation is increased by the few studies to analyze the rates of sports participation of a student population in relation to the field of academic study. Looking at 387 students at two Swiss universities, authors of one survey found that theology majors were, by a wide margin, the least involved in sports, while students of the natural and social sciences were among the most active.[75] A study of 345 students at Amherst College looked specifically at the relationship between academic major and rate of participation in sports. It was found that social-science majors participate most frequently, followed by natural-science majors. Students of the humanities were significantly less active ($t = 2.366$, $p < .01$; $t = 2.087$, $p < .025$).[76] If these findings are typical, which only empirical research can establish, the correctness of my argument about sports and a scientific *Weltanschauung* will be supported.

Henning Eichberg has pointed to the importance of a mathematical-empirical world-view, but he has also, less persuasively, attempted to find a correlation between the rise of modern sports and the Romantic Revolution which swept over much of Europe and America at the end of the eighteenth and the beginning of the nineteenth centuries. It is, in my view, more probable that Romanticism, with its pervasive antiscientific bias, encouraged the survival of premodern sports like hunting and fishing and hindered the emergence of modern sports. We can see this clearly in a movement strongest in Germany, where the Romantic Revolution was also quite intense. I have in mind the German variety of gymnastics known as *Turnen*.

The origins of *Turnen* are conventionally traced to the innovative educational work of Johann Christian Friedrich GutsMuths and Friedrich Ludwig Jahn. Both men believed in the importance of physical education. Both set up systems which included a wide range of gymnastics and what we know as track and field sports. Both were ardently nationalistic. When GutsMuths republished his *Gymnastik für die Jugend* (1793) in 1817, he dropped the Greek word from the title and replaced it with a German word, he substituted a nationalistic for a universal reference, and the book became *Turnbuch für die Söhne des Vaterlandes*. In it, he wrote, "We must give our youth a patriotic education for the spirit and a truly paramilitary education for the body."[77] In the foreword to his *Deutsches Volkstum* (1810), Jahn proclaimed, "A state without a people is nothing, a soul-less artificiality; a people without a state is nothing, an airy, disembodied abstraction."[78] Jahn himself was committed enough to become an active participant in Germany's national revolution against the Napoleonic occupation of the fatherland.

From Jahn's *Turnplatz* in the fields near Berlin, established in 1811, the movement spread quickly throughout Germany and from Germany to the rest of Europe and even to the United States. The movement was always political as well as athletic. Although the early *Turner* were often Liberal nationalists, which brought them into a protracted conflict with the Prussian authorities, the political orientation of the movement gradually shifted to the right, especially after the failure of the Liberal revolution of 1848 and the flight of the more radical *Turner* to America.[79] The *Turner* became increasingly committed to Romantic nationalism, to the celebration of the mysterious German spirit, which is born of the mystic unity of Volk and Vaterland. The mysticism reaches a kind of crescendo in Hermann Burte's novelistic evocation of the ideal Turner in Wiltfeber: Der ewige Deutsche (1912), surely one of the most Romantic novels ever written.

Although GutsMuths and Jahn had not been immune from the tendency to quantify, to seek records, or to encourage competition, the Turner became increasingly hostile to what their most famous twentieth-century leader called "the anti-spirit of noisy championships."[80] The Turner, as defenders of Romantic nationalism, became the enemies of modern sport, which they perceived as Liberal, rational, international, and un-German. "Der Sport ist undeutsch."[81] This rejection of modern sports by the Turner is of crucial importance. Their journal, Die Deutsche Turnzeitung, condemned boxing and running and they denounced modern sports as semitic.[82] When word of the revived Olympic games reached Germany, the Rheinische-Westfälische Zeitung voiced opposition: "A sports club or any individual German who embarrasses his country by furthering or even visiting these games deserves to be cast out by his morally indignant people."[83] When the invitation to Athens arrived, the Deutsche Turnerschaft rejected it.[84] When a group of gymnasts went anyway, they were subsequently expelled from membership.[85] Four years after the first modern Olympics, the Deutsche Turnerschaft's chairman announced that sport was "a passionately pursued form of physical exercise as alien to German behavior as its name, for which there is no German word."[86] As late as 1933, a writer in Die Schar called for the renunciation of "concrete stadium, cinder track, tape-measure, stopwatch, manicured lawn, and track shoes. . . . In their place comes the simple meadow, free nature."[87] Even the Turner of the working class, despite their Marxist vision of a modern, social-democratic Germany, declared their reluctance to endorse competitive gymnastics, especially high-level competition.[88] Competition, both team and individual, did eventually become a part of German gymnastics, but modern sport remained suspect. From the late nineteenth century until the dissolution of the Deutsche Turnerschaft under Hitler, there was the repeated accusation that sport was English, not German, a symbol of Liberal internationalism, a threat to the Romantic unity of the German *Volk* upon the native soil of the *Vaterland*. And England, birthplace of modern sports, returned the "compliment" by an almost complete neglect of *Turnen*.[89] It was, therefore, a perverse historical irony that Adolf Hitler, the personification of Romantic nationalism in its most irrational and destructive form, was persuaded to set aside his initial reluctance to sponsor the Olympic games of 1936. In order to allow *der Führer* a propaganda coup, sport finally received its German apotheosis.[90]

In Romantic nationalism's opposition to modern sport, we have seen the other side of the coin, the obverse of the scientific worldview. In our search for the roots of modern sport, we have moved in an explanatory regression from abstractions like the Industrial Revolution and the Reformation to a still more abstract formulation—the scientific world-view. And now we confront a paradox. The quest for records is in itself one of the most remarkable forms of the Faustian drive, one of the most extraordinary manifestations of the Romantic pursuit of the unattainable. Sports themselves, originating in the spontaneous expression of physical energy, have their source in the irrational. We are all familiar with the frenzy of an athletic encounter, with the atavistic enthusiasm of football fans, with the naked aggression of the boxer's punch, with the inexplicable determination of the entranced runner who staggers on despite the spasms of his tortured body. Paradox, yes. Contradiction, no. Sports are an alternative to and, simultaneously, a reflection of the modern age. They have their roots in the dark soil of our instinctive lives, but the form they take is that dictated by modern society. Like the technological miracle of Apollo XI's voyage to the moon, they are the rationalization of the Romantic.

Why Baseball Was
Our National Game

1. AMERICAN EXCEPTIONALISM

MARXIST and Weberian explanatory models of social change differ in many respects, some of which we have touched upon, but they agree in their rejection of what historians have referred to as "American exceptionalism." They agree that the historical development of the United States has followed the same general pattern as that demonstrated by other modern societies. America is no exception to the laws which govern the transition from feudalism to capitalism or from traditional to modern society.

But Americans have always liked to think of themselves as unique, have been drawn to the flattering notion that America is, indeed, an exception. "Only in America" is the demotic form of this faith. What the man in the street simply asserts, the historian in his study, and the anthropologist, the sociologist, the novelist and the poet, articulate in their more complex forms.

The Puritans of New England imagined themselves to be Englishmen with a special mission, but Englishmen still, chosen by God,

An earlier version of this chapter appeared as "Literature, Sociology, and 'Our National Game,'" *Prospects*, 1 (1975), 119–36. Used by permission of *Prospects*.

dispatched into the wilderness on a divine errand. The sense of American uniqueness faded in the eighteenth century, when the dark colors of Calvinism bleached into the somewhat lighter shades of Christian piety and even into the mild deism of the American Enlightenment. The colonists and the Mother Country drew somewhat closer together as two parts of what historians sometimes refer to as the "Atlantic civilization." It was a cosmopolitan age. The War for Independence, whether or not it was truly a revolution, raised to consciousness the problem of American identity. In 1782, Crèvecoeur published his *Letters from an American Farmer* and posed the still inadequately answered question: Who is this new man, this American? Five years later, Royall Tyler's play *The Contrast* set forth one version of the difference between the American and the Englishman, between Brother Jonathan and John Bull. From Tyler through the "international novels" of Hawthorne and James to the writers of the present day, creative minds have dramatized their conception of an American character.

Early in the nineteenth century, George Bancroft began to publish the first fully developed theory of American exceptionalism. His monumental *History of the United States* (1834–1875) presented a providential view of the American past. The United States had been destined by God to demonstrate to the world the moral and political superiority of democratic institutions. The observed difference between Europe and America was, therefore, part of a divine plan for the regeneration of the world through the agency of the common man. At the end of the century, Frederick Jackson Turner's famous essay "The Significance of the Frontier in American History" (1893) contributed mightily to the theme of American exceptionalism. His theory was secular and environmental, a kind of hymn nonetheless, a celebration of American democracy as the offspring of the frontier. In Turner's view, the frontier acted as a crucible in which age-old European customs were burned away, in which the true metal of the American character was created.

More recently, Louis Hartz has gone back to Alexis de Tocqueville's *Democracy in America* (1835–1840) in order to demonstrate another version of American exceptionalism. It is the thesis of *The*

Liberal Tradition in America (1955) that America was settled by men whose orientation if not their actual status was predominantly middle class. They came to a land which had neither a feudal aristocracy nor a peasantry. They had, therefore, the institutional as well as the geographical space in which to develop Liberal capitalism. The Liberal tradition exfoliated and flourished, unhindered by the feudal institutions which hedged in the growth of English or French Liberalism, unchallenged also by the nascent socialism of the European working class. Americans were, in Tocqueville's phrase, "born equal." They won their freedom almost without a struggle, which perhaps accounts for the American tendency to optimism and to an irksome sort of innocence.

Bancroft, Turner, Hartz—they are only three of the many scholars who have assumed a difference for which there must be an explanation. None of the major hypotheses about American exceptionalism and none of the more important efforts to delineate the American character (or characters) has dealt directly with the nature of American sports, but it is probably the case that most of the writers who *have* speculated about American sports have felt that our sports are somehow peculiarly American.

John R. Tunis, for instance, devoted most of his life to novels and essays about American sports. In *The American Way in Sport* (1958) he attempted to explain the distinctiveness of our approach to physical contests. His theory is symptomatic and deserves a moment's notice. "Sport," he wrote, "is a great clue to national character."[1] And the clue to American sports? "It was the frontier . . . that made us what we are in sport today."[2] The frontier was a source of mobility, restlessness, and change as well as equality and individualism. It was, moreover, the spirit of the frontier that led to an emphasis on organization and to the quest for records.[3] The difficulty here is that Tunis has bought Frederick Jackson Turner lock, stock, and barrel. If the frontier explains America, he reasoned, then the frontier must explain America's sports. (A similar fallacy seems to have seduced an authority on Australian cricket, who notes that the Australian version of the game "sprang from the heart and way of life of a pioneering people who had to conquer crude and challenging conditions."[4])

The lure of the frontier as an explanatory hypothesis must be power-ful. It leads to the naive conclusion that whatever we see in our sports must somehow be the product of the frontier.

It is easy enough to scoff at the simplicity of such ideas, but I must confess that I can trace the origins of my own interest in the compar-ative sociology of sports to a moment in Berlin in 1969 when I, an American sitting in the stadium built for the 1936 Olympics and watching the frenzied German crowd watching the soccer match, wondered why. Why were these Germans passionately involved with soccer while we Americans remain stubbornly loyal to baseball and football, two sports scarcely known in Europe? A few months earlier, I had watched the 1968 Olympics on German television and had been enthralled by the gymnastics competition in which Czechoslo-vakia's Vera Caslawska defeated her rivals from the Soviet Union and East Germany, i.e., from two nations whose armies had only weeks before occupied Prague and destroyed the possibility of "socialism with a human face." Gymnastics were, in 1968, a very minor sport in the United States. Was I un-American to marvel at Vera Cas-lawska and at Japan's Sawao Kato, who won the men's competition? My subsequent efforts to isolate the uniquely American element in American sports led me, unexpectedly, to the rather contrary conclu-sion that American sports are less unique than they seem. They are really modern sports, essentially the same as the sports of every other modern society. Implicit therefore in my interpretation of the rise of modern sports has been the assumption that the phenomenon is inte-gral to every industrial or postindustrial society. My examples have been drawn quite intentionally from a large number of nations, always with the sense that modern sports are the same the world over, despite whatever local variations may occur.

But local variations do occur. Premodern sports like bullfighting and curling survive into the twentieth century. Baseball and football fail to penetrate Europe while cricket and rugby are scarcely played on this side of the Atlantic. Gymnastics are the second most popular participant sport in Denmark and are still, despite the sudden burst of television-induced interest in recent years, a peripheral sport in the United States.[5] With the advantages of a lunar or a sociological perspective, the similarities in the sports of Des Moines and Düsseldorf loom large. With the closer inspection of distinctive detail, the local variations become more obvious. Let us explore them. Let us look at our "national game."

2. QUANTIFIED PASTORAL

When John J. McGraw, the cocky, colorful manager of the New York Giants in the days of their glory, toured the British Isles with his team in 1924, Arthur Conan Doyle ventured a prediction. He thought that baseball might well sweep the United Kingdom as it had the United States.[6] Doyle seems in this instance to have been less insightful than his beloved Holmes. Baseball, the American version of several English ballgames, never caught on among the British. Why not? The easy answer is that our national game is peculiarly American, fitted to American conditions and to the American character. As early as 1866, an observer of American pastimes wrote,[7]

It is a game which is peculiarly suited to the American temperament and disposition; the nine innings are played in the brief space of two and one half hours, or less. From the moment the first striker takes his position, and poises his bat, it has an excitement and vim about it. . . . There is no delay or suspense about it, from beginning to end.

Harper's noted in 1886 that "the fascination of the game has seized upon the American people, irrespective of age, sex, or other condition."[8] One of baseball's best historians has concluded that the game was "ingrained in the American psyche" by the end of the nineteenth century.[9] Beginning his book on baseball, which he entitled simply *America's National Game*, Albert G. Spalding laid down the law:[10]

To enter upon a deliberate argument to prove that Base Ball is our National Game; that it has all the attributes of American origin, American character and unbounded public favor in America, seems a work of supererogation. It is to undertake the elucidation of a patent fact; the sober demonstration of an axiom; it is like a solemn declaration that two plus two equal four.

Carl Diem, investigating American sports for the German government, reported in amazement, "Measured by enthusiasm, there really is only one game in America, baseball."[11] By 1927 Elmer Berry's *Philosophy of Athletics* contained remarks which must have even then seemed truisms:[12]

Baseball is peculiarly American in its temperament and psychology. . . . It is our national game not alone because of history and development but by nature and characteristics as well. The game "fits" Americans; it pleases, satisfies, represents us.

More recently, Allan Nevins has placed his prestige as a historian behind the proposition that baseball is "a true expression of the American spirit" and Jacques Barzun has urged foreigners to learn about baseball if they wish to understand America.[13]

Meanwhile, countless millions of ordinary citizens have found a handy metaphor in Tinker to Evers to Chance, have defended Bone-head Merkle's costly failure to touch second base, have lamented the moral lapse of Shoeless Joe Jackson, have argued about whether or not Babe Ruth called his shot in October 1932, have wept at dying Lou Gehrig's claim to have been the luckiest man in the world, have participated in angry controversies over the merits of Ty Cobb versus those of Joe DiMaggio and Willie Mays. When baseball's public image was threatened by the Black Sox scandal of 1919–1920, the grand jury summoned to determine if the players had been bribed reacted as if the case had been one of blasphemy; reporting to the judge, the foreman declaimed,[14]

The jury is impressed with the fact that baseball is an index to our national genius and character. The American principle of merit and fair play must prevail. . . . The national game promotes respect for proper authority, self-confidence, fairmindedness, quick judgment and self-control.

It was a ritual moment of self-reassurance. Doubts about the moral condition of American society were quieted. The devils were cast out.

And the Supreme Court of the United States followed the baseball returns.[15] In the Federal League Case of 1922, the court decided that baseball was an exhibition and not a business in the sense of the Sherman Antitrust Act of 1890. Oliver Wendell Holmes went on to opine that, although baseball players crossed state lines, individual games of baseball were invariably played within the borders of a single state. The game was, therefore, exempt from an act regulating interstate commerce. On the basis of these arguments, the court held that major-league baseball's monopoly was entirely legal. The position was reaffirmed in 1953 in *Toolson vs. New York Yankees, Inc.* Two years later, the monopolistic power of the International Boxing Club was broken up by the Supreme Court, which held that only Congress had the right to grant an exemption from the antitrust laws and that Congress had not done so on behalf of boxing. In 1957, the Supreme Court declared in the Radovich case that professional football is also subject to the Sherman Act and allied legislation. With some obvious embarrassment, the learned justices conceded that, if they had been asked to judge baseball's status *without* the difficult precedent of the Federal League Case, they might have been forced to conclude that a baseball game had legal similarities to a football game. Nonetheless, when Curt Flood challenged the monopoly once again and fought his way to the Supreme Court, Mr. Justice Blackmun wrote a majority decision based entirely on *stare decis*—it was up to Congress to undo what the Court had done, if Congress wished to. The most intriguing part of the unpersuasive opinion in *Flood vs. Kuhn* (1972) was the Justice's lengthy rolecall of the heroes of baseball and his evocation of the glories of the game.

Why this need to believe in baseball, which shall have no other games before it? What is it about baseball that makes it so different? Allan Nevins' reference to baseball's "strenuosity, excitement, speed, and drama" is no help at all unless we want to believe that other sports lack these qualities, but several popular explanations are worth a moment's notice, if only because they demonstrate a will to believe which gropes hopefully toward almost *any* explanation.

As early as 1867, the *Spirit of the Times*, the first of our famous sporting magazines, commented on the ease of access to the game:[16]

Of all out-door sports, base-ball is that in which the greatest number of our people participate either as players or as spectators. . . . It is a pastime that best suits the temperament of our people. The accessories being less costly than those of the turf, the acquatic course, or the cricket-field, it is an economic game, and within the easy reach of the masses.

Compared to yachting, yes, but the argument that everyone can play cannot be taken seriously as an explanation for baseball's popularity.

Two people can play catch and four can play work-up, but baseball requires at least eighteen players, a bat, a ball, and an open space. Soccer can be played with less equipment, basketball with fewer players, volleyball with less space, badminton more easily than any of the team games. For a maximum of accessibility and a minimum of accessories, it is hard to find a better sport than running. If every American has played baseball, or at least softball, it is because our culture has made this inevitable, not because baseballs cost less than footballs.

In recent years, historians have speculated not about the spareness of the "accessories" but about the role of technology in the spread of baseball.[17] It is undeniable that technological transformation has changed the context and the parameters of modern sports. The National League, organized in 1876, was made possible by the railroads, which carried teams from city to city, and by the telegraph and the rotary press, which allowed the nineteenth-century fan to follow the team's progress while it toured. Radio certainly played its part in the 1920s, and television has carried the game to millions even while it apparently has reduced the numbers of those who are brought to the turnstiles. It is plausible that modern technology has increased the number of people in any society who can be drawn to a single sporting event at a given moment, but it is not logical to maintain that *baseball* has profited more than any other sport from technological advances. Of course, some advances do favor one sport over another; gymnastics, for instance, loses its essence if one merely *hears* about what happens on the balance beam or the uneven parallel bars. Television can, in this case, provide a stimulus which radio could not. Similarly, some have argued that television has given football a competitive advantage over baseball in that the narrow focus upon the batter distorts the Gestalt of the game more than a narrow focus upon football's ball carrier.[18] But I can think of no inherent characteristics of baseball which enabled it, more than its immediate rivals, to take advantage of pretelevision technology.

Equally prevalent, but no more persuasive, are arguments that stress such psychological factors as hero worship or the occasion for nostalgia. A recent scholar has suggested that baseball flourished, at least in part, because of what he calls the "Folk Hero Factor," be-

cause legendary figures like Babe Ruth captured the national imagination.[19] Any baseball buff can add a hundred magic names to that
of the Sultan of Swat—as Justice Blackmun does in *Flood vs.
Kuhn*—but folk heroes do not seem in themselves sufficient to set
baseball apart from other sports. Boxing, too, has had its magic
names—John L. Sullivan, Gentlemen Jim Corbett, Jack Johnson,
Jack Dempsey, Joe Louis, Muhammad Ali—but boxing has never
been put forth as our national sport. There is undeniably an interaction between a game and its heroes, and I do not mean to assert that
Ruth's glory did not reinforce the hold of baseball on the sporting
public; yet, it seems reasonable to insist that baseball's heroes, from
Cap Anson to Catfish Hunter, are more the benefactors than the creators of the game's popularity. Most of them have proven to be rather
colorless men when out of uniform. They are, in other words, more
the result than the cause. The present vogue of professional football
certainly cannot be explained by the assertion that potential heroes,
for inexplicable personal reasons, began to toss pigskin rather than
horsehide.

The appeal of nostalgia is not so easily dismissed. Historian Bruce
Catton has called attention to baseball's ability to evoke rural nostalgia, and former baseball commissioner Ford Frick introduced baseball's official encyclopedia with the remark, "Baseball's position in
our way of life is due . . . to its rich history. The fan cherishes
memories of ball players of his youth."[20] Middle-aged and elderly
men continue to be faithful to the game they once played because it
brings back their own youth. No visitor to St. Petersburg can deny that
nostalgia plays a role in the game's appeal for older fans, but once
again there is the problem of causation. Can one seriously contend
that baseball is *peculiarly* suited to nostalgia? If one were to become
rational about these matters, one might maintain that the potentiality
for nostalgia is greatest in games that are most closely bound up with
youth. Baseball, which can be played at the professional level by men
in their early forties, is in this sense better suited for nostalgia than
tennis, which can be played into advanced age, but basketball's physical demands generally force an earlier abandonment of the sport.
Nonetheless, although John Updike's Rabbit Angstrom and Jason
Miller's former champions remain fixed in the toils of their basketball

memories, basketball's potential for nostalgia has never been exploited as has baseball's. Wilt Chamberlain and Bill Russell are not yet part of a national myth, at least not in the manner of the Bambino. It is because of baseball's peculiar attraction that so many have been nostalgic, not the other way around.

All four of these common attempts to explain the fascination of baseball—ease of access, the technological impetus, the presence of folk heroes, the occasion for nostalgia—share the same defect, the confusion of cause and effect. None of them offers any answer to the inevitable question: why baseball rather than another game? One is tempted to throw up one's hands and announce in despair, "It's entirely a matter of historical accident. Pakistanis play polo and Americans play baseball. Once a game is part of a culture, it's there to stay. Chronological priority becomes cultural preference." There is surely an element of truth in this line of exasperated argument. Baseball never had to compete against a doctrinaire, institutionally entrenched predecessor like German *Turnen*. In a new and relatively open country, baseball and cricket—once popular in America—rivaled each other as fulfillers of a psychosocial need, much as plants and animals struggle to occupy ecological niches. That baseball won out is due partly to chauvinism and the desire to have an *American* game, but there are other factors that enabled baseball to outdistance purely American rivals like football and basketball. Two quite dissimilar factors are at work—the place of baseball in the cycle of the seasons and the tendency of baseball toward extremes of quantification. Historians have occasionally and novelists have often explored the first factor; no one has done more than touch upon the second.

The ceaseless effort to discover rural traits in an essentially urban sport indicates the importance of the pastoral impulse in baseball. The origins of the game can be traced to "town ball" played in Boston in the eighteenth century, and the first baseball team to take the field with recognizably modern rules was New York's Knickerbockers, an urban and rather urbane team organized by Alexander Cartwright, a bank clerk, in 1845.[21] In 1897, only three of the National League's 168 players were from the rural South, while 31 men came from Massachusetts alone. The early years of the game brought forth a disproportionate number of Irish-American and German-American city dwellers. Despite the game's natal circumstances and early environment, the *imagery* of baseball has tended to be pastoral. Baseball flourishes in small towns, insisted one of Frederick Jackson Turner's followers, "and even in the remoter west whence the frontier has barely disappeared." [22] There are those who cherish memories of "the Gas-House Gang," but the true pilgrimage is to Cooperstown; and the postage stamp issued in 1939 to commemorate the game shows a sandlot, a barn, a church, a country school. The symbolic message is clear. Alexander Cartwright has been forgotten except by historians, and Abner Doubleday, who had no part whatsoever in the creation of the game, forever shares with Natty Bumppo the mythic air of Cooperstown.

Pastoralism is more than an emphasis on the rural. The Gestalt is a complex one which includes open space, grass, warm weather, the bright sun. Baseball is "a game played on a spacious green expanse in the bright light of day." [23] As Roger Angell and Roger Kahn have emphasized, it is a summer game, played by the boys of summer. The weather is a part of the folklore of a game in which one sits in the bleachers and hopes that the game will neither be rained our nor called because of darkness. Baseball cannot be played in inclement weather, as can its rivals among team sports. These factors—open space, warm, clear weather, a grass field—have been woven into the rhetoric of baseball. Thomas Wolfe expressed this as well as any writer: [24]

baseball . . . is . . . really a part of the whole weather of our lives, of the thing that it is our own, of the whole fabric, the million memories of America. For example, in the memory of almost everyone of us, is there anything that can evoke spring—the first fine days of April—better than the sound of the ball smacking into the pocket of the big mitt, the sound of the bat as it hits the horsehide: for me, at any rate, and I am being literal and not rhetorical—almost everything I know about spring is in it—the first leaf, the jonquil, the maple tree, the smell of grass upon your hands and knees, the coming into flower of April. And is there anything that can tell more about an American summer than, say, the smell of the wooden bleachers in a small town baseball park, that resinous, sultry and exciting smell of old dry wood?

Gerard McCauley echoes Wolfe: "As soon as the American earth softens mackinaws are shed for sweaters and American boys are feel-

102 WHY BASEBALL WAS OUR NATIONAL GAME

ing the sting of balls snapping into gloves, anticipating that in a very short time the trees will bud, the sun will linger, telling them baseball is here."[25] For the poet Donald Hall, the theme of nostalgia mingles with that of the pastoral, for "baseball is continuous, like nothing else among American things, an endless game of repeated summers, joining the long generations of all the fathers and all the sons."[26]

As these quotations suggest, the pastoral view of baseball appears with special clarity in American literature, especially in works by Irwin Shaw and Mark Harris. Shaw's title, *Voices of a Summer Day*, is in itself suggestive. The summer day is one spent on Cape Cod by middle-aged Benjamin Federov, who watches his son Michael playing baseball and thinks back on his own life, intertwined as it was with the American game. Shaw's language communicates both the pastoral and the nostalgic elements:[27]

The sounds were the same through the years—the American sounds of summer, the tap of bat against ball, the cries of the infielders, the wooden plump of the ball into catchers' mitts, the umpires calling "Strike three and you're out." The generations circled the bases, the dust rose for forty years as runners slid in from third, dead boys hit doubles, famous men made errors at shortstop, forgotten friends tapped the clay from their spikes with their bats as they stepped into the batter's box, coaches' voices warned, across the decades, "Tag up, tag up!" on fly balls. The distant, mortal innings of boyhood and youth.

As Leo Marx demonstrates in *The Machine in the Garden*, the pastoral genre in literature is a mode of reconciliation which seeks out and presents a middle landscape between the city and the forest. In Shaw's pastoral, the summer day becomes a moment when the hero comes to terms with himself and with what he has made of his life. When he returns to his wife and daughter, they ask, "What did you do?" He answers, "I watched a ball game"—and the answer suffices.[28]

Mark Harris's *Bang the Drum Slowly* is a more complex work in which pastoral elements interact with the *Realitätsprinzip*. The narrator is Henry Wiggen, the pitcher-autobiographer whose pastoral vision of baseball had already been chastened in Harris's earlier novel, *The Southpaw*. Henry Wiggen, author and insurance salesman as well as ball player, is beset with problems:[29]

I won 26 in 52, my best year and damn near my ruination, for between the Series money and the book I owed the United States Bureau of Internal Revenue $876 which I busted my ass over playing winter ball in Japan and Cuba and hitting the banquet circuit and selling annuities to ballplayers. . . . I wrote them and said, "It is no use. Come put me in jail. I will work it off at a dollar a day hammering rocks." They wrote again, saying, "Please remit," and they dragged us through court.

But the book is not about his problems. The book is about Bruce Pearson, of Bainbridge, Georgia, a country boy who functions as a symbol of rural simplicity—and of knowledge lost to urban types like Henry Wiggen, who writes of Bruce:[30]

He traveled according to rivers. He never knew their name, but he knew which way they went by the way they flowed, and he knew how they flowed even if they weren't flowing, if you know what I mean, even if they were froze which they were for a ways, knowing by the way the bank was cut or the ice piled or the clutter tossed up along the sides.

Henry is also impressed by Bruce's insights into that most pastoral of animals, the cow. It is with subtle irony that Harris allows Wiggen to remark of Bruce Pearson, "Bruce is not a natural."[31] The term is, of course, ambiguous. Bruce was not a natural in the baseball sense, but he is as much a symbol of man in nature as William Faulkner's Ike McCaslin or Ernest Hemingway's Nick Adams. He learned to play baseball in a field of peanut hay; he was astonished to discover that the New York Mammoths intended to pay him money to continue at the game. The big leagues are a mixture of urban and rural types, but Henry's advice to Bruce, who lacks confidence in his own abilities, is suggestive: "Half the pitchers you face are only country boys like yourself, and the other half are only country boys from the city."[32]

The plot of the novel is a pastoral version of the Lou Gehrig story. Bruce calls Henry from the Mayo Clinic in Minnesota and tells him that he has been given only a few months to live. His speech is comical: "It means I am doomded," says Bruce. But the novel is a strange combination of comedy and tragedy. Henry and Bruce spend the time just before spring training in Bainbridge, Georgia, where Bruce's family welcomes the two of them to sit on the front porch, to talk about crops and hogs, to comment on the sultry weather, to reminisce in a slow, country way. The countryside is full of memories for Bruce, who overcomes taciturnity enough to give Henry a sense of the place and of Bruce's boyhood.

The baseball season is a contrast, partly comic, partly grim. There is rough-and-tumble competition, the grate of personalities against each other as men travel and live together under tension; there is hostility and meanness as well as prankish camaraderie. Henry finds himself changed by the knowledge of Bruce's illness: "When your roomie is libel to die any day on you you do not think about bonus clauses, and that is the truth whether anybody happens to think so or not."[33] When the rest of the team learns about Bruce's fate, there is an extraordinary moment of harmony and reconciliation that begins when Piney Woods, one of the catchers, sings Bruce's favorite song:

> O bang the drum slowly and play the fife lowly,
> Play the dead march as they carry me on,
> Put bunches of roses all over my coffin,
> Roses to deaden the clods as they fall.

"It made me feel very sad," writes Henry. "Yet I knew that some of the boys felt the same, and knowing it made me feel better." He goes on to express love in the awkward, touching way appropriate to the situation:[34]

> you felt warm towards them, and you looked at them, and them at you, and you were both alive, and you might as well said, "Ain't it something? Being alive, I mean! Ain't it really quite a great thing at that?" and if they would of been a girl you would of kissed them, though you never said such a thing out loud but only went on about your business.

It is a moment of pastoral reconciliation, appropriate to the game. Baseball, writes Murray Ross in an excellent essay, "is a *pastoral* sport, and . . . the game can be best understood as this kind of art. For baseball does what all good pastoral does—it creates an atmosphere in which everything exists in harmony."[35] Mark Harris realizes that pastoral harmony doesn't last. Despite the epiphany that follows the song, Bruce dies and Henry is the only member of the club to be present at the burial.

Pastoralism is only one aspect of seasonal significance. Baseball begins in the spring and can draw upon whatever traces of primitive religion remain in modern man. In her famous study, *From Ritual to Romance* (1920), Jessie Weston drew upon the anthropology of Sir James Frazer to demonstrate that the medieval grail knight's lance is a phallic symbol associated with the resurrection of the vegetation gods of ancient religion. She inspired T. S. Eliot's poem, *The Waste Land*, but it remained for Bernard Malamud, in *The Natural*, to go Eliot one better and to blend baseball history with the rites of spring.

Malamud's hero, Roy Hobbs, comes from the Far West, rather than from the slums of Baltimore or the sidewalks of New York. In his dreams, baseballs give birth to white roses; in the novel's fantasy of diurnal reality, baseballs become birds with white flapping wings.[36] When Roy Hobbs arrives in the city, the grass of the outfield turns green and he "romped in it like a happy calf in its pasture."[37] These pastoral elements are heightened to myth. Roy Hobbs' magic bat, Wonderboy, is also his "foolproof lance," with which he terrorizes Dutch Vogelman until the luckless pitcher "Keeled over in a dead faint."[38] The ancient goddesses—Ishtar, Isis, Aphrodite—appear in the guise of the mysterious Harriet Bird, whom Malamud refers to as "a snappy goddess."[39] Her talk is mythic enough to settle any doubts about Malamud's intention; she rattles away with references to the Old Testament, to medieval quest, and to Freud's theory of the primal horde and the origins of the Oedipal complex in the primitive act of patricide:[40]

Occasionally she stopped and giggled at herself for the breathless volume of words that flowed forth. . . . but after a pause was on her galloping way again—a girl on horseback—reviewing the inspiring sight. . . . of David jawboning the Goliath-Whammer, or was it Sir Percy lancing Sir Maldemer, or the first son (with a rock in his paw) ranged against the primitive papa?

The first part of the novel ends when Roy Hobbs is shot by Harriet Bird in his Chicago hotel room. The scene mingles memories of the dead gods—Tammuz, Osiris, Adonis, Jesus—with less mythic resemblances to the hotel room shooting of Eddie Waitkus.

The stage is set for the second part of the novel, in which Malamud introduces his version of *The Waste Land*. The wounded Fisher-King, who rules over the sterile land, appears as Pop Fisher, manager of the New York Knights, who suffers from athlete's foot of the hands, who vainly waits for the symbolic rain. "Removing his cap, Pop rubbed his bald head with his bandaged fingers. 'It's been a blasted dry season. No rains at all. The grass is worn scabby in the outfield and the infield is cracking. My heart feels as dry as dirt for the little I have to show for all my years in the game.' "[41] Roy Hobbs brings rain to the parched land and an end to the team's slump. The first time he comes to bat a tremendous noise cracks the sky and "a few drops of rain spattered to the ground."[42] Moments later, the deluge. The rains turn the grass green, Pop Fisher's hands heal, "and so did his heart."[43] Unfortunately, Roy Hobbs demonstrates a selfish pride which finally renders him unfit for the task of the grail knight. His obstinate love of wicked Memo Paris, rather than earthmotherly Iris Lemon, dooms him. His recognition of love comes too late. The novel ends not with the resurrection of the fertility god but with recollections of the Black Sox. Roy Hobbs changes his mind about throwing the playoff game, but his beloved Wonderboy splits in two, he strikes out, and the newspapers expose his past and present misdeeds. "Say it ain't true, Roy," begs the newsboy, and Roy Hobbs "lifted his hands to his face and wept many bitter tears."[44]

Since the secular reader is liable to resist the notion that the fascination of our national game is somehow religiously related to the vernal equinox, it is useful to note that perfectly sober historians have speculated on the mythic origins of ball games. Five years before the publication of The Natural, Robert W. Henderson published Ball, Bat and Bishop, in which he asserts, "It is the purpose of this book to show that all modern games played with bat and ball descend from one common source: an ancient fertility-rite observed by Priest-Kings in the Egypt of the Pyramids."[45] Henderson's argument seems extreme, but we must remember the cultic origins of many games. It is also instructive to examine a strange game played by Berber tribesmen of Libya. The game is unique. It is played by one tribe, a tribe further distinguished from other Berbers by a remarkable incidence of blond hair. Ta Kurt om el mahag, "the ball of the pilgrim's mother," struck its discoverer, an Italian anthropologist, as a sort of elementary baseball. There is a home base, a base to run to, a pitcher, batters, and fielders. The captain is allowed three strikes, the others only two.

A caught fly retires the side. The game has numerous terms that the Berber players themselves cannot explain. The game is, moreover, played without the toga-like *barracan* that is almost never doffed except for ceremonial occasions. No one can say for sure how the game came to North Africa or what exactly it signifies, but the likelihood is that it was brought by Germanic invaders centuries ago and that it contains the vestiges of a primitive rain ceremony now meaningless even to the Berbers.[46]

A curious fact about baseball's ludic time and space may add to the plausibility of speculations about the force of ancient myth. A recent student of football has noted, "Sports overlie the sacred cycle of mythic time to provide a needed psychic relief from the tedium of western linear time."[47] The astute observation is even truer of baseball and cricket than it is of football, basketball, hockey, soccer, rugby, field hockey, lacrosse, and European handball, all of which are temporally organized by clock time. In a very real sense, baseball is timeless. With sufficient inequality of sides, the game might go on forever as the weaker team tries vainly to retire the side. As it is, no one can tell exactly when a game is likely to end. This frustrates television sponsors and programmers but pleases those who feel that the game is never over until the last man is out. Spatially as well as temporally, there is a theoretical openness about baseball which not even cricket shares. If a ball is hit fair, it cannot be hit too far. The foul lines radiate outward from home plate to infinity.

There is still another spatial difference between baseball and other team games. The others are organized into polarities. The movement is an oscillation between the goals. Baseball's diamond is inscribed within the imaginary circle of the runner's path as he rounds the bases. And among the popular team games its movement is uniquely circular: around the bases and back to home plate. To the degree that Mircea Eliade's anthropological disquisitions are valid, the circle and the line are perhaps the most basic of mankind's metaphors for the eternally recurrent and the temporally unique. Is it wholly accidental that the four bases correspond numerically to the four seasons of the year? Perhaps it is. And yet. . . . Although I am not ready to say that Americans have been drawn to baseball because of the persistence of myth in our collective unconscious, I am nonetheless convinced that pastoral traits are important to the game and that modern man is not totally untouched by the annual revitalization of the earth.

Is it then farfetched to suggest that one reason for the relative decline of baseball in recent years has been the diminution of the pastoral element? Baseball games are now played under electric rather than solar light. Astroturf replaces grass, and the still air of the Astrodome further insulates the fan from Zephyr and from Boreas. For the television viewer, there is neither night nor day, only the bright image of some distant, weatherless event.

The second factor, quantification, seems directly opposed to the pastoral-primitive elements that have thus far occupied us. It is almost never a part of the literary celebration of baseball and it is probably not a matter most Americans are conscious of. It is, of course, the sixth of our seven characteristics of modern sports, the one which most sharply demarcates modern sports from those of ancient and premodern times. It is worth a moment to pause for comment on the first five characteristics of sports as they relate to baseball.

Secularism can be discussed briefly. If our argument is valid, baseball has retained something of the primitive connection between sports and the sacred. It is a secular activity with adumbrations of the mythic. As for equality of the conditions of competition and in access to the game, baseball cannot be distinguished from its principal rivals. Americans have praised the democratic quality of a game open to all, a game in which personal merit can be freely displayed and richly rewarded, but baseball is certainly no more inherently democratic than soccer or rugby or golf or any other modern game (all of which have been lauded as especially democratic by *their* admirers). No distinction is possible on the basis of equality as a criterion. Specialization and rationalization are also characteristics of both baseball and its rivals among the various sports in transition to their modern form. Both characteristics are far advanced in baseball. The division into nine separate playing positions and the proliferation of the most minute regulations came early to the game, as did the conscious attempts to perfect it by experimentation with changes in the rules. Officials experimented constantly with the number of balls and strikes, with the definition of the strike zone, with the distances between pitcher's mound and home plate, with the size and shape of the bat and ball, with countless other details of the sport.

Baseball was also among the first American sports to develop a complex bureaucratic structure. Twenty-two amateur clubs joined together in 1859 to form the National Association of Base Ball Players. In 1871, two years after the Cincinnati Reds became the first openly paid team, the first professional league was organized. The National League was launched in 1876 and the owners of the teams quickly worked out such bureaucratic details as the creation of a regular 154-game schedule which enabled each team to play every other team an equal number of times.

Baseball was, in a sense, sociologically primed for the high level of quantification which quickly became a hallmark of the game. The spatial separation of the players on the field and the relative isolation of the batter and the pitcher in their one-on-one opposition facilitated the accumulation of accurate individual as well as team statistics. The numerical aspects of the game—three strikes, four balls, three outs, four bases, nine innings, 154 games—provided the opportunity for infinitely varied arithmetical calculations. The creation of the scorecard and the tabular listing of team standings were small but important innovations which enabled the fans, or "cranks" as they were then called, to keep abreast of the statistics of the game. Newspapers responded eagerly to the passion for information and quickly introduced sports pages with box scores while *The Sporting News* (1886) offered more complete statistical information on the minor as well as the major leagues. Albert Spalding pioneered with his *Guides* to the game and the quantitative mania spread. The visible symbol for this fascination with numbers is the huge baseball encyclopedia published by Macmillan. It bulks almost as large as *Webster's Unabridged* and is consulted by baseball's true believers with greater frequency. Does anyone really care what Charles Comiskey's lifetime batting average was? Yes, people do seem to care. You can look it up.

Quantification is closely related to another important aspect of the game. The flow of time is regularly interrupted. In a famous article on the popularity of baseball, Roger Kahn argued that the pauses in the action are filled by the fan's telling of anecdotes, but I wish to suggest another explanation.[48] Imagine the scene. The pitcher holds the ball and stares at the batter who waits, waggling his bat. The television screen prints out the information to be processed in the mind of the spectator—the batter has an average of .287, but against this pitcher he has hit .352. The tension rises. The pitcher throws a knuckleball and the batter misses. The television screen informs the viewer that the pitcher has won seven and lost three thus far this season. The pitcher throws to first and fails to make the pickoff. The pitcher stares at the batter. The television set indicates that the batter's average against southpaws is .299. The pitcher throws a curve which misses the corner of the plate. The American aficionado shakes his head in disapproval. The count gradually goes to three and two and the pitcher winds up slowly. The European viewer, at this point, gives up and announces that the game is an unbearable bore. But the slowness of the pace provides the space for statistics and probabilities and speculations about strategy. The pauses in the physical action are times for the fan to assimilate the information processed for him and to discuss with others the information already a part of his psychic life. Baseball, writes Roger Angell, "is the most intensely and satisfyingly mathematical of all our outdoor sports. . . . Scientists speak of the profoundly moving aesthetic beauty of mathematics, and perhaps the baseball field is one of the few places where the rest of us can glimpse this mystery."[49]

Football shares this characteristic, with its sequence of downs and huddles and time-outs, with its almost equally intense concern for quantification and statistics, but football clearly lacks the aura of the pastoral, and the structure of the game probably prohibits the degree of quantification attained by baseball. Basketball, hockey, and soccer are all characterized by a much more continuous flow of play, which precludes this special kind of interaction between the living moment and the quantified career of the player and the abstracted, printed, bound, absolutized history of the game.

From the numbers we abstract the records. Baseball's wealth of quantified information makes it absurdly easy to establish records, which can be as significant as Babe Ruth's 60 homers in a single 154-game season or as insane as Stan Musial's two consecutive years as league-leader in three-base hits. Is there a baseball fan who cannot immediately name the names associated with the numbers 511 and

2130?[50] Players list their records in the appendices of their autobiographies and they have begun to vie with each other for the record number of records, which does not, as one might think, lead to scraping the bottom of the barrel because baseball's barrel of quantification is actually an inexhaustible cornucopia.

The concern for records can produce anomalies and can even sabotage the ostensible goals of the contest. Players can, for instance, express satisfaction with their personal records set while the team lurches from one defeat to another. Players can, occasionally, abandon the notion of a fair contest in order to boost their opponents to a new record, as in 1941 when opposing pitchers avoided giving Joe DiMaggio a base on balls so that he might continue his record-setting hitting streak. Similarly, in a generous but truly unsportsmanlike gesture, Denny McLain served—in an otherwise meaningless contest—Mickey Mantle a "fat" pitch which the startled Mantle then slammed for his 500th home run.

Mark Harris has parodied the excesses of record keeping:[51]

"You set a record," said Ugly. "Up to yesterday, you probably only switched the radio off 15,738 times. Now you switched it off 15, 739."
"Officially or unofficially?" said I.
"Every day you live you live one more day," said Lawyer Longabucco. "You beat your own record."
"Officially or unofficially?" said Blondie Biggs.
"I talked 3,112 official words today," said Jonah. "That puts me 3,112 official words up on yesterday."
"Today is the first time I ever officially hung this jock on this particular nail at 4:02 P.M. in the afternoon of July 9, 1955," said Perry.
"Today is the first day we ever lost to Brooklyn by a score of 4–3 after leading 3–0 in the first inning on Ladies Day I bet," said Harry Glee.
"Are the ladies official?" said Ugly.
"Some are and some ain't," said Harry.

Humor may yet save us, even from our play.

Another novelist, Robert Coover, has dramatized baseball's strange mixture of the primitive and the modern in The Universal Baseball Association, Inc., J. Henry Waugh, Prop. (1968), a book of almost uncanny insight. Coover presents an imagined world within an imagined world. His hero, an apparently lackluster accountant named J. Henry Waugh, works in the mundane reality of Mr. Zifferblatt's firm, but he lives emotionally, secretly, in the fantasy of an invented game, a board game played with three dice and an assortment of probability tables. In the solitude of his kitchen, he throws the dice, and from the millions of possibilities come the events of the game, which he then enters in carefully kept record books. Baseball's tendency to quantification has, in the world of the novel, finally replaced the actual game. The dice roll, the numbers show, the tables report, the results are recorded.[52]

American baseball, by luck, trial, and error, and since the famous playing rules council of 1889, had struck on an almost perfect balance between offense and defense, and it was that balance, in fact, that and the accountability—the beauty of the records system which found a place to keep forever each least action—that had led Henry to baseball.

The accountability and the beauty of the records system, they are the lure. "Not the actual game so much—to tell the truth, real baseball bored him—but rather the records, the statistics, the peculiar balances between individual and team, offense and defense, strategy and luck, accident and pattern, power and intelligence."[53]

Real baseball bored him, but the game does not disappear because Henry Waugh's novelistic imagination creates a whole universe, filled with thousands of players, living and dead, whose escapades and madcap adventures and feats of athletic prowess are more real to Henry than the shadowy employees who work under Mr. Zifferblatt's unsympathetic gaze. Old-timers, long since retired from the Universal Baseball Association, gather at Jake's bar to sing the ballad of Long Lew Lydell's famous seduction of Fanny McCaffree, whose father Fenimore was league commissioner and an active leader of one of its political factions. And all of this takes place in Henry's mind.

The novel reverses the historical sequence by which statistics emerge from the antics of flesh and blood players. Here, the dice and the tables of mathematical probabilities give birth to the characters who people Henry Waugh's imagination. The specific action of the novel springs from Henry's love of his young hero, Damon Rutherford, son of good old Brock Rutherford, one of the earliest players of the Universal Baseball Association. Jock Casey's line drive kills the handsome young pitcher, against odds of 10,077,696 to 1, and the tragic event plunges Henry into despair. Eventually, he violates his own rules and rigs the dice to put Jock Casey to death—at what would have been precisely the same odds had the cast been fair. Henry reaches over to manipulate the dice which have already come to rest. It is a tribute to Coover's skill that this act is felt for what it poetically is—murder.

This impetuous action is followed by a sudden break in the narrative technique. Up to the moment when Henry interferes with chance, he had been the central intelligence of the novel—the story is told from his perspective, he is always present as the raison d'être of his imagined baseball game. Now, Henry disappears. We move forward in the last chapter to some moment in the future when the players of the Universal Baseball Association gather to celebrate Damonsday (and now we see the symbolism of the name—"daemon," "demon"). The game has become myth, myth at which some players scoff, in which others believe. Some authorities doubt "the Great Atonement Legend," some "even argue that Rutherford and Casey never existed—nothing more than another of the ancient myths of the sun, symbolized as a victim slaughtered by the monster or the force of darkness."[54] The ancient myths, of course, are those associated with Tammuz, Adonis, and Jesus. The youth who enacts the role of Damon Rutherford will die sacrificially, like the Mayan and Aztec youths whose deaths ensured the earth's fertility, but "Damon" accepts his fate. The language is an eerie combination of the awesome and the familiar: " 'It's not a trial,' says Damon, glove tucked in his armpit, hands working the new ball. Behind him, he knows, Scat Batkin, the batter, is moving toward the plate. 'It's not even a lesson. It's just what it is.' Damon holds the baseball up between them. It is hard and white and alive in the sun."[55] Damon Rutherford will die and rise from the dead. In this brilliantly conceived work of art, Coover has dramatized the interaction of modern quantification and primitive myth. Coover's achievement deserves greater recognition than it has thus far received.

Has my analysis of baseball been self-contradictory? Have I argued that baseball's special attraction among team games, all of which combine individualism and cooperative effort, lies in its primitive-pastoral elements and, simultaneously, in its extraordinary modernity, in its closeness to the seasonal rhythms of nature and, at the same time, in the rarified realm of numbers? I assume that we have here not a contradiction but a complexity, a paradoxical situation in which the special, carefully bounded and regulated conditions of a game enable us to have our cake and eat it too, to calculate the chances of a fastball or a successful bunt and, at the same time, to luxuriate in the warm sunshine of an April afternoon. The ball is swatted into the leftfield stands and the .389 hitter trots about the bases in unconscious emulation of pre-historic runners whose religious efforts brought the dead land to life again. I interpret baseball as a ludic symbol of our ambivalence about our abandoned past and about the unknown future that we are all, willy nilly, bound for. But is this interpretation correct? Alas, we cannot look it up.

3. BASEBALL AND THE PROBLEM OF CULTURAL DIFFUSION

My interpretation of baseball posits the interaction of modern with primitive-pastoral elements. If this interpretation is a valid one, we are still left with the question implied at the start of our discussion of the game. Why is it that Americans—and Canadians, Cubans, Mexicans, and Japanese—play baseball while most other nations do not? Most modern sports are, as we have noticed, thoroughly international. Baseball is neither uniquely American nor ubiquitously modern. I have no easy answer to the problem of cultural diffusion, but I am prepared to offer some speculations.

Just as soccer and a number of other modern games were spread by the British, baseball was carried abroad by American educators, missionaries, and businessmen who introduced the game wherever they went. Some nations adopted the game, others did not. I suspect that baseball spread to Canada, Japan, and the lands of the Caribbean because these nations were, in the late nineteenth and early twentieth centuries, strongly and favorably impressed with the United States as a model of modern civilization. The motive of imitation may have helped to establish baseball as the first modern team sport at a crucial historical moment, before the British bearers of soccer were able to carry out *their* "ecological invasion" of the territory. It was, in other words, the modern element in the game which attracted Canadian, Japanese, and Caribbean players.

Direct influence of this sort may be the answer to part of the difficulty, but unanswered questions remain. Our interpretation of baseball was a twofold one—modern elements appear inextricably mixed with primitive and pastoral ones. If we agree that baseball spread to certain countries because of its modernity and its American associations, what shall we say about the obvious fact that it has *not* spread to other nations? The answer, already hinted at, is that the British were, on the whole, quicker. This was the period of British cultural hegemony. The British Empire had reached a zenith of power and influence in the years immediately before World War I. It was at this time that soccer became the most widely played of modern team sports.

This answer, unfortunately, is not wholly satisfactory. If I am right about baseball, the primitive and pastoral elements cannot simply be forgotten at this point in our discussion merely because such forgetfulness may be convenient for the argument. If these elements are psychically important, they must be important to all men and not just to Americans and others who have taken up baseball. In that case, societies which do not have the game of baseball should have some equivalent with which to enact the rites of spring, with which to remind themselves of the eternal cycle of the seasons. And they do, but that equivalent is not necessarily a game. The simple answer may be that many modern societies remain less industrialized and urbanized and secularized than the United States. The routine of agricultural labor and the recurrent festivals of traditional religion both emphasize the cycle of the seasons and the death and rebirth of the earth. There is little need for sports to play the role that baseball seems to have played in the nineteenth and early twentieth centuries. There is no necessity for an urban game to remind people of their relationship to nature when people continue to live close to the land and when their religious institutions continue to instruct them that there is a time to sow and a time to reap.

Baseball may have been a vehicle for transition, a peculiar game whose combination of modern and primitive-pastoral elements helped to bring the United States emotionally into a decisively secular modern world. To speak this way is not to suggest that baseball will now decline and disappear, but it is hard not to believe that the primitive-pastoral aspects of the game are now mostly anachronistic. It seems all too likely that baseball has had its day in the sun.

The Fascination of Football

1. POPULARITY AND VIOLENCE

IS THERE an American sportswriter or broadcaster, some mute, inglorious Howard Cosell or George Plimpton, who has failed to comment upon the football boom of the 1960s? Probably not. Baseball's claim to the title "national game" seemed increasingly questionable as the paid attendance for professional football and the television audience for both the college and the professional game soared in the 1950s and 1960s. Table 6 illustrates the growth in at-

Table 6
Regular Season Attendance for Professional Team Sports
(*in thousands*)

	1950	1960	1970	1974
Major-League baseball	17,463	19,911	28,747	29,994
Professional football	1,978	4,054	9,533	10,236
Professional basketball		1,986	6,900	9,154

tendance of the three major professional team sports.[1] While baseball's attendance continues to be larger, the baseball/football ratio has shrunk from 8.83 to 2.93. Another way to indicate the shift in interests is to observe that between 1959 and 1973, the percentage of adults attending a football game at least once in the previous twelve months rose from 23 percent to 33 percent while the equivalent figure for baseball rose only from 28 percent to 30 percent (while soccer rose from 1 percent to a surprising 13 percent).[2] The statistics for the great televised spectacles—the Super Bowl and the World Series—tell the same story. A. C. Nielsen reported in 1975 that 41.6 percent of all households watched the Pittsburgh Steelers defeat the Minnesota Vikings while only 30.7 percent tuned in to watch the World Series in which the Cincinnati Reds were nearly upset by the Boston Red Sox (and only 13.5 percent saw the National Basketball Association playoffs).[3] *Sports Illustrated*, the most widely read publication of its kind in the United States, had twelve covers featuring baseball in 1958 and only four featuring football; in 1966, there were eight for baseball and fifteen for football.

What accounts for the shift in ludic interest? William Phillips, writing in *Commentary*, offers a spiritedly subjective interpretation of the various appeals of different sports:[4]

All sports serve as some kind of release but the rhythm of football is geared particularly to the violence and the peculiar combination of order and disorder of modern life. Baseball is too slow, too dependable, too much like a regional drawl. Basketball is too nervous and too tight; hockey too frenzied; boxing too chaotic, too folksy. Only football provides a genuine catharis.

Phillips speaks as an admirer of the game, as does George Stade in his remarkably perceptive essay on football:[5]

Football is first of all a form of play, something one engages in instinctively and only for the sake of performing the activity in question. Among forms of play, football is a game, which means that it is built on communal needs, rather than on private evasions, like mountain climbing. Among games it is a sport; it requires athletic ability, unlike checkers. And among sports, it is one whose mode is violence and whose violence is its special glory.

For others, the "special glory" is a species of horror. "More than twenty-five million Americans fostered their own dehumanization each weekend last fall as fans of big-time football. . . . Collegiate and especially professional football reveal the fascist streak in our society. . . . Football's totalitarian authority structure . . . reflects the militarism prevalent in our culture."[6] From a similar standpoint, Paul Hoch has argued that football surpassed baseball in popularity in the late 1960s precisely because of a basic militarism in American life which found violent expression in our games as well as on the battle fields of Vietnam.[7]

Proponents and antagonists of the game seem therefore to agree on the presence of violence, even when they agree on little else, but violence raises some vexing questions about football and society. The game's American origins are collegiate and for years the game was perceived as "the college game." Does this mean that Harvard and Yale and Princeton possessed especially violent subcultures? According to a Gallup Poll published in 1960, interest in football is associated with a college education while Americans with a grade-school education are far more likely to prefer to watch baseball (table 7).[8] Is it likely that the alleged "fascist streak" in our society is most

Table 7
Preferred Spectator Sport by Education
(*figures in percentages*)

	Grade-School	High-School	College
Baseball	40	34	21
Football	10	24	36
Basketball	6	10	13

virulent among those with bachelors degrees? Such questions are not frivolous. They may be answered affirmatively, but they must be confronted analytically, empirically, and without prejudgment of the issues. We shall return to them after looking at the primitive and the modern in football.

As a first step toward rational discussion of the issues, we must ask if it is accurate to refer to football as a violent sport. If we mean the term to refer to some sort of illegitimate, unsanctioned physical force, then football is not inherently violent, but becomes so only when the players break the rules of the game (either the written rules or the less stringent unwritten ones accepted by the players and the officials). Indeed, one of the most obvious aspects of sports is that behavior forbidden in other circumstances is perfectly acceptable within the context of the game. To grab a walker in the park about the waist and hurl him to the grass is to commit violence, but to perform a physically identical act in one's role as linebacker is certainly not violent in quite the same sense of the word. If the word were not embedded in our linguistic repertory, if there were some other word that might better be used to describe what linebackers do, we might suggest that football is *not* violent. Unfortunately, there is a kind of unleashed energy—in warfare, in nature ("a violent thunderstorm"), and in sports—that we call violent. Let us agree that many sports include legitimate, socially sanctioned forms of violence, which is quite distinct from simply saying, with approval or distaste, that these sports are violent.[9]

To go beyond the condemnatory assertion that football is full of violence is not to deny that the basic elements of the game—running, blocking, tackling, catching, throwing, kicking—involve a good deal of physical force, much of it in the form of violently aggressive "body contact." Players do block, tackle, and hit each other in ways that are technically legitimate and yet clearly intended to intimidate and cause physical pain if not injury. In the vernacular, players "hit" each other, they "stick," they enjoy "contact." Woody Hayes, famed coach of Ohio State University, boasts, "We teach our boys to spear and gore. . . . We want them to plant that helmet right under a guy's chin. . . . I want them to stick that mask right in the opponent's neck."[10] It is this sort of behavior that Vince Lombardi of the Green Bay Packers meant when he said, "Football is a violent game. To play you have to be tough. Physically tough and mentally tough."[11] What coaches preach, players practice. Asked how he felt about a jolting collision on the field, a San Diego Charger replied, "It felt warm all over."[12] An astute observer who spent a season with the Pittsburgh Steelers concluded, "A taste for contact is the common touch which all pro football players—quarterbacks and wide receivers alone excepted—must have."[13] Here is no secret. "Contact" is an integral and presumably attractive aspect of the game for players and spectators alike, college education or not. It is a game of "controlled violence," "disciplined violence."[14]

Biographies and autobiographies and novels often focus on the injuries that players receive, many of them quite intentional. Injuries are a part of the game too. In George Stade's opinion, they dignify the game and give it zest.[15] This last observation is very important. It hints that injuries are a psychologically positive facet of the sport. Presumably, athletes rarely wish to suffer crippling injuries, but there is an unmistakable element of pride in their voices when they recount the games they played despite their pain-wracked bodies. In football parlance, to "play hurt" is not to feign an injury but to continue the game despite one's physical distress. Injury for the contemporary football player is comparable to the duelling scars proudly borne by the nineteenth-century Prussian aristocrat. Injury becomes, therefore, a certificate of virility, a badge of courage—which is certainly what it is in Frank Gifford's recent book, *Gifford on Courage* (1976). Stade's term "zest" may be hyperbole, but there does seem to be a readiness to accept if not to seek injury as a way of dignifying the game. As one of the players remarks, "You have to show that you don't care about your body."[16] A sober thought to meditate upon when we are about to confuse the virtues of violent sports with those of therapeutic physical education. Whatever we wish to say about an afternoon of professional football, we cannot claim that it is conducive to the athlete's health.[17]

Football has another dimension which its critics have stressed. It is an analogue to warfare. It is, like chess, "a crazy miniature war," a playful war waged for its own sake.[18] The primary objective of this miniature war is not the physical destruction of the enemy but the conquest of his territory. The yard-markers follow the ball up and down the field as if in parody of the movement of markers on a military map. The goal is defended with the determination of men who stand between the ravaging foe and their homeland.

The heroic warriors are commanded by their general, the coach. Many observers have claimed that in all sports the coaching profession is characterized by authoritarian tendencies, but the most remarkable personifications of authoritarian and even dictatorial leadership seem to cluster along the sidelines of football games.[19] Famous coaches of the past, like Walter Camp, Amos Alonzo Stagg, and the very nearly canonized Knute Rockne, developed paternalistic styles which combined formal strictness and fatherly affection in such a way as to win devotion from students and alumni. In the 1950s and 1960s, the stress on winning and the threat of unemployment upon losing led to a new breed of coach represented by Woody Hayes, Bear Bryant, and Darrell Royall in the college game and by Vince Lombardi among the professionals. The Lombardi phenomenon is in itself worthy of the extended study which it has, fortunately, already received.[20] Everyone who came close to the man seems to agree—whether one enlisted in the army of his admirers or resisted the attraction of his flamboyant personality—the man was a *presence*. Although "he preferred to see himself as the leader of this family, as a father," the players did not fail to notice the ardor of his admiration for General George Patton.[21] Like his fellow coaches in the National Football League, Lombardi brooked no dissent, yet, despite his harshness and even brutality, the Green Bay Packers—if we can trust the published accounts—seem almost to have worshipped him. They seem to have cherished the numerous anecdotes which portray God Almighty as an envious imitator of Vincent Lombardi. Compared to Bear Bryant and Darrell Royall, Lombardi was relatively unscathed by negative criticism. One must conclude that his Nietzschean will-to-win was admired by millions of Americans. Baseball too has had its legendary managers, like John J. McGraw, Miller Huggins, Casey Stengel, and Leo Durocher, but they have been famed more for their insights or for their verbal antics than for their ability to train men, to motivate them to an almost suicidal pitch, and to lead them into the moral equivalent of war.

The bellicosity of the game and its similarities to actual warfare have been emphasized in numerous novels, including Gary Cartwright's The Hundred Yard War (1968) and Peter Gent's North Dallas Forty (1974), but the most probing literary analysis of the game is probably Don DeLillo's End Zone (1972). The book is set in a fantasy Texas which is stranger than the historical reality. The coach at Logos College, Emmett Creed, believes in pain, renunciation, self-sacrifice, and discipline. His thoughts are truly a synthesis of remarks made in hundreds of locker rooms by hundreds of real and fictional coaches:[22]

We need more self-sacrifice, more discipline. . . . We need to build ourselves up mentally and spiritually. Do that and the body takes care of itself. I learned this as a small boy. I was very sickly, a very sickly child. I had this and that disease. I was badly nourished. My legs were no thicker than the legs of that chair. But I built myself up by determination and sacrifice. The mind first and then the body. It was a lonely life for a boy. I had no friends. I lived in an inner world of determination and silence. Mental resolve. It made me strong; it prepared me. Things return to their beginnings. It's been a long circle from there to here. But all the lessons hold true. The inner life must be disciplined just as the hand or eye. Loneliness is strength. The Sioux purified themselves by fasting and solitude. Four days without food in a sweat lodge. Before you went out to lament for your nation, you had to purify yourself. Fasting and solitude. If you can survive loneliness, you've got an inner strength that can take you anywhere. Four days. You wore just a bison robe. I don't think there's anything makes more sense than self-denial. It's the only way to attain moral perfection.

Creed's speech is creed and credo, a moral statement worthy of Theodore Roosevelt, whose strenuous life is a kind of coach's paradigm. The credo is a fictive distillation and Emmett Creed is Don DeLillo's invention, but he is also the creation of American football and an embodiment of its values.

DeLillo's narrator is a thoughtful football player named Gary Harkness, a youth anxious to puzzle out the nature of the game and its relation to war. At the University of Miami, where he had also played football, he had started reading "an immense volume about the possibilities of nuclear war."[23] He was fascinated. "The problem was simple and terrible: I enjoyed the book. I liked reading about the deaths of tens of millions of people."[24]

At Logos College, Gary plays for Coach Creed and takes a course from Major Staley of the ROTC. The major is distinctly related to Norman Mailer's military philosopher, General Cummings, a brooder on the many ways in which modern technology has transformed warfare from a test of courage into a scientific competition:[25]

War is the ultimate realization of modern technology. For centuries men have tested themselves in war. War was the final test, the great experience, the privilege, the honor, the self-sacrifice or what have you, the absolutely ultimate determination of what kind of man you were. War was the great challenge and the great evaluator. It told you how much you were worth. But it's different today. Few men want to go off and fight.

What war no longer accomplishes, football does. Major Staley and Coach Creed preach complementary versions of the same monomaniacal *Weltanschauung*.

Thus does the novelist's fantasy corroborate the argument that football's similarity to warfare enables its enthusiasts to express their primitive aggressiveness, to validate their sense of manhood in a military pantomine, but the novel corroborates another insight. As William Phillips indicated, football is a peculiar combination of order and disorder, a complex game of strategy, a means to shape experience. It is, in Coach Creed's view, "a complex of systems. It's like no other sport. When the game is played properly, it's an interlocking of a number of systems." [26] In the middle of a game with an unlikely institution named West Centrex Biotechnical Institute, Gary thinks that the game provides information, details,[27]

impressions, colors, statistics, patterns, mysteries, numbers, idioms, symbols. Football, more than other sports, fulfills this need. It is the one sport guided by language, by the word signal, the snap number, the color code, the play name. The spectator's pleasure, when not derived from the action itself, evolves from a notion of the game's unique organic nature. Here is not just order but civilization.

Exactly what Woody Hayes has been saying all along. Like warfare, football requires a complex strategy. It is more than neanderthalic mayhem.

As the novel progresses, however, the impulse to order becomes overwhelmed by the chaos of expressive experience. Gary must deal not only with Coach Creed and Major Staley but also with a notably eccentric girlfriend, with a Jewish bed-wetter whose sole purpose in life is to "reject heritage, background, tradition and birthright," and with a philosophical former player who lives alone with a poster of Ludwig Wittgenstein and who reads compulsively about atrocities.[28] The psychic environment is, understandably, too much for anyone. Gary collapses. "High fevers burned a thin straight channel through my brain. In the end they had to carry me to the infirmary and feed me through plastic tubes." [29]

What does it all mean? DeLillo chooses not to say, which leaves the tantalized reader unsure about the author's final judgment of football, but DeLillo is scarcely unique among imaginative writers in his refusal to lapse from metaphoric to literalistic modes of expression. It is enough that he has suggested the primitive qualities of football's symbolic combat and its distance from the impersonal technological horrors of thermonuclear warfare. Let us explore the problem further in both its primitive and modern aspects.

How shall we relate the primitive elements of football to those of baseball? The elements are clearly not the same, which partly accounts for the indifference or hostility which enthusiasts for the first sport sometimes express for fans of the second. We have speculated that baseball's primitive traits can be traced back to the fertility rites of the ancient vegetation myths. Despite the sacrificial aspects of the myth, the significance of the fertility ceremonies is affirmative. The earth struggles successfully to free itself from winter's deadly grip, the cycle of the seasons begins anew. But football's primitive aspects are less tightly joined to religious ritual and more closely linked to the prehistoric *Existenzkampf*. "Football announces the continuity between contemporary man and his most ancient ancestors."[30] A recent issue of *Natural History*, featuring an anthropological interpretation of football as a seasonal rite, pictured a hulking, mud-splattered football player on its cover.[31] He looks like a survivor from the Stone Age, which he is. The elaborate gear seems to emphasize, almost simultaneously, the primitive and the futuristic. "The football player in uniform strikes the eye in a succession of gestalt shifts: first a hooded phantom out of the paleolithic past of the species; then a premonition of a future of spacemen."[32]

2. MODERNITY

And football is, nonetheless, a truly modern game with all the characteristics of modern sport. The emotional function of the game may be primitive and even atavistic, but the structure of the game is clearly modern, isomorphic with basketball, baseball, soccer. To understand the degree of the sport's modernity, we need to consider its historical origins and development.

Historians like Robert W. Henderson trace the beginnings of football back to the same Egyptian myths which allegedly gave birth to baseball and to all modern ball games, but our purposes require us to go no further back in time than the Middle Ages, where documentary and iconographical evidence is fairly abundant. Football developed from rugby which developed from folk-games played in France and England—circumstances which suggest a connection, now broken by the game's seasonal displacement to the fall, with the same vegetation gods that presided over the birth of baseball. Soccer was played by monks at Easter and Shrovetide, usually within the confines of a cloister. "The Tuesday before [Ash Wednesday] was so closely bound up with football that Shrove Tuesday was simply named 'Football-day.' "[33] At Auxerre, in the twelfth century, the ball was handed to the Dean of the Chapter by a clerical student, "after which the *Prosa* . . . for Easter day . . . was chanted by those in the procession."[34] Any doubts about the association of the game with fertility ritual should be dispelled by J. J. Jusserand's account of the rituals at Boulogne-la-Grasse, where the "jour du mardi gras" included a basket of eggs and a staff at the end of which was a suspended, beribboned, leather football.[35] In England, it was common for the Shrovetide game of soccer to pit married women against spinsters.[36] American football can be traced back to speculative origins far older than the fertility myths, but Medieval soccer was certainly associated with the rebirth of life after a season of deathly cold.

The game was taken up by the peasantry, but in a form far different from modern soccer, let alone modern football. The "sturdie plowman," wrote Alexander Barclay of Ely in 1514,[37]

> lustie, strong, and bolde
> Overcometh the winter with driving the foote ball,
> Forgetting labour and many a grevous fall.

The plowman was also likely to sustain many a "grevous fall" in the game, which was a rough-and-tumble struggle between opposed villages. The rules were minimal and there was no one to enforce them. Almost any sort of behavior was tolerated if the overt intent was to kick the ball rather than to maim the other players. The game frequently degenerated into a wild scuffle, with players fighting for the ball "like dogs for a bone."[38] In *The Governour* (1531), Thomas Elyot denounced the game as "nothing but beastly fury and extreme violence."[39] Small wonder that other moralists articulated their dismay. The game was frequently banned by royal edict and local legislation. James I of England barred from his court "all rough and violent exercises, as the football, meeter for mameing than making able the users thereof."[40] The rules were vague about boundaries as well as about the extent of physical abuse allowed. The ball was kicked across fields and streams, over walls, down village streets, to the distant goal, usually the portals of the parish church. The villagers participated in large numbers, but how large no one knows. How many "goals" were needed to win? We have no idea because it did not occur to medieval players to keep the statistics of the game. Needless to say, no one set any records.

This sport, half game, half free-for-all, seems to have been played continuously in France and England and, in somewhat more refined form, in Italy until the late nineteenth century. Writing in 1901, Jusserand commented, "The game of football still survives . . . in its primitive form, with the same rudimentary rules, the same sort of combattants, played on the same days, as in the time of the crusades."[41] By the early nineteenth century, many different versions of the game were played at Winchester, Harrow, Eton, and other English public schools. In 1848, a group of students, graduates of the public schools, gathered at Cambridge to formalize the rules of soccer. Fifteen years later, the game spread to the point where the Football Association was formed. The pace of rationalization increased. "Between 1863 and 1878 greater changes took place in respect to the game than in any comparable period of time either before or since."[42] Legend has it that the quantum leap from soccer to rugby had already been made, in 1823. The plaque on the wall at Rugby School immortalizes William Webb Ellis, who picked the ball up and, in bold disregard for the rules of the game, ran with it. The inspired achievement of William Webb Ellis seems to belong with that of Abner Doubleday, whose ludic inventiveness is of equally precarious historicity. (In both cases, the legend began a full two generations after the alleged deed.) It is Eric Dunning's contention that the folk versions of what became soccer never had a strict rule against use of the hands. Modern soccer actually postdates rugby, which more closely resembles the medieval game. It was not until 1849 that rules adopted at Eton forbade holding or throwing the ball.[43]

The Football Association dates from 1863, the Rugby Union from 1871. The first game spread quickly around the world, the second became popular in France, South Africa, Australia, New Zealand, and the United States, where it quickly turned into American football. While rugby remained an essentially English game, played by an elite of middle-class and upper-class schoolboys, there was little need for elaborate rationalization. The players understood the rules. They knew what was "rugby" and what wasn't. They knew, for instance, that it was proper to pick up the ball and run with it when it was "accidentally" heeled out of the "scrum." But Americans did *not* know and they required written rules for numerous details which Britons took for granted.

As David Riesman and Reuel Denney demonstrate in an excellent article, rugby's metamorphosis into football was in itself a fascinating instance of cultural diffusion.[44] Although the Princeton-Rutgers match of November 6, 1869, is conventionally given as the first intercollegiate football game in America, the encounter was more like soccer than like rugby. The latter sport, parent to American football, was first played intercollegiately on May 15, 1874, when a team from McGill University in Montreal voyaged to Cambridge to challenge the novices of Harvard. When Princeton, Columbia, Harvard, and Yale met at Springfield, Massachusetts, in 1876, they sought to regularize the rules of a game which still had too many troublesome local variations. Football moved quickly through the phase of rapid transformation. From 1880, the ball was "hiked" out by the center from a static line of scrimmage. By 1882, the eleven positions of single-platoon football were established and the "first down" was invented— three tries for five yards. In 1906 came the forward pass, which made the game recognizably football in the modern sense, i.e., *foot*ball in which the foot plays almost no role at all. Through this period, the Intercollegiate Football Association, which had been founded in 1876, tinkered with the scoring system, which went through numerous experiments.

By World War I, football was a thoroughly specialized, rationalized, bureaucratically organized example of modern sports. It was, of course, theoretically open to all young men who wished to prove their skills as runners, blockers, tacklers, passers, catchers, or kickers. In practice, the game was dominated by the elite Eastern schools until the late 1880s, when the universities of the Middle West began to throw their weight around. As time passed, Walter Camp's list of All-American players began to include Polish and Italian as well as British and German names. At least one scholar believes that Yale's early superiority over Harvard came from the former's eagerness to recruit players on the basis of skill rather than by the more ascriptive criterion of membership in an old Boston family.[45]

Like baseball, basketball, and other modern sports, football is marked by a high level of quantification. Although the stress on co-operative effort is greater than in baseball, so that it is harder to attribute a result to an individual player, the statistics of the game include figures on yards gained rushing, passes completed, first downs, etc. On the basis of such quantification, records can be calculated. Every season, new records are set, presumably to the great satisfaction of both players and spectators. Books written to immortalize successful teams conclude with appendices on won-lost records and team standings. The hagiography of individual players routinely provides a list of individual records. It is, however, probably the case that quantification and the quest for records are not so advanced as in baseball. In this way too, football is somewhat less modern than baseball, but we are once again faced by the paradoxical combination of primitive and modern elements that we found in our commentary on baseball.

We have already noticed the fact that football's time and space are unlike baseball's but like that of basketball, hockey, lacrosse, and European handball (a game combining elements of soccer and basketball), i.e., time is clock-time and spatial movement is oscillatory rather than circular. Baseball's uniqueness in this and other ways may, in part, explain its failure to spread to Europe, but what about American football? Since football's origins are even more obviously European than baseball's, why hasn't the game recrossed the Atlantic to captivate the British and the French (as it has captivated many British and French Canadians)? It may be, quite simply, that rugby provides ample instinctive satisfaction. It too is a team game which affords an outlet to the primitive desire to bang into people. It too satisfies the modern hunger for quantification. The ecological niche is filled. Where rugby is not popular, in Germany and Italy, for instance, our brand of football may yet win its bridgehead. The appearance of our Super Bowl on German television points in that direction.

3. CATHARSIS AND WAR

Having considered football's primitive substance and modern form, we can return to the vexing question of a possible correlation between football's curve of rising popularity and the escalation of America's military involvement in Vietnam, Cambodia, and Laos. Paul Hoch and others assert that the parallel is not accidental. The passion for professional football derives, they argue, from the same social-psychological factors which led the United States into its catastrophic military adventure in the jungles of Southeast Asia. The plausibility of this indictment depends largely on whether or not one accepts the theory of catharsis through sports.

Konrad Lorenz, in his influential book *On Aggression* (1963), suggests that sports can provide a cathartic experience through which aggression can be diverted from its more destructive forms and harmlessly released upon the playing field.[46]

The value of sport . . . is much greater than that of a simple outlet of aggression in its coarser and more individualistic behavior patterns, such as pummeling a punch-ball. It educates man to a conscious and responsible control of his own fighting behavior. Few lapses of self-control are punished as immediately and severely as loss of temper during a boxing bout. More valuable still is the educational value of the restrictions imposed by the demands for fairness and chivalry which must be respected even in the face of the strongest aggression-eliciting stimuli.

This attractive and widely accepted theory implies that players and spectators will achieve the emotional calmness that Aristotle claimed for the beholders of tragic drama, from whom the passions of terror and pity were "purged."[47] If this theory is true, then the diversion of aggressive tendencies into the safely controlled domain of sports diminishes the incidence of aggression elsewhere in society. The angry young man who vents his rage through blocking and tackling utilizes a socially acceptable channel for violent emotions which might otherwise have led him to commit homicide or rape. Similarly, spectators have the opportunity, through the psychological mechanism of identification, to experience vicariously intense excitement and a subsequent peace. Football decreases the likelihood of violent crime at home and of military adventures abroad.

It is a great pity that the catharsis theory is invalid. There is some evidence to indicate that the players themselves are less aggressive after the game than before the kickoff, an effect which may result mostly from the enormous amount of energy expended during the actual encounter, but there is a rare consensus among psychologists apropos of the alleged catharsis experienced by the spectators.[48] This consensus rests mainly on two types of experiment. In the first type, spectators have been tested with pencil-and-paper techniques before and after they attended athletic events of various sorts. In one study, for instance, obliging football fans submitted to interviewers who asked them thirty-six questions from the Buss-Durkee Hostility Inventory (plus "filler" items). The authors used the same technique to test spectators at a gymnastics event. They concluded, "No support for a catharsis effect is obtained in the present study."[49] In fact, the scores tended to show increased hostility after the event even when the fan's favored team won. The second type of test is one developed by Leonard Berkowitz and his associates. Although the experiment has been performed with many variations, the basic form can be described as follows: the subjects are shown violent and nonviolent films, e.g., a film of a boxing match versus a travelogue. The subjects are then tested for their willingness to express their aggressiveness in an action against another person. This is measured by the amount of electric shock they think they administer to another person in what they think is the testing of that other person's ability to respond to questions. (The other person receives no shock, but the subject doesn't know this.) The entire complicated experiment is derived from some famous studies done by Stanley Milgram and described by him in *Obedience to Authority* (1974). Subjects who observe films about violent sports are more willing to administer a high level of electric shock than subjects who see another sort of film, from which one can conclude that the alleged catharsis through watching sports did not take place.

It is wise to be cautious when speculating about peoples' actual behavior in society on the basis of pencil-and-paper tests or laboratory situations, but we have additional reason to be skeptical of the catharsis theory. We know that sporting events in Great Britain have recently been accompanied by outbreaks of destructive "soccer hooliganism" and that South-American soccer matches have enraged spectators to the point where scores of deaths and hundreds of injuries have occurred.[50] Urban authorities in America have in many cases discontinued the traditional Friday-night high-school football game because of the attendant mob violence and many such athletic events are now held in secret, with no one present other than the contestants and the officials. Persuasive evidence for the catharsis theory has yet to be gathered.

Let us return now to the possibility raised at the start of our consideration of football. If the spectator of football is psychologically more aggressive than the baseball fan, if football is at the same time more popular with the rich than with the poor, must we infer that aggressiveness correlates with a large income, a good education, and high status? The trouble with this inference is that we know from a myriad of studies that aggressive behavior and violent crime are more frequent among the disadvantaged than among the advantaged.

The way out of the apparent intellectual dilemma is not hard to locate. We must remember that the "aggressiveness" measured by psychological tests is at best a psychological disposition toward the behavior which results in social mayhem. The advantaged members of society are usually socialized to control such dispositions. They are simultaneously more "aggressive" and more restrained than are their less educated fellow citizens. Stimulated by the primitive contents of a football game, the middle-class spectator is better able than others to find a socially acceptable way to simmer down. Indeed, we may go further with the logical deductions of this argument. In a remarkable essay by Norbert Elias and Eric Dunning, "The Quest for Excitement in Unexciting Societies," it is hypothesized that there is an inverse relationship between the routinization of daily life in modern society and the prevalence of sports like soccer, rugby, hockey, and American football. "In the more advanced industrial societies of our time, compared with societies at an earlier stage of development, occasions for strong excitement openly expressed have become rarer."[51] Games like football provide Saturnalia-like occasions for the uninhibited expression of emotions which must remain tightly controlled in our ordinary lives. The role of shouting, screaming spectator compensates us for the more restrained roles of parent, employee, and citizen. And, if the excitement becomes excessive, it spills over into riotous behavior.

If this hypothesis is correct, we can explain the function of football in American education. Our high schools and, to an even greater degree, our colleges are agencies of socialization dedicated very largely to the nurture of rational behavior. In football's collegiate heyday, from the 1880s to the 1950s, American colleges were institutions which emphasized discipline and social control. Students, drawn mostly from the middle class, were supposed to study. It was also expected, since boys will be boys even when they are Amherst Men, that they would exhibit the exuberance associated with adolescence. Collegiate sports, especially football, provided a regular and socially sanctioned occasion for displays of manly courage, outbursts of drunken revelry, and the release of whatever college rules had, from Monday through Friday, suppressed. And, once the student had graduated, the force of nostalgia conspired with the calendar (games are played on weekends, when middle-class citizens turn from labor to leisure) to give football its special place among the many versions of the emotional "time out."[52]

There is, consequently, no reason to assume that the turn-of-the-century Ivy League possessed an especially violent subculture or that the "fascist streak" in American society is most pronounced among the most educated. It is rather that the most thoroughly socialized citizens most need the compensation of modern sports. It is they who most require the emotional "time out" provided by football and other violent games. They purchase the tickets priced beyond the means of most Americans, they tuck their bourbon bottles into their well-tailored coat pockets, they indulge themselves in a socially sanctioned emotional orgy. Since they *are* the most thoroughly socialized citizens, they seldom let this heightened aggressiveness degenerate into physical aggression. Sticks and stones will break my bones, but hysterical cheering for the home team hurts only my sense of decorum.

But can we reject the possibility of a catharsis for the spectator and still describe the game of football as the occasion for a Saturnalia-like emotional "time out"? We can if we consider not merely the role of spectator in its narrowest dimension—one who watches an athletic event—but rather the extended repertory of roles acted out by students during a football weekend or by middle-aged professionals before and after as well as during a game. A sedentary, passive response to the contest, like that of the viewers of films in the experiments by Berkowitz, is liable to terminate in increased hostility and aggressiveness, but an active part in the larger drama of "a big weekend" allows the release of emotions in a range of behavior including pregame levity, frenzied cheering during the game, and postgame carousing. The game itself figures as the occasion for various activities frowned upon when not associated with the football weekend. In this wider sense, some modified version of the catharsis theory may be valid. The athletic event excites the spectator and provides a context for the release of normally proscribed and inhibited behavior. The behavior sometimes goes too far, but the definition of "too far" is usually set by the middle class. Thus, the vandalism which follows victory in a football game is perceived as quite different from the "trashing" that sometimes accompanies radical political protest. And it *is* different. The symbolism of a car overturned to celebrate Ohio State's gridiron conquest of the University of Michigan is diametrically opposed to the symbolism of a car smashed in the midst of racial unrest or in the turbulent wake of an antiwar demonstration.

For further insights into social class and the "emotional time out" of sports, we can turn to a recent study of Canadian football. The Canadian equivalent of our Super Bowl is the playoff game between the winners of the Western and Eastern Conferences. Since the winners receive a trophy donated by Earl Grey, as well as considerable pecuniary benefit, the excitement accompanying the game is referred to generally as "the Grey Cup festivities." Investigating these festivities, a team of sociologists observed behavior in eleven middle-class and lower-class lounges and bars in Hamilton, Ontario, host city for the Grey Cup game. The middle-class lounges were the scenes of adolescent revelry:[53]

The atmosphere of these establishments was supercharged with a high degree of gregarious behavior and boisterous conduct, and the level of this legitimate deviance continued to rise as the evening and the drinks flowed on. Spontaneous shouts and yells and horn-blowing emanated from various parts of the bar, competing with each other in . . . volume. . . . Males engaged in spirited camaraderie and backslapping types of behavior. Sporadically spirited fights would break out.

Meanwhile, the lower-class bars operated almost as if there were no championship to be decided. "The whole lower-class bar scene could be described as 'business as usual.' "[54] The phrase, "business as usual," does not describe an atmosphere of complete tranquillity. "Fights broke out every hour or so."[55] Although the author of this study goes on to condemn the "monopoly capitalistic nature of Canadian society," it is sufficient for our purposes that we ponder the difference between the "legitimate deviance" occasioned by the football game and the unsanctioned but nonetheless "normal" violence of the lower-class bar. The fights that occurred in the lounge were unusual events associated with a special kind of celebration while the brawls in the bar were "business as usual," even when seen from a radical perspective. In plain terms, it is likely that the disadvantaged members of every society tend to express their frustrations in direct forms of deviance while the advantaged make greater use of the Saturnalia-like opportunities of the institutionalized "time out." Since football combines primitive elements with a sophisticated complex of teamwork and strategy, it seems especially well suited for its dual function as a model of modern social organization and as an occasion for atavistic release.

Let us carry our speculations one step further. If the game of football increases the spectator's hostility and aggressiveness, as implied by a rejection of the catharsis theory, then the Neo-Marxists may be correct to posit a connection between the game's popularity and an interventionist foreign policy, i.e., what they call "militarism." If, on the other hand, the game of football is an occasion for the release of dammed emotions in a Saturnalia-like "time out," as implied by the modified version of the catharsis theory, then the sport should, logically, tend to lessen the likelihood of aggression elsewhere. At least one anthropologist has attempted to test the question empirically. Comparing ten primitive cultures characterized in the ethnographic files as "warlike" with ten pacific cultures, he found that warlike behavior correlated significantly with the presence of combative sports He went on to study the popularity of baseball and football as spectator sports in the United States from 1920 to 1970, only to discover that there was no statistically significant relationship between football and wartime—football gained in popularity during World War II and the Korean War, but it gained during the intervening years as well.[56] A preference for football over baseball might have had a statistically significant correlation with support for a "hawkish" policy in Vietnam, but no one seems to have tested this hypothesis. Had this been the case, with other factors like education and income held constant, we might have inquired about causation. Did the aggressiveness stimulated by the game increase the desire to unleash emotion in the socially sanctioned (up to a point) act of war or did a mounting frustration with guerrilla warfare send the citizenry to the stadium, where one was at least able to shout and scream with one's equally frustrated peers? Research into such questions as these has barely begun.

Individualism
Reconsidered

AMERICANS LIKE to think of themselves as individualists. The word itself came into the language as "individualism" when Henry Reeve translated the French term *"individualisme,"* which Alexis de Tocqueville had employed as part of his analysis of democracy in America. Tocqueville's contemporary Ralph Waldo Emerson gave the doctrine of individualism his own Transcendental formulation and made the belief in self-reliance an article of American faith. By the time Herbert Hoover came to the presidency in 1929, the phrase "rugged individualism" had long since become a cliché. The Liberal tradition, which Louis Hartz and others have seen as the key to American political ideas, derives from the principle of maximized individual liberty. The flattering contrast between the American individualist and the European conformist has been a staple of our political rhetoric. When David Riesman and others bemoan the alleged conformism of the present-day American, it is usually with the notion that the lamentably submissive behavior of our time is in marked contrast to the distinctively individualistic ways of previous generations.

Historians of American literature have also laid special emphasis on the theme of individualism. Hester Prynne's self-reliant defiance of the Puritan community, Henry David Thoreau's disavowal of all organizations he had not expressly joined, Captain Ahab's fierce blasphemies, Huckleberry Finn's escape to the territory, Isabel Archer's insistence on her right to choose her own fate, Frederic Henry's decision to make a separate peace between himself and the Austrian army—literary critics and ordinary readers have been lyrical about such moments in our literature. Our self-image is individualistic.

Our self-image is also cooperative. As John William Ward and other historians have pointed out, Tocqueville marveled at American cooperativeness as well as at evidences of individualism. The penchant for forming voluntary associations struck the French aristocrat as more characteristically American than the quickness to defy all institutions, voluntary or involuntary. While the Transcendentalists and their heirs have always stressed self-reliance, the major institutions of the society have underlined the virtues of cooperation. Natty Bumppo might go alone into the wilderness; most pioneers sought the security and the companionship of collective effort. Although Henry Thoreau retired (for a time) to Walden Pond in order to unearth the true essentials of life, his countrymen trudged, or took the newly built railroad, to Boston or New York or Chicago, where they pursued a less lonely version of individuality. Theorists like John Dewey and George Herbert Mead explained the self not as a mysterious node of inner identity but rather as the product of social interactions. And political leaders with a colloquial bent urged Americans to join the team.

Join the team. The word originally had little to do with sports. (Consider a team of oxen.) Today it is hard to think of the word "team" apart from sports, for it has been in team sports that Americans have sought a combination of individualism and cooperation, a form of collective endeavor which nonetheless encourages the development of individuality. "Certainly," writes Allan Nevins, "the dominant theme of individualism is reflected in our leisureways."[1] But is it? Is it not true that the most popular sports in America are all team sports? Had the Thoreauvian impulse been dominant, we might expect Americans to have chosen sports like swimming, skiing, cross-country running, or even golf or tennis, where the individual is clearly separable from the team, rather than for baseball, basketball, football, and hockey, where teamwork is the *sine qua non* of achievement.

In one of the earliest inquiries into sports and national character, Joseph Strutt wrote:[2]

In order to form a just estimation of the character of any particular people, it is absolutely necessary to investigate the Sports and Pastimes most generally prevalent among them. War, policy [politics], and other contingent circumstances, may effectually place men, at different times, in different points of view, but, when we follow them into their retirements, where no disguise is necessary, we are most likely to see them in their true state, and may best judge of their natural dispositions.

Discussing baseball and football, I have attempted to do as Strutt suggests, to follow Americans into their play, into that realm of relative freedom "where no disguise is necessary," but I must admit that most attempts to interpret national character on the basis of specific kinds of modern sports have been unsuccessful for the simple reason that modern sports tend to be widely diffused and to resemble one another in their structure if not in their contents. The differences in soccer Italian style and soccer Swedish or Brazilian style are undoubtedly real, but they are probably too subtle for us to construct from them any reasonable interpretation of national character. Comments on the "lethargic" nature of Swedish players or the "fiery" temperament of Italians contribute very little to our store of insights into national character. There is, however, good reason to think that the broad difference between individual and team sports is psychologically and culturally significant. With this possibility as the lure, we can examine the rates of participation in individual and team sports in the United States and in other modern societies.

1. INDIVIDUAL VERSUS TEAM SPORTS

Asked by pollsters to name their favorite sport to watch, Americans respond as indicated in table 8.[3] For both sexes, the preference for team sports is overwhelming. There were similar results when 562 residents of Minneapolis and St. Paul were asked to give their associations for the word "sports." The replies were unambiguous. Football

Table 8
Favorite Sport to Watch
(*figures in percentages*)

	Men	Women	Men & Women
Baseball	41	27	34
Football	27	16	21
Basketball	6	12	9
Bowling	1	8	5
Wrestling	3	6	5
Boxing	4	2	3
Hockey, Ice Skating			3
Skiing			1
Golf			1
Swimming			1
Others	9	12	4
No Opinion	9	17	13

was named by 72.7 percent, baseball by 66.9 percent, and basketball by 42.6 percent while tennis—the most frequently named individual sport—was mentioned by only 21.6 percent.[4] The same pattern appears in the audience rates for sports on television. While 1975's Super Bowl attracted 41.6 percent of the audience and the World Series reached 30.7 percent, golf tournaments collectively averaged a viewership of 8.6 percent and Wimbledon reached a mere 4.5 percent of the audience.[5] Some, but not all, of this preference for team sports can be attributed to the fact that the Super Bowl takes place on a single afternoon. In contrast, the hegemony of team sports on German television is much less pronounced. While 81 percent of the audience tuned in for the 1966 soccer championships (Germany versus the Soviet Union), 52 percent watched the figure-skating championship and the cyclist's *Weltmeisterschaft*. Three years later, 77 percent tuned in for soccer (Germany versus Scotland) and 36 percent for track and field.[6]

The covers of *Sports Illustrated* represent editorial judgments about what the average sports fan cares most about. Since the magazine is a general one devoted to all sports (and some non-sports like bridge and chess), there must be some effort toward a large inclusiveness, but the distribution still shows a remarkable emphasis on team sports and a tendency for that emphasis to increase over time. As shown in table 9, *Sports Illustrated* featured football on 20.7 percent of its covers during the first twenty full years of publication while baseball accounted for another 17.8 percent.[7] Golf, the most frequently featured individual area, had a mere 8.8 percent of the total. Over the entire twenty years, the proportion devoted to team sports rises while that given over to individual sports drops, but the real surprise is that basketball shows an even greater spurt in coverage than football. Over the period of twenty years, gymnastics—one of the most popular sports in Europe and Japan—appeared only twice on the magazine's cover. In addition to the trend toward team sports, the covers indicate a marked diminution of interest in the essentially premodern sports of fishing, hunting, yachting and boating, and mountain climbing

Table 9
Sports Featured on the Cover of Sports Illustrated

	1955–58	1959–62	1963–66	1967–70	1971–74
Football	22	25	52	58	53
Basketball	6	10	18	36	39
Baseball	41	28	30	43	38
Golf	9	29	23	16	12
Hockey	4	5	6	11	11
Boxing	8	9	16	5	9
Auto Racing	5	7	4	5	6
Tennis	5	4	5	1	6
Track and Field	12	13	13	10	5
Horse Racing	13	13	7	1	4
Skiing	9	9	10	5	2
Swimming, Diving	3	8	0	1	2
Ice Skating	3	2	1	1	1
Fishing, Hunting	11	7	3	0	0
Boating	7	7	5	0	0
Other Team Sports	0	3	1	0	2
Other Individual Sports	16	7	1	0	1
Combinations of Sports	10	1	0	3	6
Non-Sports	19	11	6	7	6
Total	203	201	202	203	203

Table 10
Participation in Interscholastic Athletics, U.S.

Boys' Sports	1971–72	1974–75	Girls' Sports	1971–72	1974–75
Football[a]	878,187	1,011,809	Basketball	132,299	307,608
Basketball	645,670	688,690	Track and Field	62,211	299,215
Track and Field[b]	642,639	667,974	Tennis	26,010	84,495
Baseball	400,906	409,510	Volleyball	17,952	198,313
Wrestling	265,039	319,048	Swimming	17,229	73,946
Cross-Country	166,281	214,840	Gymnastics	17,225	61,424
Golf	120,078	135,813	Softball	9,813	110,140
Swimming	91,309	114,645	Field Hockey	4,260	59,106
Tennis	91,179	124,208	Skiing/Golf[c]	2,659	17,956
Soccer	78,510	98,482	Cross-Country	1,719	12,301
Total	3,379,798	3,785,019	Total	291,377	1,224,504

[a] Eleven-man football only.
[b] Outdoor track and field only.
[c] Skiing in 1971–72, golf in 1974–75.

(the last appeared three times during the first eight years, then disappeared from the covers). On the whole, the number of different sports to appear on the covers has declined and the decline is most noticeable in individual sports.

The same preference for team sports appears in the sports pages of newspapers and in the innumerable books published by and about sports heroes. Paul Gardiner's recent study of the social significance of American sports, *Nice Guys Finish Last* (1975), deals with baseball, football, basketball, and soccer while almost completely neglecting individual sports. The same emphasis is observable in Michael Novak's *The Joy of Sports* (1976).

In order to understand the general preference for team sports in a systematic and comparative way, it is useful for us to invent a single measurement of preferences. The ratio of participation in individual versus team sports is one such measurement. With it, we can compare European, Japanese, and American statistics even when many of the specific kinds of sport are different. If we apply this measurement to the 1,012 covers of *Sports Illustrated* from 1955 through 1974, we discover that the I/T ratio begins at .93 and ends at .31.

The data on actual participation lead to the same patterns as the evidence of the electronic and print media. Table 10 shows the total national participation of boys and girls in the top ten interscholastic sports for 1971–1972 and 1974–1975.[8] We can see that a team sport leads all four columns and that three of the four most commonly played varsity sports for high-school boys are team sports. The I/T ratio rises somewhat for boys, from .69 to .71, and increases slightly faster for women, from .77 to .81.

Table 11 shows comparable figures for the top ten sports on the intercollegiate level from 1956–1957 through 1971–1972.[9] (The

Table 11
Participation in Intercollegiate Athletics, U.S.

Men's Sports	1956–57	1961–62	1966–67	1971–72
Football	28,032	30,519	36,799	42,187
Track and Field	16,441	18,180	18,967	19,190
Baseball	16,378	16,798	17,101	19,487
Basketball	14,477	15,125	15,247	16,760
Swimming	6,524	7,913	8,269	8,667
Soccer	6,120	8,270	10,370	12,024
Tennis	6,062	6,936	7,155	7,445
Wrestling	5,720	7,630	7,889	9,437
Cross-Country	4,828	6,047	6,281	9,194
Golf	4,788	5,440	6,160	6,795
Total	109,370	122,858	134,238	151,186

Women's Sports	1971–72
Basketball	6,176
Field Hockey	5,012
Volleyball	4,124
Softball	3,185
Tennis	3,071
Swimming	2,429
Gymnastics	1,855
Track and Field	1,389
Lacrosse	827
Badminton	800
Total	28,868

NCAA surveys intercollegiate athletics every five years.) We can see several things in the numbers. Football leads in every survey and increases its share of the total participants. Baseball's share declines, but its relative position rises because track and field has fallen even faster than baseball. The men's ratios of individual to team sports are similar to those in high school—.68, .73, .69, .67. This similarity suggests a relative stability in interests, but the trend shows a slight decline in the popularity of individual sports. The figures for women are also interesting. In high school, they were somewhat more likely than males to be involved in individual sports. In college, the opposite is true and the I/T ratio sinks to .49.

For both males and females, the I/T ratio in college is lower than in high school. This strongly suggests that the educational system is biased toward team sports. Despite the talk of the importance of individual sports like golf and tennis which can be played throughout one's adult years, colleges and universities continue more strongly even than the high schools to emphasize team sports. It may be, of course, that the educational system merely responds to the demands of the students who choose sports as freely as they choose majors and courses. This notion runs contrary to the arguments of Jack Scott, Paul Hoch, and other reformers castigating athletic administrators for the excesses of intercollegiate athletics, including a culpable bias toward team sports, but the statistics on intramural sports seem to indicate that, given their own choice, the students greatly prefer team sports (table 12).[10] The figures show intramural participation, an area allegedly neglected by athletic departments and thus an area where the participants' own values are more likely to be acted upon. Team sports dominate even more starkly than in intercollegiate athletics. The I/T ratio for men's intramurals drops from .38 in 1956–1957 to .19 in 1971–1972. And this occurs while participation more than doubles. The women's ratio is .32—higher than the men's, but lower than the score for women's intercollegiate athletics. It is difficult to imagine how these lower ratios could occur if students really did prefer individual to team sports.

Unfortunately, we do not have statistics good enough to allow similar calculations for adults, but impressionistic evidence and partial statistics indicate that adult Americans do turn from team to individ-

Table 12
Participation in Intramural Sports, U.S.

Men's Sports	1956–57	1971–72	Women's Sports	1971–72
Basketball	129,005	362,375	Volleyball	61,144
Softball	106,672	309,608	Softball	51,083
Football	100,996	296,876	Basketball	49,871
Volleyball	66,375	158,769	Swimming	16,676
Bowling	35,394	57,893	Bowling	16,431
Track and Field	32,847	51,347	Touch Football	16,336
Tennis	24,038	38,043	Badminton	10,362
Swimming	22,814	45,049	Tennis	10,148
Table Tennis	22,470		Field Hockey	5,903
Golf	15,417		Table Tennis	5,767
Soccer		49,545		
Handball		31,609		
Total	556,028	1,401,114		243,721

ual sports—when they do not completely abandon sports participation. Newspapers have reported that 60,000,000 Americans now play tennis, but this estimate seems exaggerated. The U.S. Bureau of Outdoor Recreation reported in 1972 that 5 percent of all persons 12 years of age and over skied, water skied, played golf, and played tennis.[11] The Bureau also estimated that 22 percent participated in "other outdoor games or sports," which tells us less than we would like to know. If these "other sports" were baseball, softball, football, volleyball, basketball, and soccer, then team sports would once again be in the majority, but they might also have been horse-shoe pitching and croquet. We cannot tell.

Since American sports are largely organized as part of the educational system rather than through private or state-run sports clubs (as in most of Europe), adults are relatively disadvantaged. Various public and private facilities are available for adults' active participation, but the system makes it extremely difficult for American adults to keep up an involvement in team sports. If spectators in America either play or wish to play the sports they attend or watch electronically, which is certainly the case in Europe, then the increased involvement of American adults in golf, tennis, squash, and other individual sports may actually be for lack of their preferred alternative. The tennis players would really rather play basketball. But this possibility is quite speculative.

The European system, unlike the American, emphasizes participation through clubs which are generally private in Western Europe and part of the state-run industrial sector in the East (e.g., the most prestigious club in most Eastern European countries is generally *Dynamo*, the club of the secret police, of which both Roland Matthes and Kornelia Ender are members). Since facilities are *not* closely tied to high schools and colleges, one might expect that Europeans stress team sports. After all, adults need not give them up at age eighteen or twenty-two simply because they cease to be students. Nearly three million West Germans are members of soccer clubs and the *Deutscher Fußballbund* is the largest of German sports organizations. One can play as long as one can run.

In fact, however, Europeans are much more likely than Americans to be enthusiasts for individual sports. This is true despite the status of soccer as the single most popular sport for participants and for spectators. Before we look at some of the quantitative evidence, we must discuss several factors which make this kind of cross-cultural comparison difficult. In the first place, the best evidence comes from statistics on memberships in sports clubs, but not all members are athletically active. Many join for the sociability involved or even to aid their business ventures (something not unknown in the United States). In the second place, many active sportsmen—especially in individual sports like skiing—are not members of clubs. Thirdly, although European sports clubs attract a disproportionate number of their members from the young (under twenty-five), the sample is still not exactly comparable to the American student population. Fourthly, we must be alert to the definitions adopted in the various surveys. We have defined sports to be nonutilitarian physical contests. This means that swimming is a sport only when it is competitive. To go to the beach and lie in the sun and splash about or even swim for a few yards is not sport. We see the difference in practice when we examine an Austrian study in which 28 percent of a sample of 1,000 teen-aged boys and girls are listed as swimming recreationally while only 6 percent swim competitively.[12] Similarly, cycling is either a true sport or a noncompetitive recreational activity depending on whether or not the cyclist is involved in a contest. In a Czech study, 48 percent of the girls were listed as active cyclists, but only 1 percent cycled competitively.[13] Most studies, European and American, jumble together activities which are pure play or games with those that are sports under the strictest definition. Since Communist nations often list tourism and chess under the same rubric as true sports, we must be cautious. Finally, even when we are reasonably sure that we are dealing with true sports rather than with a noncompetitive physical activity like hiking, we must contend with the problems of classification into team and individual sports. Gymnastics is sometimes a massed display rather than an individual competition. (Team competitions are no problem in gymnastics because individuals perform and are scored separately; the team's score is merely an aggregate.) Tennis includes doubles play as well as singles. Rowing includes single sculls as well as double sculls, coxed and coxless pairs and fours, and coxed eights.

Fortunately, the difficulties are not crippling. Since our comparisons are not comparisons in absolute numbers but in ratios, it is the proportions we care about. If the proportion of active soccer players who join sports clubs is roughly the same as the proportion of active swimmers or weightlifters who join *their* clubs, then our ratio will not be disturbed by the fact that not every athlete joins a club. If, on the other hand, rugby clubs are filled with idle folk who simply like the congenial atmosphere while tennis clubs are composed mostly of ardent players, our ratios will be skewed—but I see no reason why this sort of discrepancy should exist. The fact that our samples are drawn from somewhat different age groups is a more difficult problem because there is a universal tendency for older people to drop out of team sports and this tendency will distort our ratios. Nonetheless, the overrepresentation of young people in our European data will largely correct this. The fourth difficulty is also a manageable one. If we proceed cautiously, we can usually determine whether or not a survey has mixed data on spontaneous play with that on true sports.

With these qualifications in mind, let us examine the pattern of sports clubs memberships in West and East Germany (table 13).[14] Although soccer leads the list in both countries, gymnastics is a

Table 13
Memberships in Sports Clubs, 1973[a]

| Type of Sport | Male and Female Members | |
	West Germany[b]	East Germany[b]
Soccer	3,197,759	487,570
Gymnastics	2,567,116	344,372
Shooting	777,049	
Track and Field	629,644	159,244
Swimming	517,951	72,187
Tennis	503,215	
Handball (European)	468,082	133,031
Table Tennis	387,056	68,353
Skiing	276,987	32,296
Horseback Riding	259,340	
Bowling		138,903
Volleyball		71,395
Judo		35,609
Total	9,584,199	1,542,960

[a] Top ten sports only.
[b] The population of East Germany is approximately one-fourth that of West Germany.

strong second. The I/T ratio for West Germany is 1.61, indicating a marked preference for individual sports. The ratio is, in fact, roughly twice what we found for the student population of the United States. Although the top ten sports are somewhat different, the figure for sports-club members of East Germany result in a similar ratio, 1.23.

The French pattern is like the German. In table 14, soccer heads the list with 38 percent of all members (compared to 33 percent for West Germany and 32 percent for East Germany), but the I/T ratio is .98, lower than in either Germany but still considerably higher than in the United States.[15] An excellent Danish survey of all active participants between the ages of 15 and 40 shows the remarkable strength of gymnastics in that country—12.1 percent of the entire population consists of active gymnasts while only 13 percent of the population goes in for soccer, but it is likely that many of the active gymnasts compete only with their inner sense of excellence.[16] The Danish I/T

Table 14
Memberships in Sports Clubs, France,
1963

Type of Sport	Male and Female Members
Soccer	443,898
Skiing	259,107
Basketball	103,601
Tennis	82,300
Judo	54,544
Gymnastics	53,004
Track and Field	51,512
Rugby	44,300
Swimming	39,084
Cycling	37,705
Total	1,169,055

Table 15
Active Participants, Denmark, ca. 1953

Type of Sport	Male and Female Participants
Soccer	199,079
Gymnastics	184,687
Handball	119,983
Shooting	47,994
Swimming	31,273
Track and Field	30,651
Badminton	30,327
Tennis	20,524
Rowing	14,259
Boxing	5,728
Total	684,505

ratio is 1.15, comparable to the French and East-German results (table 15).

The last study in this selective survey of studies sheds light from a somewhat different angle. Japan is obviously not a European nation,

but it is a modern society and it is certainly one that most Americans
are likely to think of as less individualistic than the United States.
The Japanese Amateur Athletic Association has carefully surveyed
the membership of thirty-five national sports federations. The results,
as of 1967, appear in table 16.[17] What is most remarkable is the
modernity of the sports. Judo and kendo (Japanese swordsmanship)
are in no danger of extinction, but the combined number of their
adherents is smaller than the numbers playing baseball. Sumo wrestling, which Americans often think of as typically Japanese, accounts
for a scant 0.5 percent of all organized athletics. Except for kendo
and sumo, the list of sports looks almost identical to that for the
United States, but the look is somewhat deceptive. When we calculate the I/T ratio, we come out with 1.34. The Japanese too are
much more likely than we to be involved in individual sports—and
this despite the fact that they often regard baseball as their national
game. Supportive evidence for this rather unexpected conclusion ap-

Table 16
Memberships in Japanese Sports Organizations, 1967

Type of Sport	Members	Type of Sport	Members
Baseball	824,728	Rugby	52,431
Volleyball	612,080	Rifle Shooting	50,868
Pingpong	526,035	Handball	34,585
Paddle Tennis	492,836	Sumo Wrestling	29,123
Basketball	413,770	Boating	22,835
Judo	407,782	Skating	15,113
Track and Field	386,220	Horsemanship	13,181
Kendo	329,299	Cycling	8,910
Softball	178,958	Yachting	8,711
Gymnastics	152,801	Clay Pigeons	7,661
Golf	114,178	Wrestling	7,205
Archery	103,588	Weightlifting	4,847
Soccer	103,204	Boxing	4,720
Mountaineering	101,677	Hockey	4,593
Swimming	100,408	Fencing	4,561
Tennis	92,632	Canoeing	1,094
Badminton	89,670	Modern Pentathlon	818
Skiing	63,544	Total	5,364,666

pears in a carefully conducted empirical investigation of children's games. When 120 American boys and girls were compared with 120 of their Japanese counterparts, M. V. Seagroe found a statistically significant "emphasis on informal social play in Japan and on team games in America."[18]

Table 17
A Comparison of I/T Ratios

		I/T
United States		
Interscholastic Sports, Boys,	1971–72	.69
	1974–75	.71
Girls,	1971–72	.77
	1974–75	.81
Intercollegiate Sports, Men,	1956–57	.68
	1961–62	.73
	1966–67	.69
	1971–72	.67
Women,	1971–72	.49
Intramural Sports, Men,	1956–57	.38
	1971–72	.19
Women,	1971–72	.32
Other Countries		
West German Club Members,	1971	1.61
East German Club Members,	1971	1.23
French Club Members	1963	.98
Danish Active Participants,	1953	1.15
Japanese Club Members,	1967	1.34

These five studies are national in scope. Local studies abound and their results vary from place to place and from time to time, but their tendency is clearly to support the generalization drawn from the national studies: young people in the United States prefer team sports to individual sports while teenagers and young adults in Europe and Japan are likely to be drawn in the opposite direction.[19] There is good reason to believe that Table 17, summarizing the results of seventeen studies, is an accurate indicator of American versus European-Japanese preferences.

There is also considerable impressionistic evidence to substantiate the quantified data about the United States in cross-cultural context. John R. Tunis commented in an early work that the French "prefer and do best at individual games—golf, tennis, pelota and the like"; a generation later, Robert Daley remarked that "what is really admired in sports in Europe is individual exploit." [20] Such opinions prove nothing, but they do indicate that not all sportswriters have been enamored with the theory of American individualism as expressed in sports.

Still another kind of supportive evidence can be derived from the study of psychological tests, particularly personality tests. Although the present state of scholarship makes it risky to generalize from the contradictory and sometimes confused results of the psychological studies done on athletes, one tentative conclusion does seem justified. The choice of team rather than individual sport is a manifestation of personality. Ordinary experience tells us that most people are active in more than a single sport; professional football players, for instance, seem especially drawn to golf as a recreational sport. Nonetheless, most people seem to have a preference for either team or individual sports. Instruments such as the California Personality Inventory, The Edwards Personal Preference Schedule, the Cattell Sixteen Factor Personality Questionnaire, and other widely used pencil-and-paper tests do show a significant correlation between individual sports and such personality traits as introversion, autonomy, independence, and individualism. This is especially true of women athletes, who must withstand considerable social disapproval if they display a serious commitment to competitive sports. Out of the "equivocal results" and the "mosaic of contradictions" observed in the field, out of the considerable scholarly discord, this one theme does emerge. [21]

2. FICTIVE RUNNERS

Novelists work in another mode from sociologists and psychologists and they offer another kind of witness, but their works also tend to confirm these tentative conclusions about team and individual sports in Europe and the United States.

One of the earliest American authors to make serious use of sports in his fiction was Charles Emmett Van Loan. One of his collections of stories, *Taking the Count* (1915), is devoted to the prize ring and to the world of the professional boxer. Another collection, *Score by Innings* (1919), is about baseball. This bifurcation of interests between boxing and baseball was until quite recently typical for American novelists, dramatists, and poets. From Jack London's gentle story, "The Abysmal Brute" (1913) to Leonard Gardner's grim portrayal of a battered, hopeless "pork-and-bean" fighter in *Fat City* (1969), many of America's best writers have used the ring to dramatize the unmediated struggle of man against man.[22] And from the days of Van Loan and Ring Lardner to those of Robert Coover and Philip Roth, even more of our best writers have used baseball as their metaphor for the human condition.[23] In the 1960s, a great many novelists began to explore the possibilities of football and basketball.[24] Only in the last five years have writers suddenly begun to exploit tennis and golf.[25] If we think of serious works of art intended for adult readers, the emphasis in literature as in history has been upon team sports.

It is rather different in Europe, at least in Western Europe. If we examine the corpus of "sports literature" written in English, French, and German, we discover that writers as unlike as George Bernard Shaw and Bertold Brecht have shared the American fascination with prize fighters, that a few novelists of real importance have written about team sports (mainly soccer), and that a remarkable number of first-rate writers have made significant art from the lonely effort of individual athletes.[26] While the characters of American novels collectively step up to bat, crouch down at the line of scrimmage, or dribble and pass their way toward the basket, their fictive counterparts in Europe are much more likely to be runners, cyclists, swimmers, or oarsmen—lonely, estranged men, men determined to prove themselves to a hostile world.[27] While Mark Harris and Bernard Malamud dramatize the quest for community and the dangers of egotism, the British, the French, the Germans, and the Swiss are likely to focus on the psychological drama of the long-distance runner as he acts out some inner crisis. The dominant tone of the fiction concerned with baseball is comic. The dominant tone of the European stories is tragic.

La Ligne Droite (1956) by Yves Gibeau is a partial exception to the generalizations offered above. Although it is definitely a novel about lonely effort and individual anguish, it is not a tragedy. *La Ligne Droite* is, on the contrary, the fictional equivalent of the stories of Ray Ewry, Wilma Rudolph, and other champions who triumphed over physical disabilities. Gibeau's novel is about Stefan Volker, a German athlete badly wounded in the Second World War. When discovered by a concerned trainer, Stefan is an embittered newspaper-vendor, a silent survivor who wants only to be left alone to brood over the amputation of his right arm. Thanks to the trainer's patience, Stefan begins hesitantly to run again. In the climactic contest of the novel, he competes against an international field and achieves his personal record for 800 meters. Since Gibeau is French, the obvious theme is international comity, symbolized by the international track meet where Volker ("*Volk*") represents the German people. The book ends, therefore, with the symbolic suggestion that Germany has risen like a seared phoenix from the ashes of the destruction which it brought upon itself.

Bert Buchner, the distance runner of *Brot und Spiele* (1959), is a character revised from the hero of the short story "Der Läufer," which Siegfried Lenz published a year earlier. Technically, the novel is simplicity itself—the journalist narrator describes a 10,000-meter race for the *Europameisterschaft* and thinks back to his first encounter with Bert Buchner when both were German prisoners of war. He remembers Bert's first races as representative of an obscure working-class sports-club and his swift ascent into the ranks of Europe's best distance runners. He had often run "as if his life depended on it" and this is how he runs the 10,000 meters.[28] The race is a symbolic one that the nameless narrator wants his former friend and protégé to lose in order that he might be punished for the ruthlessness of his ambition and for the betrayal of his friends. Despite the narrator's conviction—"This time he will not win"—the reader is ambivalent.[29] How can one not identify with the vividly described, beautifully characterized runner, the oldest of the eight contestants, who runs as if his life depended on it? But Lenz is an inflexible moralist. Bert falls a few meters from the tape, crawls forward, collapses completely, and smiles enigmatically—as if to accept the inevitable. He is carried off. "Where will they bring him? Where?"[30]

There is an uncanny resemblance between Bert Buchner's moral and physical failure and that of Ike Low, the working-class miler of Brian Glanville's *The Olympian* (1969). In Glanville's novel, the concern is as much for Sam Dee, Ike's fanatical coach, as for the runner himself. "Strength is not just the strength of the body," he intones, "it is the strength of the mind. The strength of the will prevails over the weakness of the body. . . . A champion is a man who has trained his body *and* his mind, who has learned to conquer pain, and to use pain for his own purposes."[31] Sam Dee, who seems clearly to be modeled after the Australian coach Percy Cerutty, is the ultimate authoritarian, the idealist who demands that Ike surpass human possibility. Through the triumph of the pupil, the teacher scorned and rejected for his unconventional theories will be vindicated. The plot is complex, but the failure—like Bert Buchner's—seems inevitable. At the Olympics, Ike chases after the African runner who leads the pack. Ike runs "through the pain barrier," hears Sam's voice urging him on, and fails to accomplish the impossible. Like Bert Buchner, he falls, "Not running any more. Just falling, falling."[32]

The last of our runners is the most famous. Colin Smith, the hero of Alan Sillitoe's novella and film, *The Loneliness of the Long-Distance Runner* (1963), is the resentful, angry son of a father who worked himself to death at a milling-machine and left his family little more than the paltry insurance that his widow quickly squanders. Colin's frustration leads him to petty crime and to imprisonment in Borstal. There he discovers a redeeming talent—he can run. "I've always been a good runner, quick and with a big stride as well, the only trouble being that no matter how fast I run, and I did a very fair lick even though I do say so myself, it didn't stop me getting caught by the cops after that bakery job."[33] Now, with the enthusiastic backing of the prestige-hungry warden of the prison, he begins to train, to run through the countryside and to experience a sense of freedom that he had never known before. His time drops and the warden begins to talk of his representing England. But this is the basic irony. "England" is the society that has imprisoned him. He has been asked to join the enemy. The warden's more immediate goal is a prize cup, but Colin is clear about what is at stake for him:[34]

The pop-eyed potbellied governor said to a pop-eyed potbellied Member of Parliament who sat next to his pop-eyed potbellied whore of a wife that I was his only hope for getting the Borstal Blue Ribbon Prize Cup For Long Distance Cross Country Running (All England), which I was, and it set me laughing to myself inside, and I didn't say a word to any potbellied pop-eyed bastard that might give them real hope.

(The film is an improvement over the novel in that the viewer is kept in suspense until the last moments of the race.) Symbolically then, Colin runs against the Borstal prison, against the class structure of English society, against the injustices that he can suffer from but not describe. He runs, approaches the finish line, hears the frenzied encouragement of everyone connected with the prison, and stops:[35]

And I could hear the lords and ladies now from the grandstand, and could see them standing up to save me in: "Run!" they were shouting in their posh voices. "Run!" But I was deaf, daft and blind and stood where I was, still tasting the bark in my mouth and still blubbing like a baby, blubbing now out of gladness that I'd got them beat at last.

He refuses the victory asked of him by his oppressors and he triumphs morally over those who have deprived and injured and humiliated him. It is a fine novel and a magnificent film.

Stefan Volker, Bert Buchner, Ike Low, and Colin Smith are all distance runners rather than sprinters. Their creators needed time, time for their creatures to suffer, to doubt, to despair, and—sometimes—to fail. From the precious moments of a sprint or a leap or a throw, poets make lyrics, but the novelists of athletic individualism need an extended motion a movement through time. They need space to extend the moment and time to study the lonely struggle with self-inflicted pain that can scarcely be endured. For these European writers, and for the exceptional American like Patricia Nell Warren, the lonely race is transfigured into a tragic metaphor for life itself, "the road all runners run." Modern sports are very different from primitive, ancient, and medieval sports, and we have come a long way from the world of the Apache youths, running from the circle of the sun to the circle of the moon, but there is, finally, despite all our distinctions, only one race, which all the others symbolize.

Conclusion

FROM THE perspective of the Neo-Marxists, modern sport is the enemy of freedom. Modern sport is, in its essential characteristics—and not just in its abuses, aberrations, or excesses—the epitome of inhumane social organization. The immense possibilities of the human spirit are crushed and flattened to the "dehumanized" outlines of "one-dimensional man." We have already considered this argument and concluded that it is exaggerated, a partial truth at best. Despite imperfections and false emphases, modern sports hold forth the possibility of a realm of relative if not absolute freedom. The testimony of athletes, beginners as well as champions, corroborates the analyses of philosophers like Hans Lenk, Michel Bouet, and Paul Weiss. In sport we can discover the euphoric sense of wholeness, autonomy, and potency which is often denied us in the dreary rounds of routinized work that are the fate of most men and women.

Do we want now, after considering the complicated problem of team versus individual sports, to modify our optimistic conclusion and to suggest that individual sports are somehow more liberating than team sports and that the American penchant for the latter reveals a strain of conformism and acquiescence in our character? Prudence calls for hesitation and further speculation.

Shall we say that individual sports express the autonomy of the athlete while team sports indicate a dependence on others? There is historical evidence to suggest that many Americans once assumed that team sports were a useful device to curb the excesses of individualism. In his Phi Beta Kappa address at Harvard in 1893, Francis A. Walker praised sports in general for their nurture of public spirit and for their opposition to "the selfish individualistic tendencies of the age."[1] A decade later, Gertrude Dudley and Frances A. Kellor, two prominent physical educators of the day, published *Athletic Games in the Education of Women*. Worried by the prevalence of what they too called "selfish individualism" among their own sex, they urged the development of a cooperative spirit, especially in school girls, who seemed maddeningly slow to learn that "social ethics is essentially the result of team work." The uncooperative girl who refused to play games at all continued "an individualist in her later activities," a fate which the authors earnestly deprecated.[2] In 1919, Walter Camp, Yale University's renowned "Father of American Football," proclaimed that sports "teach team work in opposition to individualism and selfish purposes."[3] The depreciation of individualism and the stress on the word "selfish" sound odd today, but it may be that the approach to sports then was a more realistic one than the contemporary notion that team sports develop an inner-directed self-reliance.

There does not seem to be any way to avoid the conclusion that a preference for team sports represents an inclination toward cooperation rather than toward the kind of autonomy symbolized by the long-distance runner, but we err greatly if we assume that cooperation is always the enemy of individualism. It may be that our conception of individualism has been faulty, too limited. Perhaps the choice is not between individualism and conformity but between two conceptions of the preconditions of individualism, conceptions which are in turn related to the two conceptions of freedom which contemporary philosophers sometimes refer to as "freedom from" and "freedom to."

One side of the Liberal tradition has always emphasized the individualism which flourishes under a kind of negative freedom when a man is unbound by the restraints and trammels of institutional order. Henry David Thoreau chooses to rely upon himself and to announce his complete independence from society. Huckleberry Finn departs "for the territory," where he can be free from Aunt Polly and her attempts to "sivilize" him. The other side of the Liberal tradition, the side which developed into democratic socialism, has stressed the individualism which thrives under positive freedom, when a man is free to choose among alternatives and to act upon his choice. It is the opposite of the Spartan-like reduction of wants exemplified by life at Walden Pond. For this conception of freedom, the transition from traditional to modern forms of social organization represents a net gain, an increased opportunity for each person to maximize his or her human potential. Under the conditions of modern democracy, society liberates because man in society is free to do what no man ever did alone. We can, for instance, voyage to the moon and back.

The voyage is a cramped one, and there's the rub. The difficulty is that the fullest realization of the second version of freedom and the kind of cooperative individualism it implies is frequently at the expense of the first version of freedom. Cooperation expands choices and opportunities for action, but it also imposes obligations and curtails the kind of spontaneous freedom symbolized by Natty Bumppo alone in the wilderness. We are involved, as it were, in a moral trade-off between two conceptions of freedom. Let us acknowledge that there are certainly situations where the loss of "freedom from" is greater than the gain of "freedom to." Cooperation can degenerate into restrictive conformity. There are, indeed, entire societies where individual liberties have been sacrificed at the altar of the state. But it is too easy to lose faith, to romanticize the past, to exaggerate the present ills of Liberal or social democracy, and to forget the extraordinary increase in human freedom that has occurred in the last two hundred years. We tend sometimes to accept the benefits of "freedom to" as if they were commonplace or even "natural" and at the same time to resent every diminution of "freedom from" as if we were reduced to slavery. We walk into the terminal of an airport and purchase a ticket to Tokyo or Nairobi; we complain that we must stand in line to have our baggage checked.

This trade-off between two conceptions of freedom can be seen as clearly in sports as in any other modern institution. Those marvelously individualistic Greeks whose athletic festivals excluded team sports entirely were the same fiercely quarrelsome Greeks who exhausted themselves in pointless wars and lost their independence to the Macedonians and the Romans. Modern sports, even modern Olympics, are different from the Greek games. Like voyages to the moon or flights to Tokyo, they assume a very high level of cooperation. They demand of us that we surrender a portion of that "freedom from" whose purest manifestation is spontaneous play. Indeed, it has been a principal thesis of this entire book that *modern* sports assume far more cooperation than sports as we defined them in our preliminary paradigm. On the day of the race, predetermined months in advance by an athletic bureaucracy, the runners wait tensely in their electronic starting blocks, each in his allotted lane (and each with a number pinned to his shirt). They leap forward not when *they* choose to but when the official fires his gun. The loss is real, but the gain is also real.

Words like "loss," "gain," and "trade-off" are borrowed from the language of the economists, who are professionally anxious that we not delude ourselves with the pleasant thought of getting something for nothing, but perhaps the secret of modern sports and the basis of their nearly universal popularity is that we gain a great deal more than we lose. In modern sports, as in the fine arts or the pure sciences, the result of the most intensive cooperation frequently appears to be and is accepted as individual achievement, which it surely is, although not quite in the sense advocated by Henry David Thoreau. It is actually one of the happier ironies of modern sports that we can lose ourselves in play and forget the creative and sustaining (and restricting) social organization and cultural assumptions that have been a central concern of this book.[4]

Examples are useful. Nadia Comaneci's solo *salto* is made possible by two coaches, a choreographer, a physician, an assistant music master, and a masseur, not to mention an entire civilization which imagined the sport of gymnastics and staged the international drama of the Olympic Games. But she alone performs. There she is. The New York Yankees were a symbol of championship baseball, and we are well aware of how much cooperative effort was required for them to win the 1932 World Series. But memory singles out the awkward figure of Babe Ruth, pointing (maybe) at the flag in center field, where he will, where he *did*, hit his unforgettable home run. There he was.

What is true for them is true for the rest of us at our less spectacular levels of commitment and achievement. I rush across the tennis court and return the ball with what seems to me in my enthusiasm the perfect stroke, the right stroke, the stroke dictated by the imperatives of tennis. I have surrendered myself to the rules of the game and I am, paradoxically, flushed with an ecstatic sense of amplitude and freedom.

One final observation is appropriate. We have sought to distinguish precisely and systematically among categories of play, games, contests, and sports, but the static precision of an intellectual distinction should not be confused with the ebb and flow of ordinary experience. Spontaneous play is paradigmatically separate from modern sports, but the preference for one implies no exclusion of the other from our lives. When we are weary of modern sports, when cooperation palls into conformity, there is always another option. When we are surfeited with rules and regulations, when we are tired—like Robert Frost's apple-picker—of the harvest we ourselves desired, we can always put away our stopwatch, abandon the cinder track, kick off our spiked shoes, and run as Roger Bannister did, barefoot, on firm dry sand, by the sea.

Notes

Abbreviations Used

IRSS   *International Review of Sport Sociology*
JSH   *Journal of Sport History*
RQ   *Research Quarterly*
SI   *Sports Illustrated*
SW   *Sportwissenschaft*
TPK   *Theorie und Praxis der Körperkultur*

Preface
1. Introduction to Alfred Peters, *Psychologie des Sports* (Leipzig: Der Neue Geist Verlag, 1927), p. xii.

I Play, Games, Contests, Sports
1. *The Four Minute Mile* (New York: Dodd, Mead, 1957), pp. 11–12.
2. *Wesen und Lehre des Sports* (Berlin/Frankfurt: Weidmannsche Verlags-Buchhandlung, 1949), p. 10.
3. Arthur Ashe and Frank Deford, *Arthur Ashe* (Boston: Houghton Mifflin, 1975), p. 46.
4. See Eugen Fink, *Oase des Glücks* (Munich: Karl Alber, 1957) and *Spiel als Weltsymbol* (Stuttgart: Kohlhammer, 1966); David L. Miller, *Gods and Games* (New York: World Publishing Co., 1969).

5. "The Elements of Sport," *The Philosophy of Sport*, ed. Robert G. Osterhoudt (Springfield, Illinois: Charles C. Thomas, 1973), p. 55; see also his "What Is a Game?" *Philosophy of Science*, 34 (June 1967), 148–56.

6. See F. K. Mathys, "Kultischer Fußball in Japan," *Olympisches Feuer*, 6 (April 1959), 12–13.

7. Jean Youd, "Notes on Kickball in Micronesia," *Journal of American Folklore*, 74 (1961), 64.

8. *Homo Ludens: A Study of the Play Element in Culture* (1938; rpt. London: Temple Smith, 1970), p. 98.

9. J. J. Jusserand, *Les Sports et jeux d'exercice dans l'ancienne France* (Paris: Plon, 1901), p. 58.

10. *Les Jeux et les hommes* (Paris: Gallimard, 1958), p. 32.

11. Closest to my own definitions are those of John Loy, "The Nature of Sport: A Definitional Effort," *Quest Monograph*, no. 10 (May 1968), 1–15.

12. See M. I. Finley and H. W. Pleket, *The Olympic Games: The First Thousand Years* (New York: Viking Press, 1976), pp. 31–32.

13. See Jules Gritti, *Sport a la une* (Paris: Armand Colin, 1975), p. 114.

14. See Ralph Henry Gabriel's introduction to John Allen Krout, *Annals of American Sport* (New Haven: Yale University Press, 1929), p. 3.

15. *Sports in America* (New York: Random House, 1976), p. 62.

16. See John M. Roberts, Malcolm J. Arth, and Robert R. Bush, "Games in Culture," *American Anthropologist*, 61 (1959), 597–605; John M. Roberts and Brian Sutton-Smith, "Child Training and Game Involvement," *Ethnology*, 1 (1962), 166–85; John M. Roberts, Brian Sutton-Smith, and Adam Kendon, "Strategy in Games and Folk Tales," *Journal of Social Psychology*, 61 (1963), 185–99; Brian Sutton-Smith, John M. Roberts, and Robert M. Kozelka, "Game Involvement in Adults," *Journal of Social Psychology*, 60 (1963), 15–30; Brian Sutton-Smith and John M. Roberts, "Rubrics of Competitive Behavior," *Journal of Genetic Psychology*, 105 (1964), 13–37; John M. Roberts and Brian Sutton-Smith, "Cross-Cultural Correlates of Games of Chance," *Behavior Science Notes*, 1 (1966), 131–44; Brian Sutton-Smith, "The Sporting Balance," *Soziologie des Sports*, ed. Rolf Albonico and Katharina Pfister-Binz (Basel: Birkhäuser Verlag, 1971), pp. 105–13; Brian Sutton-Smith and John M. Roberts, "The Cross-Cultural and Psychological Study of Games," *IRSS*, 6 (1971), 79–87; Brian Sutton-Smith, "Games, the Socialization of Conflict," *SW*, 3 (1973), 41–46; Brian Sutton-Smith, "Play as Adaptive Potentiation," *SW*, 5 (1975), 103–18; Donald W. Ball, "The Scaling of Gaming," *Pacific Sociological Review*, 15 (July 1972), 277–94; Donald W. Ball, "What the Action Is," *Journal for the Theory of Social Behavior*, 2 (1972), 121–43; Donald W. Ball, "Control versus Complexity," *Pacific Sociological Review*, 17 (1974), 167–84.

17. For their lack of concern for noncompetitive games, they have been faulted by Henning Eichberg, "Spielverhalten und Relationsgesellschaft in West Sumatra," *Stadion* 1 (1976), 13–15.

18. "Child Training and Game Involvement," *Sport, Culture and Society*, ed. John W. Loy and Gerald S. Kenyon (New York: Macmillan, 1969), p. 124.

19. *Ibid.*, p. 128.
20. "The Cross-Cultural and Psychological Study of Games," p. 86.
21. *Ibid.*
22. *Les Jeux et les hommes*, p. 142.
23. *Ibid.*, pp. 169–70.
24. See also Benjamin Lowe, "The Aesthetics of Sport," *Quest Monograph*, no. 16 (1971), 13–17; Lowe, "A Theoretical Rationale for Investigation into the Relationship of Sport and Aesthetics," *IRSS*, 8, no. 1 (1973), 95–101; Lowe, *The Beauty of Sport* (Englewood Cliffs: Prentice-Hall, 1977); Francis W. Keenan, "The Athletic Contest as a 'Tragic' Form of Art," *The Philosophy of Sport*, ed. Robert G. Osterhoudt (Springfield, Illinois: Charles C. Thomas, 1973), pp. 309–26; Robert Mitchell, "Sport as Experience," *Quest Monograph*, no. 24 (1975), 28–33; H. T. A. Whiting and D. W. Masterson, eds., *Readings in the Aesthetics of Sport* (London: Lepus Books, 1974).
25. "Social Implications of the Interaction between Spectators and Athletes," *Exercise and Sport Sciences Reviews*, 2 (1974), 202. The phrase "play and display" is an allusion to Gregory P. Stone, "American Sports—Play and Dis-Play," *Chicago Review*, 9, no. 3 (1955), 83–100. For a recent critique of sport as spectacle, see Christopher Lasch, "The Corruption of Sports," *New York Review of Books*, 24 (April 28, 1977), 24–30.
26. *Mythologies* (Paris: Editions du Seuil, 1970), p. 17; see also Gregory P. Stone and Ramon A. Oldenburg, "Wrestling," *Motivations in Play, Games and Sports*, ed. Ralph Slovenko and James A. Knight (Springfield, Illinois: Charles C. Thomas, 1967), pp. 503–32.
27. *Homo Ludens*, p. 32.
28. *Les Jeux et les hommes*, p. 37.
29. The best discussion of the "ludic frame" is by Alan G. Ingham and John W. Loy, "The Structure of Ludic Action," *IRSS*, 9, no. 1 (1974), 23–60.

II FROM RITUAL TO RECORD

1. Quoted by Harry Clay Palmer, "The 'Around the World' Tour," *Athletic Sports in America, England, and Australia*, ed. Palmer (Philadelphia: Hubbard Brothers, 1889), 446–47. Mark Twain's fascination with baseball and cultural contrast also appears in *A Connecticut Yankee in King Arthur's Court* (1889), where the game is played by medieval knights under the coaching of Hank Morgan.
2. See Hans Damm, "The So-Called Sport Activities of Primitive People," *The Cross-Cultural Analysis of Sport and Games*, ed. Günther Lüschen (Champaign, Illinois: Stipes, 1970), pp. 52–69. Many anthropologists deplore the term "primitive" because of its ethnocentric connotations. Unfortunately, none of their suggested alternatives seems wholly satisfactory and I fall back upon the layman's term, although I do not use it in order to make moral judgments.
3. *Weltgeschichte des Sports*, 3rd ed., 2 vols. (Frankfurt: Cotta, 1971), 1, 3.
4. *Games of the North American Indians* (Washington: U.S. Government Printing Office, 1907), pp. 31, 34.

5. Quoted in Morris Edward Opler, "A Jicarilla Apache Ceremonial Relay Race," *American Anthropologist*, 46 (1944), 78n.

6. "Wettkampfspiel und Dualorganisation bei den Timbira Brasiliens," *Die Wiener Schule der Völkerkunde Festschrift*, ed. A. Haekel, A. Hohenwart-Gerlachstein, and A. Slawik (Vienna: Verlag Ferdinand Berger, 1956), p. 509.

7. Opler, "A Jicarilla Apache Ceremonial Relay Race," 75–97.

8. N. A. Scotch, "Magic, Sorcery and Football among the Urban Zulu," *Journal of Conflict Resolution*, 5 (1961), 70–74. Scotch's experiences among the Zulu seem to have led to conclusions about baseball; see William A. Gamson and N. A. Scotch, "Scapegoating in Baseball," *American Journal of Sociology*, 70 (1964), 69–72. For other examples of the blend of primitive and modern, see J. R. Fox, "Pueblo Baseball: A New Use for Old Witchcraft," *Journal of American Folklore*, 74 (1961), 9–16; Eugene H. Freund, "The Transition of a Fertility Rite to an Indigenous Spectator Sport," *Quest Monograph*, no. 16 (June 1971), 37–41; "Orioles in 'Spirited' Race," *New York Times*, September 16, 1975.

9. "Wettkampfspiel und Dualorganisation," pp. 504–33.

10. Walter Umminger, *Supermen, Heroes and Gods*, trans. James Clark (New York: McGraw-Hill, 1963), pp. 71–72.

11. Quoted in W. A. Goellner, "The Court Ball Game of the Aboriginal Mayas," *RQ*, 24 (May 1953), 164.

12. The best studies of the game are Goellner, *ibid.*, pp. 147–68; Walter Krickeberg, "Das mittelamerikanische Ballspiel und seine religiöse Symbolik," *Paideuma*, 3 (1948), 118–90; Theodore Stern, *The Rubber-Ball Games of the Americas* (Seattle: University of Washington Press, 1949), pp. 34–45, 50–71; Kurt Weis, "Die Funktion des Ballspiels bei den alten Maya," *Die Soziologie des Sports*, ed. Günther Lüschen and Kurt Weis (Darmstadt: Luchterhand, 1976), pp. 115–129.

13. Ludwig Deubner, quoted by Ludwig Drees, *Olympia: Gods, Artists, and Athletes*, trans. Gerald Onn (New York: Praeger, 1968), p. 24. A contrary view appears in E. Norman Gardiner, *Athletics of the Ancient World* (Oxford: Clarendon Press, 1930), pp. 32–33.

14. Data for the table were derived from Gardiner, *Athletics of the Ancient World*, pp. 33–37; H. A. Harris, *Greek Athletes and Athletics* (London: Hutchinson, 1964), p. 36.

15. Drees, *Olympia*, p. 31.

16. Pierre Frayssinet, *Le Sport parmi les beaux-arts* (Paris: Arts et Voyages, 1968), p. 27.

17. Hans Kamphausen, "Traditionelle Leibesübungen bei autochthonen Völkern," *Geschichte der Leibesübungen*, ed. Horst Überhorst, 6 vols. (Berlin: Verlag Bartels und Wernitz, 1972–   ), 1, 69.

18. *Athletics of the Ancient World*, p. 49.

19. Peter L. Lindsay, "Attitudes towards Physical Exercise Reflected in the Literature of Ancient Rome," *History of Sport and Physical Education to 1900*, ed. Earle F. Zeigler (Champaign, Illinois: Stipes, 1973), p. 179.

20. See Alois Koch, *Die Leibeserziehung im Urteil der antiken und frühchristli-

chen Anthropologie (Schorndorf: Karl Hofmann, 1965); Ralph B. Ballou, Jr., "An Analysis of the Writings of Selected Church Fathers to A.D. 394 to Reveal Attitudes Regarding Physical Activity," *History of Sport and Physical Education*, ed. Zeigler, pp. 187–99; Georg Söll, "Sport in der katholischen Theologie des 20. Jahrhunderts," *Sport im Blickpunkt der Wissenschaft*, ed. Helmut Baitsch (Heidelberg: Springer Verlag, 1972), pp. 43–63; Rüdiger Schloz, "Probleme und Ansätze in der protestantischen Theologie," *Sport im Blickpunkt der Wissenschaft*, pp. 64–83.

21. See Frank Deford, "Religion in Sport," *SI*, 44 (April 19, 1976), 88–102; Deford, "The Word According to Tom," *SI*, 44 (April 26, 1976), 54–69; Deford, "Reaching for the Stars," *SI*, 44 (May 3, 1976), 42–60.

22. Keith Dunstan, *Sports* (North Melbourne: Cassell Australia, 1973), p. 1.

23. *The Joy of Sports* (New York: Basic Books, 1976), pp. xiv, 18–19, 34.

24. Dan Jenkins, *Saturday's America* (Boston: Little, Brown, 1970), p. 88.

25. See Martin Hörrmann, *Religion der Athleten* (Stuttgart: Kreuz Verlag, 1968).

26. See Christian Graf von Krockow, *Sport und Industriegesellschaft* (Munich: Piper, 1972).

27. "A Dart Match in Tikopia: A Study of the Sociology of Primitive Sport," *Oceania*, 1 (1930), 64–96.

28. James W. Vanstone, *Point Hope: An Eskimo Village in Transition* (Seattle: University of Washington Press, 1962), p. 122.

29. *The Olympic Games: The First Thousand Years* (New York: Viking, 1976), p. 58.

30. E. Norman Gardiner, *Greek Athletic Sports and Festivals* (London: Macmillan, 1910), p. 54. H. W. Pleket, "Zur Soziologie des antiken Sports," *Mededelingen Nederlands Institut Te Rome*, 36 (1974), 60.

31. Umminger, *Supermen, Heroes, and Gods*, p. 185.

32. Denise Palmer and Maxwell L. Howell, "Archaeological Evidence of Sports and Games in Ancient Crete, *History of Sport and Physical Education*, ed. Zeigler, pp. 69–71.

33. Alan G. Ingham, "Occupational Subcultures in the Work World of Sport," *Sport and Social Order*, ed. Donald W. Ball and John W. Loy (Reading: Addison-Wesley, 1975), p. 363.

34. Christina Hole, *English Sports and Pastimes* (London: B. T. Batsford, 1949), p. 40.

35. Jean Le Floc'hmoan, *La Genèse des sports* (Paris: Payot, 1962), p. 46.

36. Dennis Brailsford, *Sport and Society: Elizabeth to Anne* (Toronto: University of Toronto Press, 1969), p. 31.

37. Foster Rhea Dulles, *America Learns to Play* (New York: Appleton-Century-Crofts, 1940), p. 34.

38. Howard J. Savage, *Games and Sports in British Schools and Universities* (New York: Carnegie Foundation, 1927), p. 186.

39. "The Bifurcation of Rugby Union and Rugby League," *IRSS*, 11, Nr. 2 (1976), 54.

40. Caspar W. Whitney, *A Sporting Pilgrimage* (New York, 1895), pp. 164, 167.

41. H. Graves, "A Philosophy of Sport," *Contemporary Review*, 78 (December 1960), reprinted in *Sport and the Body*, ed. Ellen W. Gerber (Philadelphia: Lea & Febiger, 1972), p. 10.

42. The most useful historical studies of race in American sports are Edwin Bancroft Henderson, *The Negro in Sports* (Washington: Associated Publishers, 1939); John P. Davis, "The Negro in American Sports," *American Negro Reference Book*, ed. Davis (Englewood Cliffs: Prentice-Hall, 1966), pp. 775–825; Egon W. Steinkamp, *Sport und Rasse—Der schwarze Sportler in den USA* (Ahrensberg: Czwalina, 1976); Robert Peterson, *Only the Ball was White* (Englewood Cliffs: Prentice-Hall, 1970).

43. Gerald W. Scully, "Economic Discrimination in Professional Sports," *Law and Contemporary Problems*, 38 (1973–74), 67–84.

44. John W. Loy and Joseph F. McElvogue (wrongly printed as "Elvogue"), "Racial Segregation in American Sport," *IRSS*, 5 (1970), 5–23; Barry McPherson, "The Black Athlete," *Social Problems in Athletics*, ed. Daniel M. Landers (Urbana: University of Illinois Press, 1976), pp. 122–50.

45. Norman R. Yetman and D. Stanley Eitzen, "Black Americans in Sports: Unequal Opportunity for Equal Ability," *Civil Rights Digest*, 5 (August 1972), 20–34; Anthony H. Pascal and Leonard A. Rapping, "The Economics of Racial Discrimination in Organized Baseball," *Racial Discrimination in American Life*, ed. Anthony H. Pascal and Leonard A. Rapping (Lexington, Mass.: D. C. Heath, 1972), pp. 119–56; Gerald W. Scully, "Discrimination: The Case of Baseball," *Government and the Sports Business*, ed. Roger G. Noll (Washington: Brookings Institute, 1974), pp. 221–73.

46. Richard Edward Lapchick, *The Politics of Race and International Sport* (Westport, Conn.: Greenwood Press, 1975).

47. Richard D. Mandell, *The Nazi Olympics* (New York: Macmillan, 1971); Arnd Krüger, "The 1936 Olympic Games—Berlin," *The Modern Olympics*, ed. Peter J. Graham and Horst Überhorst (Cornwall, New York: Leisure Press, 1976), pp. 168–82, Karl Adolf Scherer, *Der Männerorden* (Frankfurt: Limpert, 1974), p. 132.

48. Diem, *Weltgeschichte des Sports*, 2, 631, 633.

49. Auguste Hoffmann, *Frau und Leibesübungen im Wandel der Zeit* (Schorndorf: Karl Hofmann, 1965), p. 48.

50. Frederick Rand Rogers, "Olympics for Girls?" *School and Society*, 30 (1929), 193. See also Ellen W. Gerber, "The Controlled Development of Collegiate Sport for Women, 1923–1936," *JSH*, 2 (1975), 1–28.

51. Alice Allene Sefton, *The Woman's Division, National Amateur Athletic Federation* (Palo Alto: Stanford University Press, 1941), pp. 82–84.

52. Hugo Rothstein, quoted in Hoffmann, *Frau und Leibesübungen*, p. 31.

53. Brian Glanville, "The Amazons," *Mademoiselle*, 61 (May 1965), 166–67, 228–29.

54. For an outspoken woman, see Harriet Isabel Ballintine, "Out-of-Door-Sports

for College Women," *American Physical Education Review*, 3 (March 1898), 38–43. Ballintine brought track and field sports to Vassar in 1896.

55. For changes in both attitudes and law, see Jan Felshin, "The Social View," *The American Woman in Sport*, ed. Ellen W. Gerber (Reading: Addison-Wesley, 1974), pp. 177–279; "Sex Discrimination in High School Athletics," *Minnesota Law Review*, 57 (December 1972), 339–71; Bil Gilbert and Nancy Williamson, "Sport Is Unfair to Women," *SI*, 38 (May 28, 1973), 88–98; Gilbert and Williamson, "Are You Being Two-Faced?" *SI*, 38 (June 4, 1973), 44–54; Gilbert and Williamson, "Programmed to be Losers," *SI*, 38 (June 11, 1973), 60–73; Gilbert and Williamson, "Women in Sports: A Progress Report," *SI*, 41 (July 29, 1974), 27–31.

56. For detailed empirical studies of rates of male-female participation in sports, see footnote 59 to chapter 3, below.

57. "Zur Strukturanalyse des Sports," *Die Soziologie des Sports*, ed. Lüschen and Weis, p. 65.

58. *Greek Athletic Sports and Festivals*, p. 4.

59. *Athletics of the Ancient World*, p. 103.

60. *Ibid.*, p. 115.

61. "The Structural-Functional Properties of Folk-Games and Modern Sports," *SW*, 3 (1973), 227.

62. On amateurs as those who play for the sake of play, see Paul Weiss, *Sport: A Philosophic Inquiry* (Carbondale: Southern Illinois University Press, 1969), pp. 192–211; Harold J. VanderZwaag, "Amateurism and the Olympic Games," *The Modern Olympics*, pp. 83–106.

63. For the invention and early history of the game, see Neil D. Isaacs, *All the Moves: A History of College Basketball* (Philadelphia: Lippincott, 1975).

64. For a reconsideration by H. A. Harris of views expressed in *Greek Athletes and Athletics*, see his "The Method of Deciding Victory in the Pentathlon," *Greece and Rome*, 19 (April 1972), 60–64. See also Joachim Ebert, *Zum Pentathlon der Antike* (Berlin: Akademie Verlag, 1963).

65. Quoted from Harris, *Greek Athletes and Athletics*, p. 173.

66. Roy Barton, *Philippine Pagans* (London: George Routledge, 1938), p. 38n. See also Victor Turner on the Ndembu of Zambia, *The Forest of Symbols* (Ithaca: Cornell University Press, 1967), pp. 9–11, 289–90.

67. On him, see N. G. Politis, *The Olympic Games in 1896* (Athens and London: Charles Beck/H. Grevel, 1897, pp. 31–48.

68. Jean Meynaud, *Sport et Politique* (Paris: Payot, 1966), pp. 77, 81.

69. See Henry W. Morton, "Soviet Sport: School for Communism," Ph.D. dissertation (Columbia University, 1959), p. 49.

70. See R. L. Quercetani, *A World History of Track and Field Athletics* (London: Oxford University Press, 1964), p. xvii.

71. Umminger, *Supermen, Heroes and Gods*, p. 144.

72. Hermann Josef Kramer, *Körpererziehung und Sportunterricht in der DDR* (Schorndorf: Karl Hofmann, 1969), p. 78.

73. Hermann Altrock, *Die kulturellen Aufgaben des Deutschen Sports* (Kevelaer: Verlag Butzon und Bercker, 1949), p. 9.
74. Ernst Jokl, *Medical Sociology and Cultural Anthropology of Sport and Physical Education* (Springfield, Illinois: Charles C. Thomas, 1964), pp. 56–61.
75. "Nahe der absoluten Grenze," *Rekorde aus der Retorte,* ed. Helmut Acker (Stuttgart: Deutsche Verlag-Anstalt, 1972), p. 82. On the dream of absolute comparability, see also Weiss, *Sport,* pp. 230–42.
76. See Gardiner, *Athletics of the Ancient World,* pp. 152–53. For a contrary view, see Harris, *Greek Athletes and Athletics,* pp. 80–82.
77. H. A. Harris, *Sports in Greece and Rome* (Ithaca: Cornell University Press, 1972), pp. 198–199.
78. Rufus B. Richardson, "The New Olympian Games," *Scribner's Magazine,* 20 (September 1896), 279.
79. Carl Diem, *Weltgeschichte des Sports,* 1, 352–55.
80. Kohsuke Sasajima, "History of Physical Exercises and Sport in Japan," *Geschichte der Leibesübungen,* ed. Überhorst, 4, 199.
81. *The Olympic Games,* p. 22; Maria Kloeren, *Sport und Rekord* (Leipzig: Verlag von Bernhard Tauchnitz, 1935), p. 184.
82. André Obey, *L'Orgue du stade* (Paris: Gallimard, 1924), p. 35.
83. Quoted in Morton, "Soviet Sport," p. 177.
84. *Ibid.,* p. 232. For the East-German schedule of cash payments for records, *see* Frank R. Pfetsch, *Leistungssport und Gesellschaftssystem* (Schorndorf: Karl Hofmann, 1975), p. 196.
85. *De la Gymnastique aux sports modernes* (rev. ed.; Paris: J. Vrin, 1971), p. 336.
86. Sasajima, "History of Physical Exercises and Sport in Japan," p. 199.

III CAPITALISM, PROTESTANTISM, AND MODERN SPORTS
1. Wolfgang Eichel, quoted in Horst Überhorst, "Ursprungtheorien," *Geschichte der Leibesübungen,* ed. Horst Überhorst, 6 vols. (Berlin: Verlag Bartels und Wernitz, 1972–   ), 1, 17; see also Dieter Voigt, *Soziologie in der DDR* (Cologne: Verlag Wissenschaft und Politik, 1975), pp. 29–31.
2. The best account is by Andrzej Wohl, *Die gesellschaftlich-historischen Grundlagen des bürgerlichen Sports* (Köln: Pahl-Rugenstein Verlag, 1973), pp. 9–30.
3. *Ibid.,* pp. 30–57.
4. "Coaching," *The Book of Sport,* ed. William Patten (New York: J. F. Taylor Co., 1901), p. 219.
5. Gerhard Vinnai, *Fußballsport als Ideologie* (Frankfurt: Europäische Verlagsanstalt, 1970), p. 13. Vinnai is a Neo-Marxist, but this remark is Marxist.
6. J. B. LeBlanc, quoted in Marie Kloeren, *Sport und Rekord* (Leipzig: Verlag von Bernhard Tauchnitz, 1935), p. 272.
7. The idea for such a table came from Peter C. McIntosh, *Sport in Society* (London: C. A. Watts, 1963), pp. 63, 85; the use of Rostow was suggested by Hilmi

Ibrahim, *Sport and Society* (Long Beach, Ca.: Hwong Publishing Co., 1975), p. 117.

8. For the coefficient of concordance, see George A. Ferguson, *Statistical Analysis in Psychology and Education*, 3rd ed. (New York: McGraw-Hill, 1971), pp. 312–14.

9. The fullest documentation of commercialism comes from non-Marxist sources, especially from Joseph Durso, *The All-American Dollar* (Boston: Houghton Mifflin, 1971); Bernie Parrish, *They Call It a Game* (New York: Dial Press, 1971); Peter Douglas, *The Football Industry* (London: George Allen & Unwin, 1973); Roger G. Noll, ed., *Government and the Sports Business* (Washington: Brookings Institute, 1974); Gary Davidson and Bill Libby, *Breaking the Game Wide Open* (New York: Atheneum, 1974); and Sheldon M. Gallner, *Pro Sports: The Contract Game* (New York: Scribner's, 1974).

10. Jürgen Dieckert, *Die Turnerjugendbewegung* (Schorndorf: Karl Hofmann, 1968), pp. 111–16; Horst Überhorst, *Edmund Neuendorff* (Berlin: Bartels und Wernitz, 1970), pp. 69–72.

11. Rudi Reichart, "Zur Gründung des 'Deutschen Turn- und Sportbundes,'" *TPK*, 6 (1957), 481–88.

12. See Rudolf Volkert, "Zur bürgerlichen Theorie der 'Leistungsgesellschaft' und zu dem dieser Gesellschaftstheorie unterstellten Modellcharakter des Sports," *TPK*, 24 (1975), 1082–95.

13. Quoted from James Riordan, "Marx, Lenin, and Physical Culture," *JSH*, 3 (1976), 159.

14. Cited from Hermann Josef Krämer, *Körpererziehung und Sportunterricht in der DDR* (Schorndorf: Karl Hofmann, 1969), p. 29.

15. Andrzej Wohl, "Prognostic Models of Sport in Socialist Countries," *IRSS*, 6 (1971), 26; Wohl, *Die gesellschaftlich-historischen Grundlagen des bürgerlichen Sports*, p. 181.

16. N. I. Ponomarev, "Free Time and Physical Education," *IRSS*, 1 (1966), 167.

17. *Die Frühschriften*, ed. Siegfried Landshut (Stuttgart: Alfred Kröner, 1971), p. 361.

18. Pierre Laguillaumie, "Pour une Critique fondamentale du Sport," *Sport, culture, et répression*, ed. Ginette Berthaud et al. (Paris: François Maspero, 1972), p. 41.

19. Vinnai, *Fußballsport als Ideologie*, pp. 17–18.

20. Jac-Olaf Böhme, Jürgen Gadow, Sven Güldenpfennig, Jörn Jensen, and Renate Pfister, *Sport im Spätkapitalismus*, 2nd ed. (Frankfurt: Limpert, 1974), p. 47.

21. Vinnai, *Fußballsport als Ideologie*, p. 39.

22. Jean-Marie Brohm, "Sociologie politique du sport," *Sport, culture, et répression*, p. 23.

23. Jimmy Brown and Myron Cope, *Off My Chest* (Garden City: Doubleday, 1964), p. 63.

24. Böhme, Gadow, Güldenpfennig, Jensen, and Pfister, *Sport im Spätkapitalismus*, p. 37.

25. Vinnai, *Fußballsport als Ideologie*, p. 65.

26. Paul Hoch, *Rip Off the Big Game* (New York: Doubleday–Anchor Books, 1972), p. 154.

27. Ulrike Prokop, *Soziologie der Olympischen Spiele* (Munich: Hanser Verlag, p. 21.

28. Jean-Marie Brohm, *Critiques du sport* (Paris: Christian Bourgeois, 1976), p. 23.

29. Among the best studies are John W. Loy, "Social Origins and Occupational Mobility Patterns of a Selected Sample of American Athletes," *IRSS*, 7 (1972), 5–23; Günther Lüschen, "Social Stratification and Social Mobility among Young Sportsmen," *Sport, Culture, and Society*, ed. John W. Loy and Gerald S. Kenyon (New York: Macmillan, 1969), pp. 258–76; John Eggleston, "Secondary Schools and Oxbridge Blues," *British Journal of Sociology*, 16 (1965), 232–42.

30. See George H. Gallup, *The Gallup Poll*, 3 vols. (New York: Random House, 1972), 3, 1699–1700.

31. Heinz Keßler, "Die I. Sommerspartakiade der befreundeten Armeen . . . ," *TPK*, 7 (1958), 758–63.

32. Henry Morton, "Soviet Sport: School for Communism," Ph.D. dissertation (Columbia University, 1959), p. 273.

33. Peter Sendlak, "Leibesübungen und Sport in der Soviet Union," *Geschichte der Leibesübungen*, ed. Überhorst, 4, 114–15.

34. See Jonathan Kolatch, *Sports, Politics, and Ideology in China* (Middle Village, New York: Jonathan David, 1972), pp. 148–64.

35. Krämer, *Körpererziehung und Sportunterricht in der DDR*, p. 55.

36. Dietrich Martin, *Schulsport in Deutschland* (Schorndorf: Karl Hofmann, 1972), p. 88.

37. Siegfriede Weber-Dempe, "Die Frau als Leistungssportlerin," *TPK*, 4 (1955), 820.

38. See, for example, Dietrich Denz et al., "Zur Entwicklung von Körperkultur und Sport in der DDR," *TPK*, 13 (1974), 589–601.

39. Günther Erbach, "Physical Culture and Sport in the Social Planning Process," *Sport in the Modern World*, ed. Ommo Grupe (Berlin: Springer Verlag, 1973), p. 415.

40. Paul Kunath, "Persönlichkeitsentwicklung und Sport," *TPK*, 17 (1968), 596; Fred Gras, "About the Way of Life and Development of Personality of Competitive Sportsmen," *IRSS*, 11, no. 1 (1976), 77–81.

41. See Horst Smieskol, "Sportpsychologie in den sozialistischen Ländern Europas," *Sport im Blickpunkt der Wissenschaften*, ed. Helmut Baitsch (Berlin: Springer Verlag, 1972), pp. 160–72.

42. Quoted in Josef N. Schmitz, *Sport und Leibeserziehung zwischen Spätkapitalismus und Frühsozialismus* (Schorndorf: Karl Hofmann, 1974), pp. 21–23.

43. See Jean-Marie Brohm, "Une Politique ouvrière: le PCF et la collaboration de classe," *Sport, culture et répression*, pp. 141–69; Guy Hermier, Roland Passevant, Michel Zilbermann, *Le Sport en questions* (Paris: Editions sociales, 1976).

44. Arnold Beisser, *The Madness in Sports* (New York: Appleton-Century-Crofts, 1967).

45. Hans Lenk, "Leistungssport in der Erfolgsgesellschaft," *Leistungssport in der Erfolgsgesellschaft*, ed. Frank Grube and Gerhard Richter (Hamburg: Hoffmann & Campe, 1973), p. 21. See also Hans Lenk, "Sport, Arbeit, Leistungszwang," *Leistungssport*, 1 (1971), 63–70; Lenk, "Notizen zur Rolle des Sports und der Leistungsmotivation in einer künftigen Gesellschaft," *Die Leibeserziehung*, 20 (1971), 82–87; Lenk, *Leistungssport: Ideologie oder Mythos?* (Stuttgart: Kohlhammer, 1972); Lenk, " 'Manipulation' oder 'Emanzipation' im Leistungssport," *SW*, (1973), 9–40; Lenk, *Sozialphilosophie des Leistungshandelns* (Stuttgart: Kohlhammer, 1976); Howard S. Slusher, *Man, Sport and Existence* (Philadelphia: Lea & Febiger, 1967); Michel Boutron, *La grande Fête du sport* (Paris: André Bonne, 1970); Harold J. VanderZwaag, *Toward a Philosophy of Sport* (Reading: Addison-Wesley, 1972); Karl Adam, *Leistungssport: Sinn und Unsinn* (Munich: Nymphenburger Verlagshandlung, 1975.

46. See Helmuth Plessner, "Die Funktion des Sports in der industriellen Gesellschaft," *Leibeserziehung und Sport in der Modernen Gesellschaft*, ed. Gottfried Klöhn (Weinheim: Julius Beltz, 1961), pp. 18–32; Gunter Gebauer, " 'Leistung' als Aktion und Präsentation," *Philosophie des Sports*, ed. Hans Lenk, Simon Moser, and Erich Beyer (Schorndorf: Karl Hofmann, 1973), pp. 42–66; Christian Graf von Krockow, "Selbst-Bewußtsein, Entfremdung, Leistungssport," *SW*, 4 (1974), 9–20.

47. "Zu Coubertins Olympischen Elitismus," *SW*, 6 (1976), 410.

48. *Les Motivations des sportifs* (Paris: Editions universitaires, 1969); Gabler, *Leistungsmotivation im Hochleistungssport* (Schorndorf: Karl Hofmann, 1972); Gabler, "Zur Entwicklung von Persönlichkeitsmerkmalen bei Hochleistungssportlern," *SW*, 6 (1976), 247–76.

49. *Les Motivations des sportifs*, pp. 45–55.

50. There is, of course, the other popular notion that athletes are psychologically healthier and "better adjusted" than nonathletes. Gabler concludes in the above-noted works that athletes are simply like nonathletes.

51. *The Four Minute Mile* (New York: Dodd, Mead, 1957), pp. 213–14.

52. *Ibid.*, p. 215.

53. See especially David Meggyesy, *Out of Their League* (Berkeley: Ramparts Press, 1970); Ralph "Chip" Oliver, *High for the Game* (New York: William Morrow, 1971); Gary Shaw, *Meat on the Hoof* (New York: St. Martin's Press, 1972); Franz Dwertmann, "Sporthilfe: eine gemeinnützige Einrichtung," *Sport in der Klassengesellschaft*, ed. Gerhard Vinnai (Munich: Fischer Taschenbuch Verlag, 1972), pp. 56–81.

54. Lynda Huey, *A Running Start: An Athlete, A Woman* (New York: Quadrangle, 1976), p. 209.

55. Hoch, *Rip Off the Big Game*, p. 199.

56. See Hans Bloss, "Sport and Vocational School Pupils," *IRSS*, 5 (1970), 25–56; Dieter Hanhart, "Freizeit und Sport in der industriellen Gesellschaft," *Arbeit, Freizeit, und Sport* (Bern: Paul Haupt, 1963), pp. 13–68.

57. See Helge Anderson, Aage Bo-Jensen, N. Elkaer-Hansen, and A. Sonne, "Sports and Games in Denmark in the Light of Sociology," *Acta Sociologica*, 2 (1956), 1–28; Leopold Rosenmayr, "Sport as Leisure Activity of Young People," *IRSS*, 2 (1967), 19–32.

58. See Hanhart, "Freizeit und Sport in der industriellen Gesellschaft," pp. 13–68; Urs Jaeggi, Robert Bosshard, and Jürg Siegenthaler, *Sport und Student* (Bern: Paul Haupt, 1963), pp. 119–22; Anderson et al., "Sport and Games in Denmark," 1–28; Stefan Grössing, *Sport der Jugend* (Vienna: Verlag für Jugend und Volk, 1970), p. 26; James E. Curtis and Brian G. Milton, "Social Status and the 'Active Society,' " *Canadian Sport*, ed. Richard S. Gruneau and John G. Albinson (Don Mills, Ontario: Addison-Wesley, 1976), pp. 302–29; Voigt, *Soziologie in der DDR*, p. 55.

59. See Marek Zürn, "Tourism and Motor Activity of Cracow Inhabitants," *IRSS*, 8, no. 1 (1973), 79–92; N. I. Ponomarev, "Free Time and Physical Education," *IRSS*, 1 (1966), 167–73; John P. Robinson, "Time Expenditure on Sports across Ten Countries," *IRSS*, 2 (1967), 67–87; Andrzej Wohl, "Engagement in Sports Activity on the Part of Workers," *IRSS*, 4 (1969), 83–121; Joffre Dumazedier, "Sport and Sports Activities," *IRSS*, 8, no. 2 (1973), 7–34; Ladislav Lopata, "The Structure of Time and the Share of Physical Education," *IRSS*, 3 (1968), 17–35; Kyuzo Takenoshita, "The Social Structure of the Sport Population in Japan," *IRSS*, 2 (1967), 5–18; Klaus Prenner, "Leistungsmotivation im Spitzensport," *Leibeserziehung*, 20 (1971), 370–75; Richard S. Gruneau, "Sport, Social Differentiation and Social Inequality," *Sport and Social Order*, ed. John W. Loy and Donald W. Ball (Reading: Addison-Wesley, 1975), pp. 121–84; Gruneau, "Class or Mass," *Canadian Sport*, ed. Gruneau and Albinson, pp. 108–41; Barbara Krawczyk, "The Social Role and Participation in Sport," *IRSS*, 8, nos. 3–4 (1973), 47–59; Inge Bausenwein and Auguste Hoffmann, *Frau und Leibesübungen* (Mühlheim: Gehörlosen Druckerei und Verlag, 1967); Günther Lüschen, "Social Stratification and Social Mobility among Young Sportsmen," pp. 258–76; Lüschen, "Soziologische Grundlagen von Leibeserziehung und Sport," *Einführung in die Theorie der Leibeserziehung*, ed. Ommo Grupe et al. (Schorndorf: Karl Hofmann, 1968), pp. 93–111; John W. Loy, "The North American Syndrome," *Sports or Athletics?*, ed. J. Alex Murray (Windsor, Ontario: University of Windsor Press, 1974), pp. 76–96; Raymond Thomas, *La Réussite sportive* (Paris: Presses universitaires, 1975), pp. 17–25; Hans Linde and Klaus Heinemann, *Leistungsengagement und Sportinteresse* (Schorndorf: Karl Hofmann, 1968).

60. *Homo Ludens* (London: Temple Smith, 1970), p. 223. John M. Hoberman has suggested that the rejection of records may also be typical of Fascism; see "Political Ideology and the Record Performance," *Arena Newsletter*, 1 (February 1977), 7–11.

61. *Sport and Society*, pp. 108–13.

62. Günther Lüschen, "The Interdependence of Sport and Culture," *IRSS*, 2 (1967), 132; Hans Lenk, *Werte, Ziele, Wirklichkeit der modernen Olympischen Spiele*, rev. ed. (Schorndorf: Karl Hofmann, 1972), p. 77. Both tables reproduced by

permission of the publisher. See also Paavo Seppänen, "Die Rolle des Leistungs-sports in den Gesellschaften der Welt," SW, 2 (1972), 133–55.

63. See Christian Graf von Krockow, Sport und Industriegesellschaft (Munich: Piper, 1972), pp. 28–32.

64. Foster Rhea Dulles, America Learns to Play (New York: Appleton-Century-Crofts, 1940), p. 6.

65. Ibid., pp. 10, 12. See also Robert W. Malcolmson, Popular Recreations in English Society, 1700–1850 (Cambridge: Cambridge University Press, 1973).

66. Sport and Society (Toronto: University of Toronto Press, 1969), p. 141. See also H. Mayer, "Puritanism and Physical Training," IRSS, 8, no. 1 (1973), 37–51.

67. Kloeren, Sport und Rekord, pp. 19–37, 205–65.

68. For example, William R. Hogan, "Sin and Sports," Motivations in Play, Games and Sports, ed. Ralph Slovenko and James A. Knight (Springfield, Illinois: Charles C. Thomas, 1967), pp. 121–47.

69. Social Theory and Social Structure (Glencoe: Free Press, 1957), p. 579.

70. Henning Eichberg, "Der Beginn des modernen Leistens," SW, 4 (1974), 21–48.

71. Leistungssport: Ideologie oder Mythos?, p. 144.

72. Der Weg des Sports in die industrielle Zivilisation (Baden-Baden: Nomos Verlag, 1973), pp. 135–37.

73. Edgar Joubert, "Sport in France," Sport and Society, ed. Alex Natan (London: Bowes & Bowes, 1958), p. 29.

74. Roger Boileau, Fernard Landry, and Yves Trempe, "Les Canadiens Français et les Grands Jeux Internationaux," Canadian Sport, ed. Gruneau and Albinson, pp. 158, 163.

75. Jaeggi, Bosshard, and Siegenthaler, Sport und Student, p. 27.

76. Computed by me from data gathered by Daniel Lundquist, Fall 1976.

77. Turnbuch für die Söhne des Vaterlandes (Frankfurt: Wilmans, 1817), p. xvii.

78. Werke, ed. Carl Euler, 2 vols. (Hof: Verlag von G. A. Grau, 1884–1885), 1, 160.

79. Hannes Neumann, Die Deutsche Turnbewegung in der Revolution 1848/49 und in der amerikanischen Emigration (Schorndorf: Karl Hofmann, 1968).

80. Edmund Neuendorff, quoted in Jürgen Dieckert, Die Turnerjugendbewegung, p. 20.

81. Quoted in Gerd Krämer, Wie Fern Ist Uns Olympia? (Osnabrück: A. Fromm, 1971), p. 17.

82. Carl Diem, Weltgeschichte des Sports, 3rd ed., 2 vols. (Frankfurt: Cotta, 1971), 2, 945.

83. Krämer, Wie Fern Ist Uns Olympia? p. 28.

84. Arnd Krüger, Sport und Politik (Hannover: Fackel-Träger Verlag, 1975), pp. 30–31.

85. Horst Überhorst, "Return to Olympia and the Rebirth of the Games," The Modern Olympics, ed. Peter J. Graham and Horst Überhorst (Cornwall, New York: Leisure Press, 1976), p. 14.

86. Quoted by Horst Geyer, "Stellvertreter der Nation," *Die Vertrimmte Nation,* ed. Jörg Richter (Reinbek bei Hamburg: Rowohlt Verlag, 1972), pp. 80–81.

87. Quoted in Eichberg, *Der Weg des Sports in die industrielle Zivilisation,* p. 120; see also Überhorst, *Edmund Neuendorff,* p. 19.

88. Horst Überhorst, *Frisch, Frei, Stark und Treu* (Düsseldorf: Droste Verlag, 1973), pp. 50, 136.

89. McIntosh, *Sport in Society,* p. 58.

90. Mandell, *The Nazi Olympics;* Hajo Bernett, *Sportpolitik im Dritten Reich* (Schorndorf: Karl Hofmann, 1971); Arnd Krüger, *Theodor Lewald* (Berlin: Bartels & Wernitz, 1975); Krüger, *Die Olympischen Spiele 1936 und die Weltmeinung* (Berlin: Bartels & Wernitz, 1972).

IV WHY BASEBALL WAS OUR NATIONAL GAME

1. *The American Way in Sport* (New York: Duell, Sloan and Pearce, 1958), p. vii.

2. *Ibid.,* p. 16.

3. *Ibid.,* pp. 134, 151.

4. R. S. Whitington, *An Illustrated History of Australian Cricket* (London: Pelham Books, 1974), p. 17.

5. Helge Anderson, Aage Bo-Jensen, N. Elkaer-Hansen, and A. Sonne, "Sports and Games in Denmark in the Light of Sociology," *Sport, Culture, and Society,* ed. John W. Loy and Gerald S. Kenyon (New York: Macmillan, 1969), p. 173; Deobald B. Van Dalen and Bruce L. Bennett, *A World History of Physical Education,* 2nd ed. (Englewood Cliffs: Prentice-Hall, 1971), p. 262.

6. See Joseph Durso, *The Days of Mr. McGraw* (Englewood Cliffs: Prentice-Hall, 1969), p. 187.

7. Charles A. Peverelly, *The Book of American Pastimes* (New York, 1866), p. 337.

8. Quoted in Foster Rhea Dulles, *America Learns to Play* (New York: Appleton-Century-Crofts, 1940), p. 223.

9. Harold Seymour, *Baseball,* 3 vols. (New York: Oxford University Press, 1960–), 2, 4.

10. *America's National Game* (New York: American Sports Publishing Company, 1911), pp. 3–4.

11. Carl Diem, *Die Olympische Flamme,* 3 vols. (Berlin: Deutscher Archiv-Verlag, 1942), 2, 829.

12. *The Philosophy of Athletics* (New York: A. S. Barnes, 1927), p. 183.

13. See David Q. Voigt, *American Baseball,* 2 vols. (Norman: University of Oklahoma Press, 1966–70), 1, vii; 2, 240.

14. Quoted in J. G. Taylor Spink, *Judge Landis and Twenty-Five Years of Baseball* (New York: Thomas Y. Crowell, 1947), p. 63.

15. See "Monopsony in Manpower," *Yale Law Journal,* 62 (1952–53), 576–639; Samuel R. Pierce, Jr., "Organized Professional Team Sports and the Antitrust

Laws," *Cornell Law Quarterly*, 43 (1958), 566–616; W. Clyde Robinson, "Professional Sports and the Antitrust Laws," *Southwestern Social Science Quarterly*, 38 (1957), 133–41; "The Superbowl and the Sherman Act," *Harvard Law Review*, 81 (1967), 418–35; John P. Morris, "In the Wake of the *Flood*," *Law and Contemporary Problems*, 38 (1973–74), 85–98.

16. Quoted in John R. Betts, *America's Sporting Heritage* (Reading: Addison-Wesley, 1974), p. 93.

17. John R. Betts, "The Technological Revolution and the Rise of Sports," *Mississippi Valley Historical Review*, 40 (1953), 231–56.

18. See Robert J. Kelly, "Toward a Theory of Competition and Cooperation in Sports," *Journal of Popular Culture*, 4 (1971), 604–14.

19. Ralph Andreano, *No Joy in Mudville* (Cambridge, Mass.: Schenkman, 1965).

20. For Catton, see Voigt, *American Baseball*, 1, xxviii; for Frick, see Andreano, *No Joy in Mudville*, p. 4.

21. On Cartwright, see Harold Peterson, *The Man who Invented Baseball* (New York: Scribner's, 1973).

22. Frederic L. Paxon, "The Rise of Sport," *Sport and American Society*, ed. George H. Sage (Reading: Addison-Wesley, 1970), p. 34.

23. John F. Rooney, *The Geography of American Sport* (Reading: Addison-Wesley, 1974), p. 1.

24. Quoted in Tristram P. Coffin, *The Old Ball Game* (New York: Herder & Herder, 1971), p. 183. Interrogation mark added to last sentence.

25. "The Million Dollar Infield," *Playing Around*, ed. Donald Hall (Boston: Little, Brown, 1974), p. 45.

26. "Fathers Playing Catch with Sons," *Playing Around*, p. 166. See also Frank Deford, "Rites and Wrongs of Spring," *SI*, 40 (February 25, 1974), 70–81.

27. *Voices of a Summer Day* (New York: Delacorte Press, 1965), p. 12.

28. *Ibid.*, p. 223.

29. *Bang the Drum Slowly* (1956; rpt. New York: Doubleday-Anchor Books, 1962), p. 29.

30. *Ibid.*, p. 12.

31. *Ibid.*, p. 13.

32. *Ibid.*, p. 73.

33. *Ibid.*, p. 139.

34. *Ibid.*, pp. 196–97.

35. Murray Ross, "Football and Baseball in America," *Sport and Society*, ed. John T. Talamini and Charles H. Page (Boston: Little, Brown, 1973), p. 103; see also, Peter Grella, "Baseball and the American Dream," *Massachusetts Review*, 16 (Summer 1975), 550–67.

36. *The Natural* (1952; rpt. New York: Dell, 1971), pp. 8, 23.

37. *Ibid.*, p. 66.

38. *Ibid.*, pp. 9, 185.

39. *Ibid.*, p. 25.

40. *Ibid.*, p. 26.

41. *Ibid.*, pp. 34-35.
42. *Ibid.*, p. 63.
43. *Ibid.*, p. 74.
44. *Ibid.*, p. 190.
45. *Ball, Bat and Bishop* (New York: Rockport Press, 1947), p. 4.
46. Corrado Gini, "Ritual Games in Lybia," *Rural Sociology*, 4 (1939), 283-99.
47. Michael R. Real, "Super Bowl: Mythic Spectacle," *Journal of Communications*, 25 (1975), 35.
48. "Intellectuals and Ballplayers," *American Scholar*, 26 (Summer 1957), 342-49.
49. *The Summer Game* (New York: Viking, 1972), pp. 4, 303.
50. Cy Young (most games won by any pitcher) and Lou Gehrig (most consecutive games played).
51. *Bang the Drum Slowly*, p. 147.
52. *The Universal Baseball Association, Inc., J. Henry Waugh, Prop.* (New York: Random House, 1968), p. 19.
53. *Ibid.*, p. 45.
54. *Ibid.*, pp. 220, 223-24.
55. *Ibid.*, p. 242.

V THE FASCINATION OF FOOTBALL

1. Data taken from the *Statistical Abstract of the United States*.
2. John W. Loy, "The North American Syndrome," *Sports or Athletics?*, ed. J. Alex Murray (Windsor, Ontario: University of Windsor Press, 1974), pp. 94-95.
3. *World Almanac and Book of Facts, 1976*.
4. "A Season in the Stands," *Commentary*, 48 (July 1969), 66.
5. "Game Theory," *Columbia Forum* (Fall 1966), 173.
6. Eugene Bianchi, "Pigskin Piety," *Christianity and Crisis*, 32 (February 21, 1972), 31-32.
7. *Rip Off the Big Game* (New York: Doubleday-Anchor Books, 1972), p. 7.
8. The poll was published nationally on January 4, 1960; see George H. Gallup, *The Gallup Poll*, 3 vols. (New York: Random House, 1972), 3, 1699-1700.
9. See Georges Magnane, *Sociologie du sport* (Paris: Gallimard, 1964), p. 35.
10. Quoted by Morton Sharnik and Robert Creamer, "A Rough Day for the Bear," *SI*, 17 (November 26, 1962), 16.
11. Quoted in Tom Dowling, *Coach* (New York: Norton, 1970), p. 46.
12. Quoted in Arnold J. Mandell, *The Nightmare Season* (New York: Random House, 1976), p. 19.
13. Roy Blount, Jr., *About Three Bricks Shy of a Load* (Boston: Little, Brown, 1974), p. 113.
14. Ray Nitschke and Robert W. Wells, *Mean on Sunday* (Garden City: Doubleday, 1973), p. 253.
15. "Game Theory," 174.

16. Quoted in Blount, About Three Bricks Shy of a Load, p. 117.

17. Although the structure of the game, the testimony of the players, and the witness of a number of recent novels all indicate the football player's need to express aggression in the form of physical collisions, psychologists have not been able to devise personality tests which separate football players from other athletes. Repeated experiments with the Minnesota Multiphasic Personality Inventory, the Cattell Sixteen Factor Personality Questionnaire, the Edwards Personal Preference Schedule, and the Thematic Apperception Test have provided a wealth of contradictory evidence. See William L. Lakie, "Personality Characteristics of Certain Groups of Intercollegiate Athletes," RQ, 33 (1962), 566–73; Howard S. Slusher, "Personality and Intelligence Characteristics of Selected High School Athletes and Nonathletes," RQ, 35 (1964), 539–45; Richard A. Berger and Donald H. Littlefield, "Comparison between Football Athletes and Nonathletes on Personality," RQ, 40 (1969), 663–65; Brent S. Rushall, "An Evaluation of the Relationship between Personality and Physical Performance Categories," Contemporary Psychology of Sport, ed. Gerald S. Kenyon (Chicago: Athletic Institute, 1970), pp. 157–65; William F. Straub, "Personality Traits of College Football Players," International Journal of Sport Psychology, 2 (1970), 33–41; Brent S. Rushall, "Three Studies Relating Personality Variables to Football Performance," International Journal of Sport Psychology, 3 (1970), 12–24; William P. Morgan, "Selected Psychological Considerations in Sport," RQ, 45 (1974), 374–90.

18. Mike Holovak and Bill McSweeney, Violence Every Sunday (New York: Coward, McCann, 1967), p. 17.

19. See George H. Sage, "Machiavellianism among College and High School Coaches" and "Value Orientations of American College Coaches," Sport and American Society, ed. George H. Sage, rev. ed. (Reading: Addison-Wesley, 1974), pp. 187–228.

20. Paul Hornung and Al Silverman, Football and the Single Man (New York: Doubleday, 1965); Jerry Kramer and Dick Schaap, Instant Replay (Cleveland: World, 1968); Kramer and Schaap, Farewell to Football (Cleveland: World, 1969); Dowling, Coach; Kramer, ed., Lombardi: Winning Is the Only Thing (Cleveland: World, 1970); Leverett T. Smith, Jr., The American Dream and the National Game (Bowling Green: Bowling Green University Popular Press, 1975), pp. 209–56.

21. Ibid., p. 251.

22. End Zone (Boston: Houghton Mifflin, 1972), p. 200. Copyright © 1972 by Don DeLillo. Reprinted by permission of Houghton Mifflin Company. World rights, exclusive of U.S. and its dependencies, Canada, and the Philippines, by permission of William Morris Agency, Inc.

23. Ibid., p. 20.

24. Ibid.

25. Ibid., pp. 83–84.

26. Ibid., p. 199.

27. Ibid., p. 112.

28. Ibid., p. 77.

29. *Ibid.*, p. 242.
30. Michael Novak, *The Joy of Sports* (New York: Basic Books, 1976), p. 85.
31. William Arens, "The Great American Football Ritual," *Natural History*, 84 (October 1975), 72–81.
32. Stade, "Game Theory," 175.
33. Carl Diem, *Weltgeschichte des Sports*, 3rd ed., 2 vols. (Frankfurt: Cotta, 1971), 1, 513.
34. Robert W. Henderson, *Ball, Bat and Bishop* (New York: Rockport Press, 1947), p. 36.
35. Jean J. Jusserand, *Les Sports et jeux d'exercice dans l'ancienne France* (Paris: Plon-Nourrit, 1901), p. 282.
36. Christina Hole, *English Sports and Pastimes* (London: B. T. Batsford, 1949), p. 53.
37. Quoted in Percy M. Young, *A History of British Football* (London: Arrow Books, 1973), p. 44.
38. Michel Bouet, *Signification du sport* (Paris: Editions universitaires, 1968), p. 257.
39. Dennis Brailsford, *Sport and Society: Elizabeth to Anne* (Toronto: University of Toronto Press, 1969), p. 20.
40. Young, *History of British Football*, p. 58.
41. *Les Sports et jeux d'exercice dans l'ancienne France*, p. 282.
42. Young, *History of British Football*, p. 161.
43. Eric Dunning, "Industrialization and the Incipient Modernization of Football," *Stadion* 1 (1976), 136–38.
44. "Football in America," *American Quarterly*, 4 (1951), 309–25.
45. Allen Sach, "American Business Values and Involvement in Sport," *Women and Sport*, ed. Dorothy V. Harris (University Park: Pennsylvania State University College of Health, Physical Education and Recreation, 1972), pp. 277–91.
46. *On Aggression*, trans. Marjorie Kerr Wilson (New York: Harcourt, Brace, and World, 1966), pp. 280–81.
47. For the catharsis theory in sports, see Robert A. Moore, *Sports and Mental Health* (Springfield, Illinois: Charles C. Thomas, 1966); Norbert Elias and Eric Dunning, "The Quest for Excitement in Unexciting Societies," *The Cross-Cultural Analysis of Sport and Games*, ed. Günther Lüschen (Champaign, Illinois: Stipes, 1970), pp. 31–51.
48. For evidence against the catharsis theory, see Emma McCloy Layman, "Aggression in Relation to Play and Sports," *Contemporary Psychology of Sports*, ed. Gerald S. Kenyon (Chicago: Athletic Institute, 1970), pp. 25–34; Edward T. Turner, "The Effects of Viewing College Football, Basketball and Wrestling on the Elicited Aggressive Responses of Male Spectators," *Contemporary Psychology of Sports*, pp. 325–28; Leonard Berkowitz, "Aggressive Clues in Aggressive Behavior and Hostility Catharsis," *Psychological Review*, 71 (1964), 104–22; Berkowitz, "Some Aspects of Observed Aggression," *Journal of Personality and Social Psychology*, 2 (1965), 359–69; Berkowitz and Edna Rawlings, "Effects of Film Violence on Inhibitions

against Subsequent Aggressions," *Journal of Abnormal and Social Psychology*, 66 (1963), 405–12; Berkowitz and Russell G. Green, "Film Violence and the Cue Properties of Available Targets," *Journal of Personality and Social Psychology*, 3 (1966), 525–30; Russell G. Green and Edgar C. O'Neal, "Activation of Cue-Elicited Aggression by General Arousal," *Journal of Personality and Social Psychology*, 11 (1969), 289–92; Donald P. Hartmann, "The Influence of Symbolically Modeled Instrumental Aggression and Pain Cues on Aggressive Behavior," *Journal of Personality and Social Psychology*, 11 (1969), 280–88; Meinhard Volkamer, "Sport als aggressives Verhalten—aggressives Verhalten als Sport," *Die Leibeserziehung*, 21 (1972), 409–15; Jeffrey H. Goldstein and Robert L. Arms, "Effects of Observing Athletic Contests on Hostility," *Sociometry*, 34 (1971), 83–90.

49. *Ibid.*, 89.

50. On the violent behavior of spectators, see Ian Taylor, "Hooligans: Soccer's Resistance Movement," *New Society*, 14 (August 7, 1969), 204–6; Taylor, " 'Football Mad': A Speculative Sociology of Football Hooliganism," *Sociology of Sport*, ed. Eric Dunning (London: Cass, 1971), pp. 352–77; Michael Smith, "Violence in Sport," *SW*, 4 (1974), 164–73; Smith, "Significant Others," *IRSS*, 9, nos. 3–4 (1974), 45–56; Smith, "Sport and Collective Violence," *Sport and Social Order*, ed. Donald W. Ball and John W. Loy (Reading: Addison-Wesley, 1975), pp. 281–330; Gladys Engel Lang, "Der Ausbruch von Tumulten bei Sportveranstaltungen," *Die Soziologie des Sports*, ed. Günther Lüschen und Kurt Weis (Darmstadt: Luchterhand, 1976), pp. 273–95; Clifford Bryan and Robert Horton, School Athletics and Fan Aggression," *Educational Researcher*, 5, no. 7 (Summer 1976), 2–11.

51. Elias and Dunning, "The Quest for Excitement in Unexciting Societies," p. 31.

52. A sensitive account of sport and turn-of-the-century colleges can be found in Guy Lewis, "Enterprise on the Campus: Developments in Intercollegiate Sport and Higher Education, 1875–1939," *History of Physical Education and Sport*, ed. Bruce L. Bennett (Chicago: Athletic Institute, 1972), pp. 53–66.

53. Alan Listiak, " 'Legitimate Deviance' and Social Class," *Canadian Sport*, ed. Richard S. Gruneau and John G. Albinson (Don Mills, Ontario: Addison-Wesley, 1976), p. 416.

54. *Ibid.*, p. 418.

55. *Ibid.*, p. 419.

56. Richard G. Sipes, "War, Sports and Aggression," *American Anthropologist*, 75 (1973), 64–86.

VI INDIVIDUALISM RECONSIDERED

1. Quoted in David Q. Voigt, *American Baseball*, 2 vols. (Norman: University of Oklahoma Press, 1966–1970), 1, xxiv.

2. Joseph Strutt, *Sports and Pastimes of the People of England*, 2nd ed. (London: Thomas Tegg, 1838), pp. xvii–xviii.

3. George H. Gallup, *The Gallup Poll*, 3 vols. (New York: Random House, 1972), 3, 1699–1700.

4. Gregory P. Stone, "Some Meanings of American Sport," *Aspects of Contemporary Sport Sociology*, ed. Gerald S. Kenyon (Chicago: Athletic Institute, 1969), pp. 5–27.

5. *The World Almanac and Book of Facts, 1976*.

6. Josef Hackforth, *Sport im Fernsehen* (Münster: Verlag Regensburg, 1975), p. 261; see also the French situation as discussed by Edouard Seidler, *Le Sport et la presse* (Paris: Armand Colin, 1964).

7. I have used four-year intervals to make sure that the predictable occurrence of the Olympic games didn't distort the results.

8. See John F. Rooney, *A Geography of American Sport* (Reading: Addison- Wesley, 1974), p. 69; "Participation Survey" of the National Association of State High School Federations, 1975. I have used the top ten sports.

9. National Collegiate Athletic Association *Report Number 4*, 1974, pp. 7, 13.

10. *Ibid.*, p. 17.

11. *Statistical Abstract of the United States, 1976.*

12. Stefan Grössing, *Sport und Jugend* (Vienna: Verlag für Jugend und Volk, 1970), pp. 28–29.

13. B. Petrak, "Sport Activity in the Life of the Population of the Czechomoravian Plateau," *IRSS*, 1 (1966), 146.

14. Dieter Voigt, *Soziologie in der DDR* (Cologne: Wissenschaft und Politik, 1975), p. 69; Gerd Hortleder, *Die Faszination des Fußballspiels* (Frankfurt: Suhrkamp, 1974), pp. 56–57. See also Heinz Schiele, "Ergebnisse und Erfahrungen von FDGB und DTSB," *TPK*, 21 (1972), 505–13.

15. Jean Meynaud, *Sport et politique* (Paris: Payot, 1966), pp. 12–13.

16. Helge Andersen, Aage Bo-Jensen, N. Elkaer-Hansen, and A. Sonne, "Sports and Games in Denmark in the Light of Sociology," *Sport, Culture, and Society*, ed. John W. Loy and Gerald S. Kenyon (New York: Macmillan, 1969), p. 173.

17. Kohsuke Sasajima, "History of Physical Exercises and Sport in Japan," *Geschichte der Leibesübungen* ed. Horst Überhorst, 6 vols. (Berlin: Bartels & Wernitz, 1972–), 4, 211.

18. "Children's Play as an Indicator of Cross Cultural and Intercultural Differences," *Journal of Educational Sociology*, 35 (1962), 280.

19. See, for example, Günther Lüschen, "Social Stratification and Social Mobility among Young Sportsmen," *Sport, Culture, and Society*, ed. Loy and Kenyon, p. 265; Fred Gras, "The Shaping of the Interest in and the Need for Sport," *IRSS*, 9, nos. 3–4 (1974), 77; Leopold Rosenmayr, "Sport as Leisure Activity of Young People," *IRSS*, 2 (1967), 23; Fritz Nigg and Otto Heidrich, "Young Girls and their Sport," *IRSS*, 3 (1968), 131; Peter Sendlak, "Leibesübungen und Sport in der Soviet Union," *Geschichte der Leibesübungen*, ed. Überhorst, 4, 113.

20. John R. Tunis, *Sports* (New York: John Day, 1928), p. 261; Robert Daley, *The Bizarre World of European Sports* (New York: William Morrow, 1963), p. 2.

21. Quoted phrases from George H. Sage, "An Assessment of Personality Profiles between and within Intercollegiate Athletes from Eight Different Sports," *SW*, 2 (1972), 408; Leon E. Smith, "Personality and Performance Research—New

Theories and Directions Required," *Quest Monograph*, no. 13 (1970), 74. See also Jean M. Williams, Barbara J. Hoepner, Dorothy L. Moody, and Bruce D. Ogilvie, "Personality Traits of Champion Level Female Fencers," *RQ*, 41 (1970), 446–53; Walter Kroll and William Crenshaw, "Multivariate Personality Profile Analysis of Four Athletic Groups," *Contemporary Psychology of Sports*, ed. Gerald S. Kenyon (Chicago: Athletic Institute, 1970), pp. 97–106; Evelyn I. Bird, "Personality Structure of Canadian Intercollegiate Women Ice Hockey Players," *ibid.*, pp. 149–56; Theresa M. Malumphy, "The College Woman Athlete—Questions and Tentative Answers," *Quest Monograph*, no. 14 (1970), 18–27; Sheri L. Peterson, Jerome C. Weber, and William W. Trousdale, "Personality Traits of Women in Team Sports versus Women in Individual Sports," *RQ*, 38 (1967), 686–90; Abraham P. Sperling, "The Relationships between Personality Adjustment and Achievement in Physical Education Activities," *RQ*, 13 (1942), 351–63; Lance Flanagan, "A Study of Some Personality Traits of Different Physical Activity Groups," *RQ*, 22 (1951), 312–23; William L. Lakie, "Personality Characteristics of Certain Groups of Intercollegiate Athletes," *RQ*, 33 (1962), 566–73; Carl E. Klafs and M. Joan Lyon, *The Female Athlete* (St. Louis: C. V. Mosby Co., 1973), p. 87.

22. Joseph Moncure March, *The Set-Up* (New York: Covici-Friede, 1928); Clifford Odets, *Golden Boy* (1937; rpt. in *Six Plays of Clifford Odets* [New York: Modern Library, n.d.]); Nelson Algren, *Never Come Morning* (New York: Harper & Bros., 1942); Budd Schulberg, *The Harder They Fall* (New York: Random House, 1947); Francis Pollini, *The Crown* (New York: Putnam's, 1967); Michael Shaara, *The Broken Place* (New York: New American Library, 1968). Stories about boxers by Ernest Hemingway and others are too many even to list.

23. In addition to Van Loan, Lardner, Harris, Malamud, and Coover, see Heywood Broun, *The Sun Field* (New York: Putnam's, 1923); Eliot Asinof, *Man on Spikes* (New York: McGraw-Hill, 1955); Ed Fitzgerald, *The Ballplayer* (New York: A. S. Barnes, 1957); Martin Quigley, *Today's Game* (New York: Viking, 1965); William Brashler, *The Bingo Long Traveling All Stars and Motor Kings* (New York: Harper & Row, 1973); Philip Roth, *The Great American Novel* (New York: Random House, 1973); Jay Neugeboren, *Sam's Legacy* (New York: Holt, Rinehart & Winston, 1975); Lamar Herrin, *The Rio Loja Ringmaster* (New York: Viking, 1977).

24. Football: William Manchester, *The Long Gainer* (Boston: Little, Brown, 1961); Robert Daley, *Only a Game* (New York: New American Library, 1967); Gary Cartwright, *The Hundred Yard War* (Garden City: Doubleday, 1968); David Scott Milton, *The Quarterback* (New York: Dell, 1970); Don Jenkins, *Semi-Tough* (New York: Atheneum, 1972); James Whitehead, *Joiner* (New York: Knopf, 1971); Don DeLillo, *End Zone* (Boston: Houghton Mifflin, 1972); Peter Gent, *North Dallas Forty* (New York: Signet, 1974); Sam Koperwas, *Westchester Bull* (New York: Simon and Schuster, 1976). Basketball: Jeremy Larner, *Drive, He Said* (New York: Dell, 1964); Jay Neugeboren, *Big Man* (Boston: Houghton Mifflin, 1966); Charles Rosen, *Have Jump Shot, Will Travel* (New York: Arbor House, 1975).

25. Tennis: Wright Morris, *The Huge Season* (New York: Knopf, 1954); Robert Barker, *Love Forty* (Philadelphia: Lippincott, 1975); Archie Oldham, *A Race through*

Summer (New York: Dell, 1975); Jane and Burt Boyer, *World Class* (New York: Random House, 1975); Edwin Fadiman, Jr., *The Professional* (New York: David McKay, 1973); Ralph M. Demers, *The Circuit* (New York: Viking, 1976). Golf: Dan Jenkins, *Dead Solid Perfect* (New York: Atheneum, 1974).

26. Shaw, *Cashel Byron's Profession* (1885–1886; rpt. Carbondale: Southern Illinois University Press, 1968); Brecht, "Der Kinnhaken," *Scherls Magazin*, 2 (1926), 48–50. On team sports, see Friedrich Torberg, *Die Mannschaft* (1935; rpt. Vienna: Verlag Fritz Molden, 1968); David Storey, *This Sporting Life* (1960; rpt. London: Longman's, 1968); Peter Handke, *Die Angst des Tormanns beim Elfmeter* (Frankfurt: Suhrkamp, 1970); Dieter Krusche, *Obenauf* (Munich: Metaverlag, 1973); Alfred Behrens, *Die Fernsehliga* (Berlin: Rotbuch Verlag, 1974).

27. In addition to the four works discussed briefly in the text, see Henry de Montherlant, *Les Olympiques* (1920, 1938; rpt. Paris: Gallimard, 1954) and *Le Songe* (Paris: Gallimard, 1923); Knud Lundberg, *The Olympic Hope* (London: Stanley Paul, 1958); Hugh Atkinson, *The Games* (London: Cassell, 1967); Georges Magnane, *La Trêve Olympique* (Paris: Albin Michel, 1950); John Henry MacKay, *Der Schwimmer* (1901; rpt. Treptow: Bernhard Zacks, 1911); Pierre Naudin, *Les Mauvaises Routes* (Paris: Gallimard, 1959); Uwe Johnson, *Das Dritte Buch über Achim* (Frankfurt: Suhrkamp, 1961); Ralph Hurne, *The Yellow Jersey* (London: Weidenfeld & Nicolson, 1973).

28. *Brot und Spiele* (1959; rpt. Munich: Deutscher Taschenbuch Verlag, 1964), p. 19.

29. *Ibid.*, p. 7.

30. *Ibid.*, p. 173.

31. *The Olympian* (1969; rpt. London: Secker & Warburg, 1974), pp. 6–7.

32. *Ibid.*, p. 310. An African runner also wins in Hugh Atkinson's novel, *The Games* (London: Cassell, 1967), but this thematically similar work is artistically much less impressive than Glanville's book. In an earlier novel about soccer, *The Rise of Gerry Logan* (New York: Delacorte, 1965), Glanville portrays a ruthless athlete successful both at sports and in the world of television.

33. *The Loneliness of the Long-distance Runner* (London: W. H. Allen, 1959), p. 7.

34. *Ibid.*, p. 39.

35. *Ibid.*, p. 52.

CONCLUSION

1. Quoted in George M. Frederickson, *The Inner Civil War* (New York: Harper & Row, 1965), pp. 223–224.

2. *Athletic Games in the Education of Women* (New York: Holt, 1909), pp. 9, 15–16, 37. See also Frances A. Kellor, "Ethical Value of Sports for Women," *American Physical Education Review*, XI (1906), 70.

3. *Athletes All* (New York: Scribner's, 1919), p. 277.

4. On the emancipatory possibilities of sport, Ommo Grupe is especially persuasive; see "Bewegung und Sport—Möglichkeit der Erfahrung und Selbstverwirklichung?" *Der Mensch im Sport*, ed. Gerhard Hecker, August Kirsch, Clemens Menze (Schorndorf: Karl Hofmann, 1976), pp. 16–29.

Index

Gladiatorial combats, 24, 29
Glanville, Brian, 155, 168, 184
Goellner, W. A., 166
Goffman, Erving, 12, 76
Goldstein, Jeffrey H., 181
Golf, 4, 12-13, 59, 108, 138, 140-45, 150, 153
Grace (Princess), 31
Graham, Peter J., 168, 175
Gras, Fred, 172, 182
Graves, H., 168
Green, Russell G., 181
Grella, Peter, 177
Grenade throwing as sport, 72
Gritti, Jules, 164
Groos, Karl, 2
Grössing, Stefan, 174, 182
Grube, Frank, 173
Gruneau, Richard S., 174, 181
Grupe, Ommo, 172, 174, 185
Güldenpfennig, Sven, 171
Gulick, Luther, 40
GutsMuths, Johann Christian Friedrich, 87-88
Gymnastics, 11, 34-35, 42, 48, 50-53, 63, 87-89, 94, 98, 141-43, 147-50, 160; see also Turnen

Hackforth, Joseph, 182
Hadrian, 45
Haekel, A., 166
Hainault, Margot de, 30
Hall, Donald, 102, 177
Hamburg Rowing Club, 60
Hamburg Sport Club, 61
Hamill, Dorothy, 39
Hammer-throwing, 66
Handball, American, 145; European, 107, 129, 148-50
Hand-fives, 59
Handke, Peter, 184
Hanhart, Dieter, 173
Hannibal, 24
Harris, Dorothy, 180

Harris, H. A., 166, 169-70
Harris, Mark, 102-04, 111, 153
Hartmann, Donald P., 181
Hartz, Louis, 92-93, 137
Hawthorne, Nathaniel, 92
Hayes, Woody, 120, 122, 124
Hecker, Gerhard, 185
Heidrich, Otto, 182
Heinemann, Klaus, 174
Hemingway, Ernest, 103, 183
Henderson, Edwin Bancroft, 168
Henderson, Robert W., 106, 126, 180
Henry VIII, King, 30
Herakles, 21-22, 50
Hermier, Guy, 172
Herodes Atticus, 45
Herrin, Lamar, 183
Highjumping, 33-34, 49, 66
Hiking, 147
Hippodamia, 21
Hitler, Adolf, 63, 88-89
Hoberman, John M., 174
Hoch, Paul, 69, 119, 130, 172-73
Hockey; see field hockey and ice hockey
Hoepner, Barbara J., 183
Hoffmann, Auguste, 168, 174
Hogan, William R., 175
Hohenwart-Gerlachstein, A., 166
Hole, Christina, 167, 180
Holmes, Oliver Wendell, 96
Holovak, Mike, 179
Hoover, Herbert, 137
Horkheimer, Max, 65
Hornung, Paul, 179
Hörrmann, Martin, 167
Horseback riding, 148, 150
Horse racing, 7-8, 30, 32, 97, 141
Hortleder, Gerd, 182
Horton, Robert, 181
Howell, Maxwell L., 167
Huey, Lynda, 173
Huggins, Miller, 122
Hughes, Thomas, 60
Huizinga, Johan, 4, 6-7, 13-14, 80

Patten, William, 170
Patton, George, 122
Pausanias, 7
Paxon, Frederic L., 177
Pelé, 37
Pelops, 21-22
Pentathlon: ancient, 42; modern, 150
Peters, Alfred, 163
Peterson, Harold, 177
Peterson, Robert, 168
Peterson, Sheri L., 183
Petrak, B., 182
Peverelly, Charles A., 176
Pfetsch, Frank, 170
Pfister, Renate, 171
Pfister-Binz, Katharina, 164
Phayllus, 49
Phillips, William, 118, 124
Piaget, Jean, 2
Pierce, Samuel R., Jr., 176
Pig Latin, 4
Pindar, 23
Plato, 23
Platonism, 24
Play, theory of, 1-14, 69, 161
Playing "doctor," 5
Playing "house," 4
Pleket, H. W., 28, 51, 164, 167
Plessner, Helmuth, 173
Plimpton, George, 117
Poincaré, Henri, 86
Politis, N. G., 169
Pollini, Francis, 183
Polo, 38, 59, 100
Ponomarev, N. I., 171, 174
Poseidon, 21
Prenner, Klaus, 174
Primitivism, 104-05, 113-16, 125, 130
Professionalism, 31-32, 39
Prokop, Ulrike,
Propertius, 28
Protestantism, 24-25, 82-86
Puritanism, 83-84, 91-92
Pythagoras, 49

Quantification, as aspect of sports, 16,
  47-51, 54-55, 67-68, 74, 81, 108-13,
  129-30
Quercetani, R. L., 169
Quetzalcoatl, 20
Quigley, Martin, 183
Quoits, 83

Race and racism, 32-33
Racing-Club de France, 61
Racquets, 59
Rapping, Leonard A., 168
Rationalization, as characteristic of
  sports, 16, 40-44, 54-55, 66-67, 108-9,
  128-29
Rawlings, Edna, 180
Real, Michael, 178
Records, as characteristic of sports, 16,
  51-55, 68, 74, 81, 129
Reds, Cincinnati, 118
Red Sox, Boston, 118
Reeve, Henry, 137
Reichart, Rudi, 171
Richardson, Rufus B., 170
Richter, Gerhard, 173
Richter, Jörg, 176
Riefenstahl, Leni, 25
Riesman, David, 128, 137
Rigauer, Bero, 65
Ring-around-the-rosie, 5-6
Riordan, James, 171
Roberts, John M., 8-11, 14, 164
Robinson, Jackie, 33
Robinson, W. Clyde, 177
Rockne, Knute, 121
Rogers, Frederick Rand, 168
Roman Catholicism, 24-25, 82-84, 86
Romanticism, 87-89
Rooney, John F., 177, 182
Roosevelt, Theodore, 123
Rosen, Charles, 183
Rosenmayr, Leopold, 174, 182
Ross, Murray, 104, 177
Rostow, W. W., 61, 170-71

Roth, Philip, 153, 183
Rothstein, Hugo, 168
Rowing, 30-31, 39, 147, 149-50, 153
Royall, Darrell, 122
Rozelle, Alvin "Pete," 45
Rudolph, Wilma, 76
Rugby, 25, 31, 38-39, 107-8, 127-30,
   147, 149-50
Rugby Football League, 31
Rugby Football Union, 31
Running, 1-3, 10, 16-19, 22, 25, 36, 43,
   49, 52, 58, 66, 77-79, 138, 142-43,
   152-57, 160
Rushall, Brent S., 179
Russell, Bill, 100
Ruth, Babe, 52, 77-78, 96, 99, 110,
   160-61

Sach, Allen, 180
Sage, George H., 177, 179, 182
Sasajima, Kohsuke, 170, 182
Savage, Howard J., 167
Schaap, Dick, 179
Scheler, Max, vii
Scherer, Karl Adolf, 168
Schiele, Heinz, 182
Schiller, Friedrich, 4
Schloz, Rüdiger, 167
Schmitz, Josef N., 172
Schulberg, Budd, 183
Scientific world-view, as explanation for
   modern sport, 84-89
Scipio Africanus, 24
Scotch, N. A., 166
Scott, Jack, 65
Scully, Gerald W., 168
Seagroe, M. V., 151
Secularism, as characteristic of sports,
   16-26, 54-55, 65, 80, 108
Sefton, Alice Allene, 168
Seidler, Edouard, 182
Sendlak, Peter, 172, 182
Seppänen, Paavo, 175
Sexuality, 33-36, 68-69, 78-79

Seymour, Harold, 176
Shaara, Michael, 183
Sharnik, Morton, 178
Shaw, Gary, 173
Shaw, George Bernard, 153, 184
Shaw, Irwin, 102
Sheard, Kenneth, 31
Shintoism, 83
Shooting, 72, 148-50
Shotputting, 72
Shuffle board, 83
Siegenthaler, Jürg, 174-75
Sillitoe, Alan, 155-56
Silverman, Al, 179
Sipes, Richard G., 181
Skiing, 138, 142, 146, 148-50
Slawik, A., 166
Slovenko, Ralph, 175
Slusher, Howard S., 173, 179
Smieskol, Horst, 172
Smith, Leon E., 182
Smith, Leverett T., Jr., 179
Smith, Michael D., 12, 181
Soccer, 18, 27, 37-38, 46, 48, 58-61, 66,
   70-71, 79, 94, 98, 107-8, 110, 114-15,
   118, 125-28, 132-33, 139-40, 142-43,
   147-50, 153
Socialism, 63-64
Socrates, 23
Softball, 142-43, 145
Söll, Georg, 167
Sonne, A., 174, 176, 182
Spalding, Albert G., 15, 95, 109
Spear-throwing, 45
Specialization, as characteristic of sports,
   16, 36-39, 54-55, 65-66, 80, 108,
   128-29
Sperling, Abraham P., 183
Spink, J. G. Taylor, 176
Squash, 59
Stade, George, 118, 121, 180
Stagg, Amos Alonzo, 40, 121
Steelers, Pittsburgh, 118, 120
Steinkamp, Egon W., 168